REAL
MEN
WEAR
BLACK

REAL MEN WEAR BLACK

By Trevor McKewen

rugby press ltd
Auckland, New Zealand

© 1994 Trevor McKewen and Rugby Press Ltd
First published in 1994
Reprinted 1995
Rugby Press Ltd
P.O. Box 100-243, North Shore Mail Centre, Auckland 10.

ISBN 0-908630-45-X

Typesetting/design by Sportz Graphics Ltd, 14 Como Street, Takapuna.
Printed in Hong Kong through Colorcraft Ltd.

Dedicated to my wife Robyn and children Jolene,
Tammy and James who have long indulged their
husband and father's obsession with sport.
Thank you.

ACKNOWLEDGEMENTS

Among the many books used to help research
Real Men Wear Black were the following. I heartily recommend all.
- *Modern Rugby League Greats* by John Coffey
- *Colin Meads, All Black* by Alex Veysey
- *Grizz: The Legend* by Phil Gifford
- *The Game, The Goal* by Alex Veysey
- *Tiger, Tiger, Kiwi, Rooster* by Richard Becht
- *Mark My Words: The Mark Graham Story*
- *Famous Fullbacks* by Joseph Romanos
- *Famous Flankers* by Joseph Romanos
- *Rugby Greats* by Bob Howitt
- *Straight From the Hart* by Paul Thomas
- *Buck: The Wayne Shelford Story* by Wynne Gray
- *All Blacks versus Springboks* by Graeme Barrow
- *Black, Black, Black* by Morrie Mackenzie
- *Old Heroes* by Warwick Roger
- *On the Lions' Trail* by Don Cameron
- *Hughie: The Hugh McGahan Story* by Todd Nicholls

The author and publishers are grateful to the following for the use of
pictures: Peter Bush, Fotopacific, Photosport and News Media.

CONTENTS

INTRODUCTION

Fight one more round. When your feet are so tired that you have to shuffle back to the centre of the ring, fight one more round. When your arms are so tired that you can hardly lift your hands to come on guard, fight one more round. When your nose is bleeding and your eyes are black and you are so tired that you wish your opponent would crack you one on the jaw and put you to sleep, fight one more round – remembering that the man who always fights one more round is never whipped. – James J Corbett, boxer.

There is something about the blackness of an All Black jersey that sends a shudder through your heart. – Gareth Edwards.

ONE statistic that has always intrigued me is the number of registered rugby players in New Zealand compared to other countries. New Zealand has 148,000 registered players. Compared to other major rugby-playing nations, we are not particularly well off. For example, England boasts almost 200,000 registered players, South Africa has nearly 260,000, France 175,000. Even Australia, despite the competition of Aussie Rules and rugby league, has 150,000 registered players on its books.

So why then do the All Blacks boast the finest record in international rugby? Why has New Zealand been able to lift itself above the numbers and consistently rank among the top three rugby nations in the world?

I witnessed the answer at Eden Park on a sunny afternoon in 1993. On that day, Sean Fitzpatrick's team were in danger of becoming only the second All Black side to ever lose a series to the British Lions. All week the coach, Laurie Mains, had mercilessly ridden his team. They were playing not only to win the series, but also for the pride of the All Blacks, railed Mains. For every man who had ever worn the black jersey. If they failed in that vital third test, they were not only letting themselves and their country down but also an entire heritage. New Zealand turned in a barnstorming performance and the Lions were repelled.

A young Auckland second five-eighth named Lee Stensness had made his debut that afternoon. And a stirring debut it was too. In my capacity as a sports reporter I spoke to Stensness only moments after the fulltime whistle. One thing struck me in our conversation. Despite the individual pressure he was under, one single dictum had driven him on. "We couldn't let down the blokes who had worn this jersey before us," he said while fingering the silver fern.

His comment reminded me of something Mike Brewer had also said. On his first tour away with the All Blacks, in France in 1986, Brewer was duelling with the grizzled veteran Mark "Cowboy" Shaw for the blindside flanker's role. Shaw sensed his time was at hand and that the likes of Brewer and Alan Whetton were the men of the future. Cowboy was ready to pass the torch on. But first a few home truths had to be made known. "Before my first match on tour, Cowboy came up to congratulate me," recalls Brewer. "Then he fixed me in the eye and said: 'Son, you've got to be willing to piss blood to wear this jersey'. He was dead right. And I've never forgotten that."

Indeed, I am convinced certain All Black teams have triumphed in internationals they had no right to win simply because of this rich heritage; this fear of bringing shame to the famous black jersey. It is the reason why Wallaby coach Bob Dwyer says there is no such thing as a bad All Black side. "Some are just better than others," notes Dwyer. All Black rugby has always been built around a rugged, uncompromising commitment to putting one's body on the line.

It seemed to me that the real essence of All Black pride coursed through the veins of men like Mark Shaw. In a fierce, confrontational game such as rugby union, unless players in the crucible of the forward battle were unbending in their approach, no amount of elaborate backplay or individual brilliance will salvage a test. These men were the unsung heroes. They often received little publicity yet were crucial to the team's performance. If anything, they were often viewed negatively. This was essentially because such men are not backwards in taking on the enforcer's role should they feel it is necessary. And while many times their predilection for taking business into their own hands was often scorned, I believe many of us secretly admired them. It was a comforting thought to know that if the opposition was trying on the All Blacks, the likes of Shaw, Frank Oliver, Kevin Skinner and Colin Meads would deal with it in their own way.

I discovered many other New Zealanders felt the same way, including the publishers of this book. We wanted to tell the tales of those men who helped construct the mystique of the black jersey that Gareth Edwards so eloquently expressed in his timeless one-liner.

I fully expect criticism from some areas for supposedly promoting violence. And I'm equally sure this book will be dismissed by some as macho posturing. Others will perhaps quibble over the choice of my subjects, claiming some don't deserve to be there while others do. For those people, I will state quite clearly my criteria. While some of the subjects in this book have occasionally undoubtedly committed deeds on the rugby field they are not proud of, they generally played within the laws of the game. Indeed, when I spoke to many of their rivals – even those who had been on the end of some of the bush justice handed out – they praised the commitment of their opponents. Rarely was a subject ever accused of a cheap shot.

For the same reason of not wanting to glorify violence, certain so-called All Black "strongmen" have been deliberately left out of this book. I am certain their absence will be noted by some readers and reviewers but I make no excuse for that. In my opinion, they let down the All Black jersey rather than added lustre to it. For that reason, I have not accommodated the Richard Loes of the rugby world.

While the original idea of this concept was to base it entirely on All Blacks, I had often noted the gallant efforts of many New Zealand rugby league representatives. League is a game whose strongest virtue is its movement. Rugby instead appeals as a more complex tactical struggle. Both codes have their strengths and weaknesses. I find both equally interesting. Yet when Auckland Warriors coach John Monie expressed a belief that New Zealanders do some of their greatest rugby league players an injustice when they don't place them on the same high pedestal as the All Blacks, I found myself agreeing.

New Zealand's unexpected rugby league victories over the world champion Australians during the 1980s were built on the same unyielding physical commitment and refusal to bow that marked many of the All Black heroes I wanted to write about. And anybody who did not appreciate the skill and courage the likes of Mark Graham brought to New Zealand rugby league has no real understanding of what team sport is all about. So after discussion with the publishers, we decided to widen this concept to include some of the outstanding Kiwi rugby league players of recent vintage.

We also believed several other players of merit were worthy of having their stories told. Forwards do not have a mortgage on courage and physical commitment. And nor is all adversity overcome on the field. The story of gifted former Kiwi utility back Dennis Williams is testimony to that. And the input of men like Fergie McCormick with the All Blacks and Dean Bell with the Kiwis were central to the success of the New Zealand national teams of their era.

Writing a book like this required, of necessity, exhaustive research. Much of that important sifting of facts, statistics and anecdotes came from reading articles and books previously devoted to many of the subjects included in this book. I am indebted to the authors for their fine work. They have my admiration and out of respect to them, I have listed their names and the titles of their books in a page at the back of this book. Some of the books listed are still available. I heartily recommend them.

I must also thank the subjects. Without exception, they were helpful and courteous. And never once was I asked for money for the privilege of speaking to them. Sadly, I cannot say this has been the case with other sportsmen I've dealt with on other projects. But these men were cut from a different cloth. The two quotes that precede this foreword go together. The attitude of the former is epitomised in the men this book is about. The latter quote is the result. It's my fervent wish that the words penned about the 13 men profiled in this book do them justice. If I have even gone halfway towards capturing the pride and commitment these players felt when they pulled on the black jersey, I will have succeeded.

WAYNE SHELFORD
'Buck'

The game was only a few minutes old but already Wayne Shelford was overwhelmed with the fury of the Frenchmen. "This is going to be one helluva rugged Test match," he told himself. In the next ruck, Shelford found out just how tough. A well-aimed French boot thumped into his jaw. He felt four teeth loosen in his mouth. For most players, that would have been enough to end their game. Not Shelford. More was to come. Shelford snatched up a loose ball and turned to set it. Behind him, French prop Daniel Dubroca let fly with a mighty kick designed to dislodge the ball from Shelford's hands. He missed. Instead his boot connected with the Shelford family jewels. The big No 8 felt a stinging sensation. But the game was in full flight and he wasn't stopping for anybody. Finally, it took a full-blooded charge from the other French prop, Jean-Pierre Garuet, to put Shelford out of the game. Garuet flew into a ruck like an errant Scud missile, thumping heads against Shelford. The New Zealander went down like a log, knocked unconscious. It was to be the first of only two occasions in his 22 tests that Shelford failed to see out a game with the black jersey on his back. When they finally got him into the dressing-rooms and persuaded him to "check the damage downstairs", the medical staff were mortified. Dubroca's boot had sliced Shelford's scrotum open and one of his testicles had literally fallen out! The medicos took him off to be stitched up, marvelling at the courage of the player who has been called the hardest man to ever play rugby.

THAT last – and probably most fitting – description about Buck Shelford was penned by leading British rugby critic Steve Jones. Jones was previewing the 1990 All Black tour of France, the first trek overseas by the New Zealanders since the monumental and devisive dropping of Shelford. Jones informed his readers that there would come a time, somewhere on the French tour, where the All Blacks would again confront the fury of Nantes, in 1986, where the New Zealanders had been virtually physically mugged. And against one of those French selections, out to soften up the All Blacks before the tests, the New Zealand players would look in vain for the man who had carried them through such difficult circumstances so often in the past. It was then, Jones predicted, that New Zealand would miss the "hardest man to ever play the game".

Jones was to be proved uncannily accurate. The All Blacks struggled in their opening game against a Côte d'Azur selection and were overwhelmed 15-19 in an ill-tempered match where the French took extreme liberties unchecked. The All Blacks, of course, rallied to win the French test series 2-0 despite losing a second provincial match in Bayonne. But it was a result that masked major problems within the All Black machine. A year later, the World Cup would be surrendered.

Whatever else is said about Wayne Shelford, it remains a tragedy that his All Black career ended in such acrimonious circumstances. Even from a young age, Shelford had been a born leader, a man who showed the way through deeds rather than words. He was born in Rotorua in 1957 and by the time he was a few years into school was already besotted with football. Not that his first position for Western Heights Primary School was an accurate portent for the future. There was Shelford at first-five-eighth!

It didn't take long to graduate to the forwards – where Shelford would line up for rugby on Saturdays and rugby league on Sundays. Already very powerful physically, he thrived in both codes, easily gaining selection in the local Bay of Plenty rep sides. Ironically, such was his prowess at league he could easily have trodden the path to Kiwi honours rather than the All Blacks. In at least one national league junior tournament in Greymouth, he found himself trading hit-ups with the likes of Dane and Kurt Sorensen, also running into Olsen Filipania and Fred Ah Kuoi at differing times.

Shelford had another motivation for continuing his association with league. His junior coach was Pat Bennett, well known in New Zealand schoolboy league circles. Shelford, who had by then picked up the nickname of Buck because of his protruding front teeth, wasn't just interested in Bennett's coaching skills, though. Pat had a rather cute daughter named Joanne that Shelford had had his eye for some time. And Joanne Bennett is now Joanne Shelford.

Eventually, it was rugby Shelford concentrated on rather than league. His other interest was the Navy and at 17, he enlisted with the intention of ultimately becoming a PTI (physical training instructor). During his basic training he turned out for the Navy club in sixth grade (under 18s) in the Auckland competition. The following year, Shelford found himself selected in the Auckland Under-18 rep side, along with two other youngsters by the name of Nicky Allen and Joe Stanley, before he headed to sea for the first time onboard the HMNZS Otago. He played for the ship side whenever Otago called into port that year, namely Australia, the Philippines and other Asian stops.

The next year, Shelford was back in Auckland, this time playing for Navy's senior side in the third division. Further recognition came with selection in the Auckland Under-21s. In 1978, he was chosen in the New Zealand Colts. It was to be a breakthrough in Shelford's career.

"I suddenly realised I could go a bit further in the game if I applied myself," recalled Shelford. "But I also knew I had to change my attitude. I'd always been pretty aggressive. When I was 18, 19, 20, I wasn't afraid of anybody. Plus the rugby in those days was bloody tough. The Auckland club scene used to have some rugged customers and you had to stand up for yourself. I didn't mind that. League had taught me a bit and I was pretty good at the old stiff-arm tackles when I had to be," he grins. "But I knew I'd have to pull my head in if I wanted to get any further in the game. So I decided to start playing more disciplined rugby."

Shelford's Navy career continued to stymie his rugby progress, though. He spent most of the 1979 season at sea and most of 1980 stationed in the United States. "When I came back for the '81 season, I decided that if I was going to have a real crack at going places I had to switch to a first division club in Auckland, so I left Navy and joined North Shore," Shelford says. The move paid instant dividends. Shelford was selected for the national Maori trial and sat on the reserves bench when New Zealand Maori fought out a gripping 12-all draw with South Africa in Napier.

In 1982, Shelford made further gains. He broke into the Auckland

Rising star on the rampage…Shelford first began to make an impact on the first class scene as a dominant No 8 for Auckland in 1983-84.

team and then found himself called up as a replacement early in the New Zealand Maori end-of-season tour to Wales and Spain. He got only two games on the tour – one against Llanelli and the tour finale in Spain. It was an unhappy tour with Shelford claiming the side was stuck in a conflict between "playing winning rugby and the traditional Maori style of football". He also felt the touring party lacked discipline. He resolved there and then that if he ever got the chance to lead a Maori side in the future, things would be different.

In 1983 and 1984, Shelford cemented his position in John Hart's Auckland team. But it was 1985 that became Shelford's breakthrough year, even if it did hold one particularly frustrating setback. The North Harbour union had just been formed and Shelford and Frano Botica spearheaded the drive to make the new province successful. He and Botica led Harbour to victory in the national third division, while Shelford also won the Tom French Trophy for the most outstanding Maori player of the year.

Shelford's multi-skilled and abrasive game was also coming to the notice of the national selectors who included him in Bryce Rope's All Black sevens squad to play in the Hong Kong and Sydney tournaments. The selectors were obviously of the belief that Shelford could bring those same skills to the All Blacks in the 15-man game. He was delighted to hear his name called out for New Zealand's planned tour of South Africa.

Shelford was devastated when the tour was called off and although pleased to earn his All Black spurs on the Argentine tour hastily arranged to replace the South African trek, he was left with a hollow feeling that not even leading the Emerging Players and Combined Services side on a tour to the United Kingdom immediately upon returning from South America could atone for. It was on that tour, the highlight being a 41-0 walloping of British Combined Services in the solitary "test", that Shelford first gave an inkling of his leadership abilities.

If '85 was a heady season, '86 was tumultuous. Shelford, still feeling aggrieved at the cancellation of the official tour, agreed to be part of the Cavaliers to tour South Africa. "Our reasons for going on that tour were to play rugby and I look back now and realise that if I hadn't gone, I would have ended my career without having played against any South African teams. So I don't regret it," he says forcefully.

Although he couldn't force Murray Mexted out of the "test" side, Shelford had a successful tour, including scoring two tries while captaining the Cavaliers to a 42-13 walloping of the South African Barbarians. He also led the side in another midweek match and by tour's end such greats as Colin Meads, Ian Kirkpatrick and Andy Haden were predicting they had a future All Black captain in their midst.

The tour opened Shelford's eyes. "It made me understand what touring sides go through when they come to New Zealand because there were no easy games on that tour. Physically, the South Africans are the hardest men I've ever played. It was a tough tour because the South Africans did seem intent on taking some of our key people out. There was Andy Dalton being hit from behind and Dave Loveridge was taken out. They were key people. Quite often they would start taking cheap shots and suddenly there would be an all-in stoush. On that tour, we had to stick so close together because everybody was against us. We had to stick together, especially on the field, so if something happened, we all got in, sorted it out quickly and got on with the game."

While the Cavaliers came home losers (at least on the scoreboard), Shelford is adamant the lessons absorbed by the young players thrown into such a difficult tour such as himself, the Whetton brothers, Steve McDowell and Grant Fox were to prove vital to the golden years just round the corner for the All Blacks. But before the heady heights of the 1987 World Cup were to be scaled, the All Blacks had an end-of-season tour to France. While others like Alan Whetton and McDowell broke through to make their All Black Test debuts against the touring Wallabies (after serving a token two-match ban for touring South Africa), Shelford was kept waiting in the wings as the selectors instead used a youthful Mike Brewer at No 8 against France and the Australians.

But on the end-of-year tour, Brewer was shifted to the openside flank and Shelford finally got to wear the black jersey in a test – at the ripe old age of 28! He gave a typically powerful performance in New Zealand's 18-7 win at Toulouse. The All Blacks lost the second test in Nantes 16-3 in a rugged encounter in which Shelford's injuries are recounted at the beginning of this chapter.

A couple of years ago, Shelford caused a stir by alleging on an Australian television programme that the French were on some kind of stimulants that day. He took considerable flak for the allegation

Putting the mana into the Maori team. Shelford charges forward in uncompromising fashion, backed up by Mark Brooke-Cowden.

but remains steadfast in his contention the French had chemical help in dealing so emphatically to the All Blacks. "I will always believe they were on something that day," he says. "I know the type of commitment and excellence it takes to go 80 minutes the way they did in Nantes. It's just not possible to keep up that sort of aggression for that long without having a flat period. I mean they just kept coming and coming. It was the most rugged test I ever played in."

With his position in the test line-up cemented, Shelford began to assert himself as a dominant international No 8 in the 1987 World Cup. New Zealand played sublime football throughout the inaugural tournament, although Shelford did find himself the unwanted centre of attention after the semi-final against Wales in Brisbane. Welsh lock Huw Richards grabbed Gary Whetton by the family jewels during a lineout and the pair ended up grappling. Richards quickly got the upper hand and was planting a couple of solid punches on his All Black opposite when Shelford intervened.

The punch was short but awesomely effective. Richards hit the deck while Shelford himself took a punch from behind by another Welshman, breaking a tooth. When Richards came to, he suffered the double indignity of being sent off by Australian referee Kerry Fitzgerald. Some say Shelford was lucky to stay on the field himself. He shrugs his shoulders when that is put to him. "I'm not proud of what happened but it was short, sharp and all over in a few seconds. And," he adds, "it did stop all the nonsense straight away. The Welsh got on with playing football after that and quit all the rubbish."

The Ballymore incident and several others, notably a similar dose of punishment dealt out to Newport club flanker Andy Pocock on the 1989 tour of Wales, earned Shelford what he believes was an erroneous reputation as an enforcer.

"I was never really an enforcer," he says. "In five years with the All Blacks, I was only involved in three punch-ups. And all of them were under provocation. In each case, the bloke who was causing the problems wasn't making any attempt to stop. You can push your luck too far."

New Zealand went on to win the World Cup, of course, with Shelford an outstanding contributor with his powerful surges off the back of the All Black scrum. In every respect, the Webb Ellis Trophy conquest was a PR dream for New Zealand rugby, in no small measure thanks to the cherubic features of David Kirk. But with Kirk pursuing life after rugby, the All Blacks needed a new skipper in 1988.

In many respects, Shelford was a controversial choice. He wasn't as educated or as articulate as Kirk and some feared his rough edges would be a potential embarrassment to the All Blacks after the slickness of his predecessor. Shelford resolved not to let any public debate over his suitability for the job influence either his personality or his philosophy.

He quickly became an inspiring on-field leader, revelling in the role of showing the way by bold example and particularly relishing restoring the haka to an act of All Black pride, rather than a crowd gimmick. Off-field, he slowly but surely grew comfortable with the enormous demands placed on an All Black captain.

Always renowned for calling a spade a bloody shovel, some feared Shelford was too blunt. Indeed, then coach Alex Wyllie, hardly a shrinking violet himself, asked pressmen to tone down Shelford's assessment of the 1988 Welsh tourists after the first test. Shelford had been asked whether the Welsh were committed enough. In typically blunt fashion, he responded by saying he had been worked over far worse in a North Harbour club game when caught at the bottom of a ruck that weekend than he had ever experienced in the first test. Wyllie, fearing the Welsh would be riled by this slight on their manhood, felt his skipper was unnecessarily waving a red flag in front the tourists. "I've never seen the sense in dodging a straight question," Shelford says simply. "I tell it how I see it."

Shelford's outstanding form continued through 1988 as he led the All Blacks on a triumphant trek through Australia. He was especially dominant in an awesome New Zealand third test performance where the Australians were totally overwhelmed by the All Blacks' commitment. Shelford ended the game with blood all over one side of his head from a serious cut. But as he stood, defiant, holding up the giant Bledisloe Cup with just one huge hand, he looked invincible.

Shelford ended the season by successfully leading New Zealand Maori through a difficult tour of France, Italy, Spain and Argentina. With vivid memories of the fateful '82 tour in the back of his mind, Shelford was determined to ensure Maori rugby regained its mana. The tour featured one of the more controversial incidents in Shelford's career; the day he was supposed to have almost led his team off the field in protest over the refereeing.

It happened in a match against a cantankerous Southern French Selection in Rodez and Shelford and his players were becoming increasingly frustrated at the locals' consistent breaching of the laws come scrum time, not to mention the numerous late hits. The French were continually charging over the mark at the scrums and Shelford was concerned that a major blow-up wasn't far away unless the ref took action. Unfortunately, the whistle-blower didn't speak English. Near the sideline, Shelford called his players over and earnestly yelled out for the tour intepreter to come down from the stand to mediate in a two-minute "discussion" among Shelford, the ref and the opposing skipper. Shelford told the ref through the interpreter that unless he sorted out the problem, he risked the Maori walking off.

The threat worked and the French got back to playing football. The only print journalist covering the tour, the New Zealand Press Association's Peter Hallwright, didn't feel the stoppage warranted major attention but, as occasionally happens, his story was "rejigged" by the Wellington-based sporting desk and an inaccurate suggestion that Shelford had tried to lead his team off the park was printed for New Zealand consumption. The then NZRFU chairman Russ Thomas was furious and although the misunderstanding was eventually cleared up, Shelford wondered whether this apparent misdemeanour would be held against him in the future.

The tour featured some daunting physical encounters, notably against French club champions Toulon, who had Eric Champ running round like a loose cannon, and formidable Argentine club Tucuman. Plenty of observers on the tour suggested the Maoris would have lost both matches but for Shelford's leadership. Toulon were dispatched 22-9 while a madcap match against Tucuman ended up being called off five minutes from the final whistle with the Maori leading 12-3. "That game was actually quite frightening," says Shelford of the latter encounter. "It was about 40 degrees for starters and Steve McDowell got sent off early in the piece which really fired the crowd up. All he'd done was spin the ref around and yell at him after their first-five had decked Brett Iti. We had bottles and oranges thrown at us by the crowd, who were actually separated from us by wire cages that surrounded the whole ground. The ref had to call the game off early and Jasin Goldsmith was hit by a beer bottle as we walked off. It was out of control. Tucuman was thrown out of the game for two years as a result of all the carrying on."

Despite the dramas, the tour was considered a great success with Shelford's captaincy skills making a major contribution.

In 1989, the All Blacks were again impressive, although not quite as dominant as the previous years as they sent France, Argentina and then Australia packing. There were some mumblings about Shelford's form, most notably from television commentator Keith Quinn. Those in the know were also saying former Auckland coach and current national selector John Hart was pushing hard for Zinzan Brooke's inclusion.

Then, when the end-of-season tour of Wales and Ireland rolled around, the New Zealand Rugby Football Union did something rather strange. For the first time in decades, they named an All Black vice-captain, with Gary Whetton gaining the nod. Quinn and several others interpreted that move as safety insurance by the selectors should Shelford's form fall away in Wales. Shelford himself says he was told that with so many young new All Blacks on the tour, and so many of them Aucklanders, the selectors felt it was wise to appoint a deputy

The glory years. Shelford holds aloft the Bledisloe Cup after a win over the Australians in 1989.

to help take the load off the busy captain. Shelford accepted that, although he felt uncomfortable about Whetton being in the role he was. The rugged No 8 was worried that a split was developing within the All Black machine among Hart and the Auckland players and Wyllie and the rest. He was shocked in 1993 when a former All Black whom he greatly respected told him he'd been approached by Whetton on the '89 tour to bolster a campaign to remove him as captain.

"Whetton was lobbying for support on that tour to unseat me," Shelford alleges. "I wasn't dumb, I had a feeling it was going on. He was very keen on getting the captaincy. He was telling people to side with him." Shelford said he had clashed with Whetton early in his All Black captaincy career. "On the tour to Australia in '88, Gary came to me and told me several of the guys were concerned 'Grizz' (Wyllie) was training us too hard and they wanted me to ask Grizz to tone it down. It was well known among the other All Blacks at the time that Gary, Grant Fox and the others ran Auckland training. I just looked at him and said: 'Gary, this is the All Blacks, not Auckland. We train for as long as Grizz wants'."

Shelford's form was so captivating on the '89 tour that any realistic bid by either the selectors or anybody else was quickly doomed. It was a far more difficult tour than most had expected. The Welsh test side may have been in tatters, but the club sides played with a passion and verve of their great national teams of old. It frequently took Shelford's leadership to pull the All Blacks out of trouble, notably against Llanelli, where his inspiring performance in welding the forwards into an inpenetratable defensive mass into the teeth of a 100 mile per hour gale saved a game that should have been lost.

The tour also featured a controversial incident in the match against Newport where Shelford felt obliged to "sort out" opposition loose forward Andy Pocock. "When you have a team of the standing of the All Blacks, you find so many teams feel their only way of staying in touch with you is by playing negatively," Shelford explains. "We ran into a lot of teams on that tour who set out to blatantly obstruct us, and Newport was probably the worst. Pocock took me out in the first lineout and I warned him there and then what would happen if he tried it again. He kept doing it, so I whacked him."

To Shelford, there is no controversy. An opposing player was cheating, the ref was doing nothing about it, so Shelford took matters into his own hands. "He was probably lucky he got a warning first.

'Pinetree' [Colin Meads] and Frank Oliver never used to bother," smiled Shelford. Despite his outstanding personal displays, the tour ended on a jarring note for Shelford when he was forced off the field (for only the second time in his All Black career) in the traditional finale against the Barbarians at Twickenham when a painful neck injury was aggravated.

The injury had been sustained in the opening stanza of the Irish international a week earlier. Shelford was so grievously injured at a maul that it seemed the All Blacks would lose their captain. The All Black doctor, John Mayhew, said that such was the extent of the damage, caused by a knee to Shelford's neck, that he expected him to come off. "But Buck had a huge pain tolerance, and he just waved us aside and played out the game." Not only that, but he scored a cracking try in the final minute of the game.

The following year, 1990, was to be the most tumultuous in New Zealand rugby since 1985. It began with a series of unexpected switches to rugby league which were to prove devastating to the upcoming World Cup campaign; first John Gallagher, then Matthew Ridge, then Frano Botica and finally John Schuster. Zinzan Brooke almost went too, only a late change of heart stopping him joining Ridge at Australian club Manly. Still, the national selectors were optimistic of a successful series against the touring Scots and Australians.

But there was concern when the All Blacks won the first test against Scotland at Carisbrook rather unimpressively. The concern deepened when Grant Fox's boot was the only thing that kept New Zealand from falling over in the second international at Eden Park. From here, the details begin to get murky. One thing was crystal clear, though: The dropping of Shelford – after captaining the All Blacks in 14 successive tests without defeat – was a bombshell of Hiroshima proportions dropped on a rugby public who had come to admire the full-blooded commitment of a player they considered special.

There have been many theories and explanations given for Shelford's demise. The only ones that really count are those provided by the selectors. The truth will probably never be known. All this book can do is give Shelford the opportunity to provide his version and point out several incongruities in the selectors' explanations.

"I had no real inkling of what was going on," Shelford says. "The first idea I had was when North Harbour had a game against North Auckland in Whangarei. At about 10 in the morning, we were doing

The Shelford haka...a sight to stir All Black fans and intimidate the opposition's.

lineouts when somebody came out to get me." Harbour coach Peter Thorburn had received a phone call from Grizz Wyllie warning him that the selectors were thinking seriously of dropping Shelford for the first test against Australia.

It's difficult to fathom what Wyllie was up to in making the call. Certainly, he was a loyal coach whose intentions were often misunderstood. It could be he knew Thorburn would pass on the news to Shelford and perhaps was simply punting that it would inspire the No 8 to a mighty game against North Auckland. Even so, it is strange that Wyllie would dispatch the other two selectors, John Hart and Lane Penn, to Whangarei while he himself went to Hamilton to watch the Aussies play Waikato. Not only did a decision as monumental as dropping a skipper of Shelford's standing demand the convenor being at the game where the panel was finally going to make up its mind, but surely, as the only former loose forward on the panel, Wyllie was the man who should have been at Whangarei.

Shelford vividly remembers Thorburn calling him in before the game. "'Thorbs' had tears in his eyes and I guessed right away what was happening. I knew I was going to be dropped from the All Blacks. I just said to him: 'Them's the breaks, Thorbs, I can't do anything about it'. We had a bit of a talk and he suggested that if I had a big one against North Auckland I might still get in. But the whole thing had rocked me a bit. It was a helluva thing to have hanging over your head going into any match."

The other puzzling aspect of the decision was how it appeared to be common knowledge among the All Blacks themselves that night, even though the team wasn't being announced until the morning. Indeed, I remember having pre-arranged an interview with Grant Fox at his Auckland office the following morning. Running marginally late, I had just parked the car when the 9am news bulletin led with the stunning news of Shelford's sacking. Two minutes later, I was in Fox's office, recounting how I couldn't believe what I'd just heard. Fox didn't miss a beat. He explained how Buck had been carrying an injury and the decision was probably the right one. The mere fact he wasn't surprised at the news indicated to me he'd received prior warning. Not that I have ever subscribed to the nonsense about an alleged fist fight between Fox and Shelford...or that Fox issued Wyllie an ultimatum – 'him or me'. Fox is not that sort of person. But certainly I gained the impression he knew ahead of time about the sacking.

At the same time I'd been driving to Fox's office, Shelford's phone had rung. "It was 8.45am when Grizz called," says Shelford. "He said: 'We're standing you down for this first test'. He told me he didn't think I was playing to my best form and that the selectors believed I was carrying an injury. He said: 'Have you got an injury?' And when I said no, he asked me: 'Then why do you wear that knee band?' I just said: 'Lots of players wear knee bands as precautions.' By this time, I was starting to get a bit pissed off about the whole thing so I just said: 'Well, Grizz, you do whatever you bloody like'. I didn't want to talk about it anymore and it was obvious he wasn't going to change his mind. I hung up and not 30 seconds later the phone went again. It was Grizz again. He said: 'By the way, what was that injury again?' I just replied: 'You can tell the press whatever you want, Grizz'."

Undoubtedly, given his past service (and possibly with a certain degree of self-preservation given the enormity of their decision), the selectors chose to tell the media that Shelford was injured, therefore allowing him a shred of dignity. It was a gesture that backfired, though. They should have realised Shelford's pride would never allow for a smokescreen. "I was never injured," he steadfastly maintains. Both Wyllie and Hart (and also Fox) in their books claim Shelford's sacking was related entirely to form. The selectors say they acutely analysed the two tests against Scotland on video and discerned that the All Black back row wasn't performing as it should and that Shelford in particular wasn't getting as wide as he had in previous years.

Hart was known to have long championed the cause of Zinzan Brooke and among Shelford followers, it was the dapper Auckland selector who was fingered as the hatchet man among the selectors. Hart willingly admits he pushed hard for Brooke's inclusion in the test team, but in his book claims the final decision was made, virtually unilaterally, by Wyllie. He told his biographer that upon he and Lane Penn's return from the Whangarei match, Wyllie had asked them how Shelford had performed. Hart says he demurred to Penn, who replied, "Very averagely," to which Wyllie is said to have replied: "Right, we'll drop him then." Hart, in fact, says he was surprised at Wyllie's decisiveness over such a momentous decision and upon learning that there hadn't been any dialogue between Wyllie and Shelford that his position was in jeopardy, that he had serious misgivings about the dumping.

Shelford's version of the entire episode is naturally coloured by his own perception of how he was treated. He clearly sees Hart as the instigator in his sacking, although he's not overly enamoured about Wyllie's role either. Shelford's fundamental problem with the entire saga of his dropping is what he perceives as a lack of honesty, loyalty and consistency in the selectors' decision. Even though the selectors were undoubtedly looking to let Shelford down lightly and retain a semblance of dignity by coming up with a fabricated injury excuse, the mere fact the three wise men were willing to mislead the public makes their former captain wonder just how often he was told the truth throughout the whole sorry affair.

Nor is he willing to accept assurances that Zinzan Brooke's courting by rugby league scouts wasn't a factor in his sacking. "When I look back on it all, I saw the whole situation as John Hart's way of getting Zinzan into the team," says Shelford. "The selectors were under pressure from rugby league chasing him. I know for a fact that during the 1989 tour that Hart had promised Zinny he was going to become the Test No 8 because Zinny told me that himself. In 1990, 'Harty' was really winding up and pushing for Zinny."

Shelford says he had always felt uncomfortable about Hart, believing the Aucklander revelled in his reputation as an extraordinary talent spotter. "What you must understand when you look at this whole thing is that Zinny was one of John Hart's boys," he says. "Harty found John Kirwan, Harty found Michael Jones and Harty found Zinny. He wanted his own boys in there and I was in the way. I'm reading between the lines, admittedly, but I've been given a lot of information over the years from people and I've been able to put two and two together. Even now, it's difficult to get to the bottom of it ."

Another factor of his dropping that rankles with Shelford is his apparent failure to get a straight answer from any of the selectors on their reasons for his demise. "In 1991, when I took New Zealand B to Australia with Lane Penn, Lane told me I should have been in the All Blacks that year. I couldn't believe it. What upsets me is that none of the three of them had the balls to front me. All they had to say was 'We want to sit down with you and talk about what we feel you're not doing'. None of that ever happened. There was no loyalty shown at all."

Given Shelford's record and his commitment to the black jersey, it certainly wasn't unreasonable to expect the selectors to sit him down and explain their decision. Shelford has read the earnest tactical dissertations in Wyllie and Hart's (and even Grant Fox's) books over why he had to be dropped. Essentially, they boiled down to the allegation that he wasn't performing the wide-ranging game the selectors wanted; that he wasn't hard enough on the heels of Michael Jones as he had been in previous years.

Which brings us to the third point of consistency. Shelford believes the All Blacks lost their way tactically, significantly in the 1990 season and in the lead-up to the World Cup. "I believe there was a knee-jerk reaction to the loss of so many players to rugby league," he says. "All of a sudden there was this fixation with playing a brilliantly exciting style of game that compared well on television to the Winfield Cup. The way I saw it, I thought we were already doing that. But the loss of the likes of Gallagher, Ridge and Schuster took key guys out of our backline who were central to the style of game we had been playing in '87, '88 and '89. What happened in 1990 and 1991 was that the All Blacks tried to keep playing a game the team no longer had the personnel to achieve.

"At the same time, we kept getting this 'play it wide, play it wide' edict from Grizz and Harty because they wanted All Black play to compare well to league. As a result, we stopped doing the basics right. The All Blacks were going wide just for the sake of going wide and everything was breaking down. They got so obsessed about going wide that they forgot about the second phase and blindside football. All our guys out wide were getting smashed and when that happens, you've got to bring the ball back in again. That's where Grizz and Harty lost the plot. They were so interested in entertaining the crowd, they forgot they were out there to win. They lost their focus."

Admittingly, Shelford would have been hard pressed to have made the 1991 World Cup. His form was slowly falling away. But by the same token, so was the performance of several other forwards and Shelford is quite justified in complaining about lack of consistency in the selectors' decision-making process. Gary Whetton was hardly inspiring during the 1990 season and many New Zealanders were dismayed during the World Cup when he was embarrassed in the lineout by American part-timer Kevin Swords. Whetton was perhaps fortunate there was a dearth of locks, as opposed to No 8s, around in 1990. Alan Whetton and Steve McDowell were two other veteran forwards clearly past their use-by date at the World Cup, yet never subjected to the same selection scrutiny Shelford was exposed to.

**An icon beyond the realms of rugby. Shelford plays a role in Sir
Howard Morrison's Command Performance.**

Shelford's dumping was the most devisive subject in New Zealand
rugby since the Cavaliers tour. Rightly or wrongly, he was an icon at
the time of the fateful decision. The public had long admired his full-
blooded commitment and his stirring leadership. Overnight, he went
from an icon to a martyr. Emotion clouded the selectors' fruitless bid
to have the decision viewed objectively. A massive "Bring Back Buck"
campaign was launched as Shelford's fans sought to embarrass the
selectors. Shelford was gratified for the public's support. "I like to
think New Zealanders are pretty educated about their rugby. They
know the game. The fact they felt I should have been in the team was
encouraging but in the final analysis, they had no say."

As the All Blacks toured France at the end of 1990, Shelford played
the off-season for English club Northampton, spurning the opportunity to play in the prestigious Pilkington Cup final so he could return
in time for the 1991 All Black trials. It was all in vain, however. He
missed out on the World Cup squad and watched as a spectator as the
All Blacks surrendered the Webb Ellis Trophy to Nick Farr-Jones'
Wallabies. "I was saddened to see them lose," he says. "But that '91
team was split. There was an Auckland camp with Harty and the rest

Even hard men have their soft side. 'Dad' with daughter Lia and son Eruera the year he was first named All Black captain.

of them with Grizz."

There was a perverse irony in Shelford's dumping. With the wave of public sympathy over his sacking, he suddenly became hot commercial property. He had work coming out of his ears. What's more, now he was no longer an All Black so he wasn't obliged to give a slice of his earnings to All Black Promotions, the company formed to ensure an equitable sharing of commerical funds among all players. A hot item on the public speaking circuit both here and in the United Kingdom and with no shortage of products to endorse, Shelford has made himself a tidy sum on top of his coaching duties. Yet when he says he would have gladly given away all the monetary benefits for the chance to have played in the World Cup, you don't doubt it.

After three years as a player and assistant coach at Northampton, Shelford accepted a two-year post with Italian club Roma. He spent the first season as a player-coach but will this season restrict himself to coaching only, finally hanging up his well-worn boots. He says he and his family will eventually return to settle permanently in New Zealand and admits to a hankering to one day coach his beloved North Harbour province.

All very appropriate in a province where he is still quaintly referred to as "God".

MARK GRAHAM
'Sharko'

Mark Graham had never known a game like it. He was playing out of his skin, enjoying one of those freakish matches he'd heard one of his heroes, the great Australian loose forward Johnnie Raper, speak of when he said every top footballer has at least one game where everything he attempts comes off. Graham had certainly picked the right match to produce it. The first test against Great Britain at Headingley was the match in which Graham Lowe was determined his Kiwis would steal a significant psychological march over the Poms. And his skipper was delivering. The opposition didn't like it, though. Graham was tackled after one stupendous burst and Pommie winger Des Drummond blatantly dropped his bulky frame on the Kiwi captain's prone head as he lay on the ground. The body slam fractured a bone near Graham's cheek and within minutes one side of his face had ballooned to frightening proportions. Worse was to come. Just before halftime Graham was gang-tackled and was shocked when he heard a shrilling "pop" followed by searing pain. He had severely torn the ligaments in his ankle. What's more, there was no doctor on hand to administer a pain-killing injection at halftime. Mark Graham's game was over when an apprehensive Graham Lowe approached and pleaded: "Mate, I need you to go back out there. You've been braining the Poms and psychologically they'll be gone if they see you come back for the second half. Just stay on for five minutes and I'll get you off." Graham went back on, defying the excruciating pain. New Zealand won a tense match 24-22. Lowe describes Graham's feat as "the most courageous thing I've ever seen on the football field".

DURING his outstanding rugby league career, Wally Lewis often struggled to find anything kindly to say about New Zealanders. For some reason, we seemed to rub "The King" the wrong way. He bagged us relentlessly in an infamous Penthouse magazine interview and delighted in rubbing Kiwi noses into the dirt whenever he got the chance.

But one New Zealander quite literally has Lewis's undying respect. So he should too. But for the prompt action of Mark Graham during a key Brisbane premiership match in 1980, the then prince of Queensland football may never have inherited his kingdom.

Graham's Brisbane club side Norths were facing Valleys in the preliminary final in the premiership play-offs when the tall Auckland loose forward broke the line and surged upfield. Lewis, then a 19-year-old whiz kid also packing down at the back of the scrum, sprinted across in cover defence for Valleys. He nailed Graham with a superb ball-and-all tackle and both men hit the solid Lang Park turf awkwardly. Graham quickly jumped to his feet to play-the-ball and keep the attacking movement rolling. But as the game swept further upfield, Lewis lay writhing on the grass clutching his throat. Nobody took too much notice. Lewis already had a somewhat deserved reputation as a prima donna who often put on a Hollywood in an attempt to attract the referee's attention. Graham immediately knew differently. "I knew Wally wasn't up to his old tricks when he began to go blue," said Graham in a massive understatement. "He was in big trouble. It turned out he had taken a decent whack to his windpipe when he tackled me and he just couldn't breathe. I ran to the sideline to get the touch judge's attention so he'd get the referee to stop the game. We got to Wally pretty quickly and we were able to fix him up. But he wasn't good for a while there."

Lewis was to later publicly thank Graham for his swift actions, reasoning that his protagonist could easily have followed the football upfield to stay in the action rather than stay back and look after him. Intriguingly, there was a degree of bad blood between Graham and Lewis leading up to this incident. In his first match for Norths that same season, Graham had extracted some revenge on Valleys' cagey captain Ross Strudwick after the man known as "Ross the Rat" had dropped his knees into the back of Norths' halfback. Graham decked Strudwick for his trouble and found himself in the middle of a major brawl before noticing "a blur" out of the corner of his eye. It was the fiesty Lewis, sprinting from some distance away – straight at Graham.

Having had to learn to look after himself during his Otahuhu days in an Auckland competition full of hard-headed wharfies, rugged Maori and Islander fowards and veteran brawlers, Graham was ready. Lewis hit the ground and got up nursing a broken jaw. It was one of the rare times a New Zealander got the better of Walter Lewis, Australian superstar. And Mark Graham was one New Zealander who had the King's respect forever.

Australians quickly came to appreciate Graham's footballing abilities (as well as his pugilistic skills!). In just his single season in Brisbane, he made a major impact. He had originally been wooed across the Tasman on the strengths of his deeds for Otahuhu, Auckland and New Zealand. His rise had been startlingly swift: from third grade at Otahuhu in 1974 as a sixth former under the guidance of a rookie coach named Graham Lowe to playing for Auckland against the likes of Australia and Wales in '75. He was a Kiwi trialist the following year and then in '77, at only 20, he was playing for New Zealand.

After helping the Lowe-coached Norths side win the Brisbane grand final over a Southern Suburbs side coached by Wayne Bennett and including a giant teenage centre named Mal Meninga, Graham went on to grind out a distinguished eight-year career with North Sydney in the Winfield Cup. But it was the rangy loose forward's feats as a Kiwi that earned him his greatest fame. It is no understatement to suggest Mark Graham did more than any other individual player to win New Zealand rugby league the respect it craved for so long but never seemed capable of earning.

The code had always laboured under a stigma of second-class status, consistently sneered upon by rugby fans who scorned it as a game for Maori, Islanders and hotel bouncers. But during the Lowe era, attitudes began to shift. The 1983 and 1985 victories over Australia captured the country's attention. One man drew the focus more than any other. While we admired Kevin Tamati's confrontationalist edge, Clayton Friend's cheekiness and Kurt Sorensen's raw power, it was Graham who consistently showed consummate skill – the sort of pure footballing ability narrow-minded rugby fans had previously believed was solely the domain of their code.

At peak form, Graham was a sensational athlete blessed with dynamic skills. He could gallop like a centre when in the clear, sabotage opposition attacking movements with his clever ball-and-all tackles where he would wrap his elastic frame around his opponent to pre-

Early days in the career of a legend. Making an impact with Otahuhu and Auckland.

vent him passing, and inspire his team in the most stressful of situations. But it was his deft ball-playing skills that earned him his lofty standing in world league. Graham could get a pass away in the most impossible of situations. Even the most organised and rugged defences could not cope with him. "He was a freak in that respect," says Lowe. "Mark, probably more than any other player, made New Zealanders appreciate that we could produce performers the equal of the very best Australians. In fact he was better than most of them. The only Australian loose forward I've seen come close to him for skills in the past 10 to 15 years is Bradley Clyde. Nobody else is even in the same ball park."

Many of Graham's Kiwi team-mates agree. "Mark was Mr Rugby League," says Kevin Tamati. "If we'd had another 12 players like Mark Graham we would have been like the Aussies – invincible. He had all the attributes: size, pace, vision, skill and determination."

Graham's Kiwi debut came in 1977 in two World Cup matches. He came on as a replacement for Wellington's Whare Henry in a loss to Great Britain before winning a start against France. His first full match was also to be marked by a try. Graham made his first overseas tour the following year when called into the Kiwi touring squad in Australia when Barry Edkins broke his jaw. He played all three tests on tour and showed potential while still feeling his way.

Great Britain toured in 1979 and Graham was called into the third test after captain Graeme West was dropped. Ces Mountford had taken over as Kiwi coach and the players were still coming to grips with his demands. "There was a bit of a revolt at the time because we felt Ces was limiting us in attack," recalls Graham. "In the end, we got a concession out of him that if we defended the way he wanted us to defend, we could attack the way we wanted to. In the first 15 minutes, we'd scored three tries and we won the test 18-11."

Typically, Graham omits to mention he was named man of the match. Already he was gaining a reputation as a superb ball player. It didn't take long for the Poms to go after him in that same Test. "One of their forwards got a hold of me and headbutted me a beauty," he recalls. "My eye was stinging. It was a really muddy ground and I remember going over to 'Butch' (Tony) Coll and asking him if it looked all right. He looked at both eyes and asked me what the hell I was talking about. I felt really embarrassed because I thought I had a serious injury and there was nothing wrong with me. But at halftime

I had a look in the mirror and saw this massive hole in my head caked with blood and mud. As I was getting stitched up, I vowed I'd never ever ask a West Coaster about an injury again!"

The Pommie forward who dealt to Graham was just the first in a long queue of rivals who used foul means in an attempt to reduce his impact on a game. Graham's silky skills have always carried with them an unwanted burden. Unlike rugby where a team functions with four or five key decision-makers, league reduces the emphasis to one or two important playmakers. The temptation for opponents is always there to hobble these crucial men through fair means or foul. Graham often felt like he was playing football with a giant bullseye on his jersey. During his days at North Sydney, the dictum that 'if you stopped Mark Graham you stopped the Bears' was standard fare.

At international level, it was even more important that his influence be blunted. Indeed, it was to the undying shame of the Australians that they felt the need to employ unseemly tactics during the 1988 World Cup final at Eden Park when Kangaroo forward Steve Roach blatantly hit Graham from behind early in the match, reducing the Kiwi matchwinner to a dazed passenger for the rest of the game. 'Sharko' was seen as a danger by the Aussies every time he played against them, and plenty of times they nailed him, wrote Gary Freeman in his book *Tiger, Tiger, Kiwi, Rooster*. "That's what happens to great players. They become targets."

With his status as a marked man came an inordinate number of injuries. In fact, rarely in his lengthy career did Graham ever play without some form of a niggling problem. And some of his injuries were horrifying. Early in my sports journalism career in New Zealand, I wrote a feature on Graham's injury problems for the now defunct *Auckland Sun*. No other story I have written during my 15-year career has evoked as much comment and discussion. I'd like to think it was because the piece was wonderfully crafted. In truth it wasn't. But it did contain a frightening run-down of the injuries Graham had suffered during his career.

We headlined the story "The Hit Man" (in a play on the obvious) and featured a giant photo of Graham standing, hands on hips, in a pair of underpants. His impressive physique was captivating enough (female readers certainly thought so!) but we then overlaid small graphic boxes arrowed towards the different parts of his body that had been severely injured during his career. Those who read of the toll league had extracted on Mark Graham's body were staggered. They learned that for several years of his career Graham had to roll out of his bed to get up in the morning because of the debilitating injuries he was suffering from. And that he couldn't bend one arm to drink a glass of water because of the nerve damage in his battered shoulder.

The list of attrition suffered by Graham is frightening: a burst eardrum, nerve damage to his neck, concussion, a broken nose, six smashed teeth, a fractured cheekbone, both shoulders dislocated, a collarbone sheared, muscle wastage in one shoulder, an entire ribcage broken, pelvic bone and sciatic nerve damage, a broken hand, a broken thumb, snapped quad muscle in his right thigh, torn knee and ankle ligaments and torn achilles tendons.

Graham remembers being on the receiving end of a vicious elbow jolt during a club match against Parramatta in 1986. "It knocked me senseless," he recalled. "I was as crook as three people but I eventually got up and staggered around. I could feel something rolling around in my mouth. My mouthguard was on the ground and when I went to put it back in it wouldn't fit. It was then I realised half my teeth had been shoved back down my throat. I lost six in one hit. Then everytime I breathed, the air would hit the exposed nerves. It was like an electric current that kept zapping me every time I opened my mouth."

There was further ignominy to come. "Nobody seemed to know who did it," explained Graham. "I watched the video later and you wouldn't believe it but a bloody TV commercial came on right before the tackle. I never did find out who did it." Graham recently had a nasty reminder of that incident. "The dentist didn't do the right job," he says. "My capped teeth had abscesses in them and I ended up with diseased gums. I've had to pay out big money to have my teeth and gums fixed up."

It was this side of the so-called glamour sport that few were aware of. In Graham's biography *Mark My Words*, his North Sydney teammate Fred Teasdell recalled one terrifying incident when Graham suffered a severe concussion in a match in 1983. Teasdell related how, after the heavy blow, Graham was finally persuaded to leave the field. Teasdell was also in the dressing room because of an injury and was stunned when the normally mild-mannered Graham suddenly attacked him. Graham then started punching giant holes in the wall with his bare knuckles. Teasdell raced off to get help and he and several club officials eventually restrained Graham and made him lie down.

A few minutes later Graham hauled himself off to the showers, turned on the hot water only and stepped under the scalding spray oblivious to what he was doing. Fortunately, an official got to the taps before Graham caused some serious damage to his skin. Taken to hospital, he was later told exactly what he'd done. To this day, he doesn't remember anything of the episode and remains eternally embarrassed at having tried to hit Teasdell, a good friend. The most remarkable aspect of the entire story, though, is that moments before he went off – and still in his groggy state – Graham had put away a Norths team-mate for a try that ultimately proved the difference in the match!

Graham's worst injury came in 1984 when he severely dislocated his left shoulder, crushing nerves and destroying a vital muscle in his back. The surgeon recommended retirement. Predictably, Graham would have none of that. The injury left a gory legacy. Graham has a "hollow" in his back where the muscle has completely wasted away. Due to the nerve damage in his shoulder and neck, his left arm was restricted in movement towards the end of his career. To drink with it, he used to have to project his elbow at right angles to his shoulder and rotate his wrist.

In the last few years of playing, Graham would always tackle on his right side to protect the "dickey" shoulder. The injuries then compounded his problems. His right forearm, which had had to be taped with padding since the 1982 season, developed worrying calcification of the bone because of the constant tackling. He also encountered lower back problems created from the stress of his upper body injuries. And near the end of his career, if he even attempted to kick a football he would double over in agony because the cartilage around his pelvic bone had almost totally worn away.

Yet despite this astonishing toll extracted on his body, Graham would always attempt to stay on the field after taking a big hit and regarded playing with some form of injury as part and parcel of being a professional. "I thought that was pretty fair," he rationalises. "The clubs were paying me good money to do something I was supposedly pretty good at so I had no problem with playing with the odd injury."

Tall, powerful, committed...and always looking to get the ball away.
Mark Graham at the peak of his powers.

At the time I penned the *Auckland Sun* article I wondered in print what sort of shape Graham would be in 10 years after retiring from league. Happily he is a rare case in that his body has responded positively to retirement. "It must be my metabolism," he grins. "My shoulders have come right and generally I'm in good shape."

Graham's ability to inspire made him a natural leader. Indeed, Ces Mountford named him Kiwi captain for the 1980 end-of-season tour of Great Britain when Graham was still only 23. The series was squared when the Poms won the third test but Graham feels the Kiwi forward pack from that tour was the best New Zealand unit he was ever involved with. "It was a really hard no-frills pack, he recalls. "We had Mark Broadhurst, Alan Rushton, Butch Coll, Graeme West. I was off the back, not that they needed me for the hard stuff, not with those guys around. If someone was whistling up around my ears with tackles, I'd just give the other blokes a number. 'Get rid of No. 10', I'd just say, and next thing you know the bloke was being stretchered off! Geez, they were hard bastards, that lot. The harder the game got the more they enjoyed it. That was back in the days when the packs used to back off five yards or so and just charge into one another in the scrums. I don't think we ever lost anything in comparison to any pack back then. If the opposition wanted to stand up and throw 'em, 'Broadie', Kevin Tamati and Alan Rushton would go absolutely mad and there usually wouldn't be enough left for Butch and 'Westie'."

Graham retained the captaincy against France in 1981 and on the tour of Australia the following year. When Graham Lowe took over in '83, he invested even more responsibility in Graham. The Kiwis lost the first test 16-4 against Australia at Carlaw Park. Graham was carried off with a knee injury and watched New Zealand's brilliant 19-12 second test victory at Lang Park from the sidelines. 1984 was a frustrating season for Graham. He was belted from pillar to post playing for Norths and had particular problems with shoulder injuries.

Graham was back to his defence-defying best in '85, though. He was inspiring in the hard-fought series against Australia and turned in one of his greatest performances in the historic 18-0 third test shut out of the Kangaroos at Carlaw Park, his first and only win over the world champions. Halfback Clayton Friend delighted in running off Graham and scored two tries.

At the end of the season, Graham reaped the honour of becoming the first, and still the only, New Zealander to captain the side on two tours of Great Britain. His first test performance where he defied Des Drummond's cheap shot and popped ankle ligaments was his greatest in a Kiwi jersey as New Zealand won 24-22. The injuries kept him out of the second test and his leadership was badly missed as the Poms won 25-8. Knowing his team needed him, he spurned medical advice to play at Elland Road, home of the Leeds United soccer team, in the series decider which ended in a 6-all draw (with a disgraceful refereeing performance where the Poms were helped no end by a 22-7 penalty count in their favour).

"That was the most painful match of my career," he recalls. "I did it real tough with the ankle through that game. Even before the match, they had to give me pain-killing injections to get me off the bus. Then they had to inject me again through the tape at halftime. I had to have more injections after the game just to get the tape off. I went straight to hospital to get the ankle X-rayed again. I couldn't go to the after-match function because it was so sore, so I just bought a bottle of whiskey, went back to my room and got motherless. It was the only way I could sleep because the pain was so bad."

If his ability to defy continual injury horrors that would have prematurely ended the career of most other players was one of the hallmarks of Mark Graham, another striking one was his compelling loyalty and honesty. Graham played for only one club in Sydney, despite a host of tempting offers from big-spending clubs like Manly and Balmain. He also stood out of international football for a year in protest over the New Zealand Rugby League's ill-considered treatment of Graham Lowe when he was dumped as Kiwi coach. And he walked away from the golden handshake of a single season with Wakefield Trinity when the English club tried to dud fellow Kiwi Brent Todd out of a portion of his contract money.

Raised a Catholic and still a religious if somewhat earthy, man, Graham's staunch principles were also further shaped by his long relationship with Lowe which dates back to 1974 when they were pitched together in Otahuhu's third grade side. "'Lowie' and I always had this philosophy that you had to look in the mirror and be happy with the bloke staring back at you. And that means that if you make a deal you stick to it no matter what," says Graham.

He was true to his word throughout his career. Shortly after he arrived at Brisbane Norths in 1980 on a deal which earned him a $A500 sign-on fee, $A200 a win and $A100 a try, Graham indirectly discov-

Three men who put Kiwi league on the map: Mark Graham, Graham Lowe and Kevin Tamati.

ered that most other players in the club were on significantly more money. And few of them were performing as well as he was for the Devils. "A few people felt I should make a song and dance about it but I figured that if you were happy with the money when you signed, which I was, and then you find out somebody else is getting twice as much as you it's their good luck," he says. "If you were happy with the terms before you knew you should be happy afterwards. You don't say 'I'm outta here'."

Certainly a commendable attitude. But woe betide anybody who regarded Graham as a soft touch or tried to take him for a ride. He was involved in a celebrated dispute with Sydney Norths after signing one contract. "The secretary at the time told me he would build a superannuation element into the contract," Graham recalls. "Fortunately I was smart enough to get him to put it in writing in a letter. Not long after, one night after training this same bloke walked past me as I was heading to the showers and just casually told me he didn't intend honouring those things in the letter. I told him that was why I signed. He said: 'Too bad, it's gone'.

"I couldn't believe it. I ripped into him and went straight to the board of directors to sort it out. When I showed them the letter they said they would think about honouring it. I replied by telling them that while they were 'thinking about' honouring it, they could look for another loose forward because I was outta there."

A stand-off ensued and quickly developed into a massive media event. "I had Channel Seven, Nine and Ten all camped in my driveway. It was like a 24-hour circus," recalls Graham. Yet because he was also in dispute with the Norths coach of the time over his antiquated training methods, Graham was worried he might still get shafted despite being legally and morally in the right. Ever cautious of the game's image, the New South Wales Rugby League got involved as mediators and Graham and the Norths directors were summonsed to appear at the league's Phillips Street headquarters.

"The bloke who ordered us in there was Tom Bellew who had ties to the Norths club, so I wasn't overly optimistic of a fair hearing," said Graham. "I put forward my case and then the lawyers with the Norths directors put forward theirs. Bellew looked at everything and then announced that Norths had until noon the next day to deposit the disputed amount of money into the NSWRL's account for me or he would fine them the same amount of money, pay it to me and grant me a free transfer. I won that battle."

Graham was always steadfast on what he regarded as matters of principle, even if it cost him financially as it did when he went to England to wind down his playing career at the end of 1988 after retiring from Norths. He had always been earnestly sought by English clubs who admired his game-breaking skills which were ideal for the more open game in the United Kingdom. The English clubs also didn't lack cash. The struggling Wakefield Trinity club approached him to join fellow Kiwi forward Brent Todd and former Kangaroo backline whizz Steve Ella as their three overseas imports.

The money was good so Graham said 'what the hell'. It was to turn into a disaster. Graham could not believe how antiquated Wakefield's training methods were. He had already endured a messy personal battle at Norths with former coach Greg Hawick over the same issue years earlier. Always a visionary and innovator, Graham knew the days of players running round the field lap after lap were long gone. He had unashamedly helped engineer the dumping of Hawick, whom he considered totally out of his depth, and had been instrumental in the introduction of modern training methods at the Bears den which, not coincidentally, have made Norths remarkably more competitive in recent years. Yet here he was in the north of England running into the same old problems.

Graham wasn't sure he still had the stomach for another fight. He largely kept quiet and tried his best. But a different issue brought things to a head. "They were trying to dud 'Toddy' (Brent Todd) on some of his contract money and I wasn't going to cop that," says Graham. "They were getting on Toddy's case because he wasn't scoring tries. That's the mentality over there. They expect their imports to do the impossible. They want them to bail them out in every match and they weren't happy Toddy wasn't getting over the line enough. But I pointed out to them who was topping the tackle count and hit-ups. He was doing his job and I told them not to blame him for the faults of the others."

Graham made it clear to the club board that if they reneged on any part of their deal with Todd, he would join his fellow New Zealander in quitting and returning to Australia. "They thought I wouldn't go through with the threat because they were paying me such big money," Graham recalled. He can still remember the aghast faces of the directors after they called what they thought was his bluff. Graham walked out. He had played only four months of the season. It was the last football he was to play.

The Wakefield Trinity experience soured Graham's attitude towards English league which he has always regarded as 'Mickey Mouse anyway'. He believes that any New Zealander who is serious about making his mark in international league is much better off playing in the Australian competition. "If I had my way, I wouldn't allow any New Zealanders to go to England," he says earnestly. "I don't believe it's hard enough over there. There have been some great Kiwi players who have gone over to England when they would have become better players if they had come to Australia."

He is disappointed, for example, that Kevin Iro quit Australian league and returned to English league. "Kevin wasn't really a success at Manly and would have had to take a pay cut to stay there. He opted not to and I can understand that. League is his profession. But I've always felt that no matter how much money I was paid now, in 20 years it was always going to seem a pittance. So I'd rather they gave me the cup any day of the week."

The perfect athlete…"he could do anything," says Graham Lowe.

Graham believes that Dean Bell has been such a stunning success for Wigan in England because "he got such a solid grounding at Eastern Suburbs in Sydney during the mid-eighties…The way I see it is that any Kiwi good enough to hold down a first grade spot in Sydney is good enough to play for New Zealand. That's how big I feel the difference is between Australian and English football."

The Wakefield experience led to Graham doing what many had never believed him capable of. He completely walked away from league, cutting all ties to the game. Having returned to Sydney, he was eager to establish his own business and threw all his energies into his pest control agency which has developed into a great success. Occasionally, Graham would drag himself off to North Sydney Oval to watch his beloved Bears go around. Nobody would know he was there. "I'd just go and stand on the hill with all the hard-core fans and watch from there," he says. "I doubt any Norths officials even knew I was there."

Graham Lowe did, though. Lowe had left the Wigan club, being wooed to Sydney by a Manly club desperate to regain its old glories. Lowe believed Graham still had a season left in him as a player. "I hounded the hell out of him trying to get him to play for Manly," said Lowe. "I thought he retired prematurely but I couldn't get him to change his mind. So I changed tack. I asked if he was interested in becoming my assistant coach at Manly."

Graham was totally surprised by the offer. He didn't expect to be tempted but was intrigued when he found he was. "I told Lowie I'd do it for a couple of months to see if I enjoyed it or not," he said. Lowe says Manly's players, particularly the Sea Eagle forwards, responded extremely positively to Graham's input. "He's a hands-on coach," said Lowe. "He gets in there and talks to players, particularly youngsters, through all the skills. He had a big input at Manly."

The Australian club saw it that way too. Even when Lowe was forced to step down through ill health, Manly asked Graham to remain on under new coach Bob Fulton. Graham did. But at the end of the 1993 season, he was approached by his old club to take over as coach of North Sydney's President's Cup (Under-21s) grade team. The Bears believed Graham was the perfect man to raise their talented young cubs. He jumped at the offer 'to go home'. "My heart was always at Norths and it was also an opportunity to have control of a team myself. This way I get to find out whether I've got it as a coach or not."

The fact that Graham was listed among the contenders for the newly-created position of an Australian-based Kiwi selector (he withdrew from consideration and the job went to Hugh McGahan) indicates the NZRL is at least big enough to put its previous difficulties with their former captain behind them. Graham admits to an interest in becoming the Kiwi coach, but only if he feels he has proven himself at Norths.

Relations between the NZRL and Graham could never be described as harmonious. It always irked Graham that Kiwi league officials seemed so intent in putting obstacles in front of its leading players and coaches. He could never understand why it was that they demanded professionalism and commitment from their players but never showed the same qualities themselves as administrators. "The difference between rugby union and rugby league in New Zealand has always been that rugby union is an amateur game run by professionals and that rugby league was a professional game run by amateurs. You can't put it any simpler than that really," he says.

It amuses Graham that the NZRL is taking so much credit for the current boom in the game here. "They've failed to realise they've had nothing to do with it," he says. "The growth of interest in league in New Zealand has come from the Winfield Cup and the Winfield Cup alone. Nobody's interested in the competitions they've got running at home, and they're kidding themselves if they think any differently. They've ridden entirely on the coat-tails of the Australian game."

Nor does Graham have any regrets over his voluntary one-year self-exile from the Kiwi jersey in response to the NZRL's dumping of Lowe as coach. "Had I been into records and all that sort of stuff, I might have hung in there," he says. "But I had to do what I felt was right and I believed they had done the wrong thing by him [Lowe]. He'd done so much for league in New Zealand. Without him, you didn't have the game. And I think jealousy came into it. They didn't like the attention he was getting. People bag 'Lowie' but let's face it, we haven't been too successful since he left. We might have won the odd test but we haven't been as consistent. Back in Lowie's era we were consistently the world's No 2 league power. We're kidding ourselves if we think that way now."

For those reasons, Graham is pleased there has been such a strong Australian influence in assembling the Auckland Warriors. He be-

The calm after the storm. Graham with son Luke following a Norths game in 1983.

lieves Auckland's future is immense, provided the Warriors put in place similar philosophies to those that have seen the Brisbane Broncos become such a juggernaut in the game. "Geez, there's going to be some pressure on the Warriors but if they do it right and tap into the amazing resources New Zealand has with their juniors, they're going to do very well. Most of the league players in New Zealand are either Maori or Pacific Islanders. And they are built for rugby league.

"If you ever sat down to design a game specifically for Maori and Islanders, you'd come up with rugby league. They have the inherent skills and they thrive on physical confrontation. If the Warriors can harness that, they'll be very powerful. The Maori are naturally a very big people. And they're fast too. The Warriors must utilise sports science, fitness regimes, mental agility and skills training and ally it all to that natural ability. Hell, you're going to have some awesome athletes then."

Indeed. And if they're good enough, they may even find themselves being mentioned in the same breath as Mark Graham. If that happens, they'll know they really have arrived.

COLIN MEADS
'Pinetree'

"I'm the first guy to try my opposition out. If I come across a fellow who's going to let me get a moral advantage over him I'll carry on doing it. It's not for any personal satisfaction or gain. It's for the team's sake. I'm conscious when it's being done to me and move quickly to overcome it. If these activities are causing trouble then you call it quits. Look, I'm no bloody angel. If I can gain the advantage by a bit of gamesmanship I'll be the first to do it for what it can mean to the team. You play this game on a manly basis and you expect the opposition to try for the same sort of advantage. I'll let no one persistently put one over me. The player who beats you at playing the game is another matter. But no one will beat me by the constant use of dubious tactics."– Colin Meads, 1972.

TWICKENHAM can be a daunting place. Sixty thousand Englishmen singing 'Swing Low, Sweet Chariot' is intimidating for even the most experienced rugby teams. It was like that on the opening day of the 1991 World Cup. England were to kick off the tournament by taking on the defending champions, New Zealand. But first the International Rugby Board had organised what passed as an opening ceremony. Actually it was pretty lame. The Poms might fancy themselves as organisers par excellence. In reality, they're not. Still, the Twickenham crowd were right into the spirit of things. The 16 nations competing were introduced to the English crowd by virtue of one of their rugby greats. All legends. There were Ollie Campbell, Paul McLean and Gerald Davies among others.

New Zealand were left to be introduced last, a mark of respect for the defending champions. Predictably, the jeering began the moment the ground announcer boomed: "And last of all, the defending champions New Zealand". The noise was deafening. Then suddenly the Twickenham crowd recognised who was dwarfing the William Webb Ellis trophy in those huge hands. Colin Meads. Hell, it's 'Pinetree'! The greatest All Black of all time. A wave of reverence swept around the massive stadium. Within moments the booing was replaced by respectful clapping. It's debatable whether any All Black other than Colin Earl Meads could have had such an impact on the crowd. After all, he had his moments of controversy in the United Kingdom, not to mention other parts of the rugby world. Yet Meads has risen above any such stigmas to attain an aura no other All Black can match.

When Gary Whetton erased Meads' record as the most capped All Black test player, he almost felt compelled to apologise to the great man. "I feel a bit awkward in taking his record," said Whetton at the time. "I don't consider myself to be in the same category as Pinetree. He was the greatest of them all. Even now, whenever I see him, there's still reverential qualities about him. Everybody looks up to Colin Meads."

Indeed. When major touring teams like the British Lions come to New Zealand, overseas journalists feel compelled to make a trip to the Meads farm for the obligatory feature story. Colin Meads is still big news internationally. Even Meads' flirtation with South Africa as coach of the 1986 rebels, the Cavaliers, could not dim the affection New Zealanders held for him. The unsanctioned tour to the republic cost him his position on the national selection panel. But by the beginning of the 1990s, he was back in an influential position as a councillor within the New Zealand Rugby Football Union. By 1994, he had been named as manager of the All Blacks.

Perhaps the greatest compliment that can be paid to Meads' enduring popularity comes from grass roots rugby fans and, strangely enough, the commercial sector. When leading company Vogels wanted an icon to help sell their bread, they didn't seek out a grinning Va'aiga Tuigamala or pasty-faced Jeff Wilson. Instead the Queen Street marketing men packed themselves and their shoe phones into their BMWs and sped south to that certain King Country farm.

Time has not dimmed Meads' deeds either. The 'Mud and Glory' television series of a few years back exposed a whole new generation to the Meads legend. Young kids, convinced yesterday's rugby heroes could not hold a candle to today's superstars of a modernised and demanding game, suddenly learned their fathers weren't exaggerating when they talked of a rampaging Meads powerfully scattering Springbok and Lions defences. Finally, they could see it for themselves. It might have been in black and white and the images occasionally grainy, but not even the inferior pictures could dim the excitement of seeing Meads, magnificently striding upfield, the ball stitting in one giant hand ("I always got into trouble for doing that," he says now) as if it was merely an oversized pinecone. Little wonder one rival said he would rather tackle a front-end loader than Meads on the burst.

When Meads goes to any rugby ground, or indeed makes a public appearance anywhere, he invariably draws as many autograph seekers as the top players. His first season as All Black manager (1994) represented Meads' 40th year of involvement in top class rugby as either a player, coach or administrator. Even though those in the Waitete club knew they had something special on their hands when a raw-boned farmer's son almost made the King Country representative team at the age of 17, few could imagine just how bright his star would ultimately shine.

The only thing that kept Meads out of provincial rugby that year was King Country selector Eddie Walker's contention that Meads was simply "too young". Physically, he was already a daunting specimen, having experienced a phenomenal growth spurt, tipping the scales at almost 15 stone and standing 6ft 4ins. His rep debut came the following year against Counties where Meads made an impact in more ways than one. Playing flanker, he arrived late for a ruck and found himself receiving the ball in a first-five position. Although he still maintains he simply didn't know what to do, Meads calmly potted a goal!

It was no surprise when he was selected for the New Zealand Colts trials that same year. But before the trial Meads was to endure the first of several brushes with the rugby law – namely referees, coaches and administrators. He had deliberately tripped a stroppy opposition lineout forward during a heated club match and found himself hauled before the King Country judiciary committee just three days before the Colts trials. Eddie Walker gave him a fearful dressing down and then informed the ashen-faced teenager he wanted to see him out-

Famous families...Stan and Colin Meads alongside two other great All Black brothers, Don and Ian Clarke.

A colossal sight on a rugby field...the great Pinetree storms upfield against Wales.

side. "Take no bloody notice of what I said in there," Walker whispered. "Get down to Palmerston North and get stuck into them." Meads did exactly that and made a New Zealand Under-21 team named to tour, of all places, Ceylon. Also in the team was Wilson Whineray, a man Meads quickly came to admire.

But moments of indiscretion did dog Meads throughout his career to the extent that long-time rugby journalist Terry McLean has felt obliged several times to publicly express his belief that the great All Black possessed a cruel streak that sometimes surfaced. Certainly, when writing this book, if I expected any one player to be challenged under the criteria I set out in the foreword, it was Meads, simply because of the celebrated Ken Catchpole incident. Indeed, when Richard Loe was evoking Australian ire by wreaking havoc on the 1992 tour, one Sydneysider wrote to a leading newspaper wondering why his fellow countrymen were so surprised by the All Blacks' behaviour. "After all," he wrote, "this was the same country who produced Colin Meads, the All Black who ended the great Ken Catchpole's career by pulling his legs apart like they were chicken bones."

It wasn't the first time it had happened. After the Test against the Wallabies in Sydney in 1968, Meads received a letter from a former Australian forward Keith Cross. Inside was a newspaper clipping which described the rehabilitation Catchpole was going through. Attached was a note from Cross saying: "Are you proud of this effort,

Colin?" Reality is that Meads has been unfairly tainted over the Catchpole affair. The superb Australian halfback, caught in a ruck, tried desperately to stop the ball coming out the All Black side by trapping it with his free foot. Meads legitimately grabbed Catchpole's leg to pull it away so the All Blacks could ruck the ball. What he didn't know was that Catchpole's other leg was trapped by the mass of bodies. As Meads pulled, the muscles in Catchpole's upper leg and groin tore badly. The players around Meads from both sides could see it was unintentional and the referee did not penalise the New Zealander. "But in the eyes of the Australians I was just a dirty bastard," Meads told his biographer Alex Veysey. "I knew 'Catchy' well as a man and he was a fine halfback, yet I could feel no guilt about it because it was the sort of thing that happens in any club match. All Australia thought I was a bloody criminal and I know Australia has still got this against me."

The other incident that dogged Meads throughout his career – and which he feared would be the only thing he was remembered for – was his sending off against Scotland on the 1967 All Black tour of the United Kingdom. Fred Allen's '67 All Blacks were a special team. Old-timers will tell you that the only All Black side of recent vintage to even remotely challenge them for world dominance was the brilliant New Zealand side of 1987 to 1989.

Before the All Blacks had reached Murrayfield, they had already seen off England 23-11, Wales 13-6 and France 21-15. Scotland were no match either and with New Zealand leading 14-3 with just a couple of minutes on the clock, spectators were beginning to file out of Murrayfield thinking little else could happen now. The Scots were defending when a ball shot wildly out of a ruck towards the home team's flyhalf David Chisholm. Meads detached from the ruck and sped after it. Meads takes up the story courtesy of Veysey's book: "I could see Chisholm rushing across to clear the ball. I thought I could get a foot to the ball before he got to it. I had to stretch to it and actually kicked the ball as he stooped to it. I kicked it into his body. Frank Laidlaw (Scotland's hooker) yelled: 'Did you see that ref, the dirty bastard'. Chisholm had gone to ground but obviously wasn't hurt. The referee arrived. To this day I am positive he did not see what happened. I am just as sure it was the commotion Frank Laidlaw was making that made up his mind for him. He ordered me off. I was shocked, couldn't believe it. My mind sort of tumbled. I took a couple of paces away, stopped and half-turned back thinking, 'He can't mean it'. Brian Lochore, our captain, was talking to the referee. Vaguely I thought, 'Thank God, now it will be all right'. Ken Gray and Chris Laidlaw seemed to be arguing with him too. But he said, 'You're off', and once they say that, you're gone. As I walked I was conscious of the close crowd booing me. I thought, 'I'd like to get a hold of one of you'. Mostly, though, I had this terrible feeling of shame. 'That's the end', I thought. 'That's finished everything'."

After the match, Chisholm came into the All Black dressing room to express his sympathy to Meads. "I'm very sorry," he said. "You kicked the ball." The great Welsh commentator and former flyhalf Cliff Morgan emphatically stated that Meads should not have been sent off. And even TP McLean, often Meads' greatest critic, claimed the Irish referee, Kevin Kelleher, had over-reacted. The All Black manager, Charlie Saxton, and coach Fred Allen backed Meads to the hilt and were just as angry as the big man himself when he was suspended for two matches. Saxton was on the three-man judicial committee but could not sway the Englishman and Welshman who sat in judgement alongside him. Meads' greatest fear was that he would only ever be remembered for the sending-off.

Fortunately, that didn't happen. The incident remains only a minor blight on a magnificent career. The irony of the Murrayfield episode is that Meads probably wouldn't have played Scotland had he not been, in the words of fellow team-mate Alister Hopkinson, "such a hard bastard". In the previous international, he had been viciously dealt to by a thuggish French side at the Colombes Stadium in Paris. In a shameful incident, a French forward callously and blatantly kicked Meads in the head. Meads had taken the ball from a Willie Away lineout and driven it on. As play moved on, a Frenchman swiftly kicked the prone Meads.

All Black winger Tony Steele, a National Party MP up until the 1993 election, witnessed the brutal assault. "The sight of him lying there was such a shock," Steele told Veysey for Meads' book. "He was Colin Meads who just never got hurt. I couldn't believe it. When finally he got up there was a big gash on the side of his head." Meads needed a mass of stitches to seal the wound and had to have it taped for the Scottish match for protection. Ironically, the referee for the Paris international, Englishman Bob Burrell, failed to send the Frenchman off. Yet the same Mr Burrell ran the line at Murrayfield and inflamed that incident by saying he would not referee again if the judiciary committee did not endorse Kelleher's decision to send Meads off.

The other occasion when Meads was dealt an injustice came on the 1970 tour of South Africa. Meads was considered crucial to the All Blacks' hopes of winning their first series on South African soil. The South Africans obviously thought so too. Early in the tour, in a match against Eastern Transvaal, the locals turned in a performance which will always be a blight on South African rugby's reputation. Alan Sutherland's nose was broken by a kick to the face and other All Blacks were victims of cheap shots as well. But it was Meads who literally suffered the most demoralising blow. A well-aimed kick cracked Meads' left forearm. It was delivered by Eastern Transvaal captain Skip Henderson, said to be the same man who broke Sutherland's nose.

In testimony to Meads' granite qualities and undying determination, he played out the match. Only afterwards did he have X-rays which revealed "a dirty big break". Many New Zealanders felt the All Blacks' chances of rolling the Springboks ended there and then. It is to Henderson and Eastern Transvaal's eternal shame that they were responsible for Meads' injury which had such a dramatic effect on the outcome of the '70 series. The irony is that no high-profile All Black has fought harder for South Africa's right to remain in international rugby than Colin Meads. In many respects, it has cost him dearly. He lost friends because of it; he lost respect in the eyes of some who had idolised him. And he lost his position as a national selector – and with it any chance of ever becoming the All Black coach – when he led the Cavaliers to the republic in 1986.

Meads has always felt an affinity with South African rugby. But for the country's standing in the game, Meads almost certainly would have made his test debut against the Springboks in 1956. He'd played for the North Island that same year but at 19, the selectors felt he was too young to be thrown into a series that had assumed war-like importance for New Zealand following the 4-0 humiliation of Fred Allen's tourists in 1949. "A number of years later Tom Morrison [an All Black selector at the time] told me that was the only reason they didn't pick me," confirmed Meads. Instead he played for the combined King Country-Wanganui team against the tourists.

Meads remembers graphically the tension of the Boks tour. "It

A break felt around the world...Colin Meads and the arm injury that
was to have a major impact on the 1970 tour of South Africa.

wasn't political tension because that hadn't become an issue yet," he recalled. "When the South Africans arrived, it was like they had to be beaten. The provinces were virtually told it was their responsiblity to soften up the Boks before the tests. I remember we had a number of games as a combined side to get our teamwork and spirit up, which was unheard of back then." Meads' next confrontation with the South Africans was to come wearing the black jersey four years later on the tour of the republic. He was in his fourth year wearing the silver fern after having made his debut on the 1957 tour of Australia. Chosen as a loose forward, he played five games at lock, three as a flanker and one as a No 8. That was to be the pattern of Meads' early All Black career. Not until Nev MacEwan retired in 1961 did Meads become a permanent lock.

The 1960 tour was as difficult as Meads had anticipated. The canny South Africans had arranged 11 lead-up matches before the first test which gave them more than ample opportunity to earnestly study the All Blacks. It was a mistake New Zealand was to repeat 10 years later. They showed their hand completely in the lead-up matches and the South Africans knew exactly what they were going to do at any given time. The first test was lost 13-0 and Meads admitted to growing self-doubt. "We were comprehensively hosed out in the first test and after it I was uncomfortable," he said in his book. "I wondered what the people back home thought of it – the Tiny Whites, the Bob Duffs, the Kevin Skinners, the Bill Clarks who had performed such great deeds against the Springboks in 1956. But after the second test (won 11-3 by the All Blacks) we felt we could live with those players; we had beaten the Springboks when all seemed stacked against us."

The third test was to be a classic, drawn 11-all after Don Clarke, in a performance lauded as the finest of his career, landed a sideline conversion of Frank McMullen's try with just minutes left. Meads had also made a marked contribution, scoring a valuable try for the All Blacks. But the series decider was lost 8-3 in a howling weather conditions in Port Elizabeth.

By 1965 when South Africa next toured New Zealand, Meads was firmly entrenched as an All Black legend. He'd been dropped for his brother Stan for one test against Australia in 1962 but other than that had been immovable since, his stature growing on the 1963-64 tour of the United Kingdom where he played 24 of the 36 matches and first locked horns with Irish foe Willie-John McBride. This Springbok side was not the match of previous South African sides. The All Blacks won the first two tests but blew their chance of a clean sweep to avenge the 1949 whitewash when complacency helped the tourists win the third international at Lancaster Park 19-16 after New Zealand had led 16-5 at halftime. "We were over-confident," said Meads. There were no such mistakes in the fourth test, won handsomely 20-3, the heaviest defeat the Springboks had suffered in an international until Australia beat an inexperienced side upon the country's return from isolation in 1992.

Meads was surprised at the timidity of the '65 Boks. "It was so out of character for them," he said. "I've always admired their rugby because like us, they were proud of their achievements. Every game counts to them, like it does to us. They're not like Australia or France who drop provincial games and think nothing of it. They have a pride in their performance, just as we do. That's what makes them such formidable foes. And they recognise it in us too. That's why they respect us far more than any other rugby nation."

The 1970 tour of South Africa was to be Meads' last tangle with the old enemy as a player. Like the tour of 10 years before, there were to be many regrets. There was much hype before the tour. The All Blacks had stitched together a remarkable record since the successful 1963-64 tour of the UK, winning 25 tests and dropping just two – one against Australia in 1964 and the third test against the South Africans the following year. Many New Zealanders believed this was the All Black team that could finally defeat the Springboks in a series on South African soil. Meads was named vice-captain to Brian Lochore. But when Lochore suffered a hand injury in a match in Perth on the way to South Africa, Meads found himself leading the All Blacks in the early provincial games.

Although not a man who warmed to captaincy, Meads proved an inspirational leader as the All Blacks played some scintillating rugby early in the tour. According to pressmen covering the tour, Meads' form was near the best of his career, matching his commanding dominance produced against the 1966 British Lions. But then came the tragedy of Eastern Transvaal in the sixth tour match. After that, things quickly began to unravel. The depth in the squad did not match previous tours during the '60s, several players complained coach Ivan Vodanovich over-trained the side and by the end of the tour 27 of the selected 30 players had played in a test at some time of the series. The

Watch your step!...Meads offers a not-so-quiet warning to Springbok great Frik du Preez in the Northern Transvaal game in 1970.

Springboks won the first test 17-6 but New Zealand fought back gamely to take the second international 9-8.

Meads returned shortly after, leading the tourists against South Western Districts with his arm solidly strapped. He was named in third test team, something he now regrets. "I don't think I should have played in the third test...the arm was not right and I knew it," he said in his book. "The week leading up to the test was arm, arm, arm instead of rugby, rugby, rugby...people would simply not let me forget it. The morning of the match I was hooked up to the BBC for an interview not about rugby but about my damned arm...I was so conscious of it that I played accordingly...afterward I felt I had let the team down by playing."

Even despite the problems on the tour, the All Blacks came close to achieving the impossible. Meads says the third test was lost only because of New Zealand's high unforced error rate while the fourth, won 20-17 by the Boks, was eminently winnable.

After the great feats of the 1960s, the seventies opened with disappointment for the All Blacks and Meads. Tragically, his final two years as an All Black were disappointing in terms of the team's results. Meads had been outstanding against the 1966 Lions but the '71 tourists were to prove of deeper character than their predecessors. Meads had the added responsibility of captaining the All Blacks against the Lions following the unexpected retirement of Brian Lochore (although he was to be wooed back by the desperate national selectors come the third test). The Brits won the first test 9-3 when Fergie McCormick missed several kicks at goal. But Meads and the All Blacks stormed back to win the second 22-12. The home team performed poorly to lose the third test 13-3 before the historic 14-all draw in the fourth international, giving the Lions their only ever series victory over New Zealand.

Despite scoring eight tries to six, the All Blacks had lost to the educated boot of Welshman Barry John. Meads believes New Zealand fell into the trap of trying to run the ball too much against the Lions when the forwards hadn't done the necessary graft.

The All Blacks also found the Lions a formidable outfit up front. At different stages of the series, things often became heated. Meads recalled one incident in the second test when Irish prop Sean Lynch was at loggerheads with his All Black opposite Richie Guy. At one scrum, the All Blacks heeled the ball but found themselves going backwards at a great rate of knots following an enormous Lions heave. "Lynch was giving it his all and yelled out: 'How do you like this for scrummaging, you *$%[&!'. I said to him: 'Bloody impressive. But if you pull your head out of the scrum you'll find we've just scored a try'. Sid Going had nipped round the back."

General opinion is that while Meads had an outstanding career for the All Blacks, he reached his peak form in 1965 and 1966 in the home series against the Springboks and then the Lions. His dominance of the Lions lineout forwards is legendary and, in the open, he was frequently dynamic. Never one to suffer fools gladly, his intolerance of poor referees and spoiling tactics often saw him resorting to jungle justice. He did not like other players taking liberties with either him or his side.

Once in a King Country-Taranaki match, lock Ian Eliason spiralled dramatically out of a lineout, winning the favour of the referee who assumed Meads had felled him. In fact, Meads had not touched him. Eliason had performed a classic Hollywood and won a penalty for his side. At the next break in play, Meads quietly but persuasively informed Eliason that if he fell out of another lineout again it would be because Meads had knocked him out.

While Meads' magnificent All Black career ended after the fateful Lions visit, he was to continue playing for his beloved King Country. But only after recovering from an horrific car accident. Always the consummate clubman, he had been out painting roofs in a fund-raising exercise for Waitete in December, 1971. For a fortnight beforehand he had been working 16-hour days in the shearing shed, rising at 4.30am each day. That night, as Meads drove home to his Te Kuiti farm, it all caught up with him. He dozed off, his Landrover skewed up a bank and cartwheeled end over end. The wrecked vehicle was found 15 minutes later when a neighbour spotted the tail-lights. He found Meads unconscious.

The great forward had been thrown clear but he was badly hurt. Rushed to hospital, Meads did not regain consciousness until the next morning. He had broken three vertebrae. In the bluntest medical terms, he had broken his back. His body had to be encased in plaster over the entire summer. It wasn't until the end of March that he was finally released from the body cast. By June he was playing for King Country and harbouring hopes of touring to the United Kingdom with the All Blacks at the end of 1972.

Ultimately though, recognising his rugby philosophy was at odds with the newly-appointed All Black coach Bob Duff, he made himself unavailable for the tour. Several leading rugby writers of the time expressed the belief that if ever Meads' steadying influence was needed on an All Black tour, it was on that troubled visit to the UK in 1972-73 which resulted in Keith Murdoch being sent home.

Meads was determined to play one more year in the black jersey, however. The Springboks were scheduled to tour New Zealand in 1973 and Meads trained the house down during the off-season in preparation for one last tilt at his respected enemy. He was crushed when the New Zealand Government postponed the tour. The blow sapped him and he made himself unavailable for provincial play in 1974, his final year of club football before retiring.

It wasn't long before Meads, so influential on the field, became equally influential off it, however – he has a lengthy and impressive record as an administrator. In 1986, he spent a year as an All Black selector only to be predictably dumped following the Cavaliers' excursion. Sent to purgatory for the South African trek, Meads was happy to pay his penance with King Country. He took over as the

Meads in the plaster case he had to wear over the summer of 1971-72 after breaking his back.

struggling union's chairman in 1987 and still holds the post now. His impact has been immense. Not only did he streamline the administration but he helped draw major sponsorship and cleared the way for provincial coaches to provide a professional approach to training and co-ordinating players.

Meads' finest moment in the role came in 1991 when King Country won promotion to the first division. He learned the news when phoned in London during the World Cup. Against all predictions, King Country has remained a first division union since its elevation. Meads can take a large slice of the credit.

Recognising his administrative skills, a new-look New Zealand Rugby Football Union headed by men of greater vision such as Eddie Tonks and Rob Fisher moved to encourage Meads to stand again. He was duly appointed a councillor in 1992 and has stayed since, a moderating voice whose views are greatly respected.

Often those views are controversial. For example, Meads is a staunch critic of the continual tinkering with rugby's rules by the lawmakers at International Board level. "We shifted house this year and while we were rummaging through all the old cupboards, I found a rule book from back in 1954," he said. "It was tiny. The 1994 one is 10 times as big and twice as complicated. I really feel rugby has got to get back to realistic laws because I don't think we've achieved what the lawmakers set out to do."

Meads is particularly disappointed with player attitudes over changes designed to make the game more entertaining. "The players and coaches have become more skilled at working round rules rather than getting on with the game. The rulemakers made them for the right reasons but if they're going to stick with them, they need to say to the players: 'You make them work'." Meads has also been a regular vocal critic of the Super 10 series. It greatly concerns him that club rugby has been eroded of both prestige and players in the past decade while he believes the Super 10 has simply increased provincial union and player greed. "We're creating frictions within New Zealand because leading players now have the attitude that they must be in Super 10 teams," he says. "If the Super 10 is going to do that to us, where will it end? Once upon a time, it was everybody wanting to get into a first division team. Now it's gone past that to everybody wanting to be in a Super 10 team."

Another strong conviction Meads holds comes from what he believes has been an over-reaction within New Zealand rugby to the threat of rugby league. He feels it is fundamentally wrong for rugby to change its rules and conditions simply because of what another code is doing. "It concerns me that our future direction is being governed by reports that are prepared on the basis of what other sports are doing," he says in a none-too-subtle reference to the NZRFU's

Farewell to a hero...an emotional Meads gathers himself before speaking to a sea of fans after his last big match in 1973.

controversial Boston Report, commissioned last year. "These people don't know what rugby means to New Zealand. Let's forget about league and other sports. Every sport has its ups and downs. Back in the early 80s, every kid was going to play soccer. What kids are playing soccer now? Let's get on with playing rugby and let's just play it better. If we're good at it, it'll look after itself. We don't need to copy the Winfield Cup. And just because a couple of our players go to league, we don't have to panic. Australia have had that problem for years. They responded by making rugby more and more attractive and they're not losing players anymore. You'll always lose one or two to league. We've got enough depth to cover it, and we'll still be just as good. Let them go".

I asked Meads to categorise both the rugby-playing nations and countries he had met during his lengthy career. Not surprisingly, the South Africans rate No 1 in both areas. "I guess in many ways it's because of their similarity to New Zealand," he responded. "The other thing was New Zealand had never really beaten them over there. They have this do-or-die attitude. They study you, they really put the acid on you in the sense that it's a national effort to beat the All Blacks. I don't think we do it as much. South Africa had a grapevine that just went in front of you. If you had one move one week, the next team knew it straight away. And this was in the days before television. I always said that we perhaps showed our strength too early on both tours. We played all our moves before the first test, didn't hold anything back and gave them too much of a look at us...In my era, Australia weren't the nation they are now. The modern player would probably say he respects Australia as much as any other country. The two countries I personally found the hardest were the French and the South Africans. The greatest quality of the French was their brilliant backs. They had the likes of Jo Maso who was probably the greatest back we ever played against. And before that were the Boniface brothers who were also brilliant. They would leave you for dead. They were a great side then, but very volatile. They're getting their act together now but back then they always had one or two rogues in their team and you encountered the odd incident. But I always admired their flair. And they were aggressive people too. You didn't knock the French around as much as you did a lot of other teams. If you charged at a Frenchman, he'd come up to meet you whereas some of the Home countries, they didn't come and meet you.

"The Welsh, before we even played them, were the country we feared the most because of their history and the great battles that had gone on before. So they were feared a lot. But take away their great fervour and the spirit of the crowd with their singing, the Welsh never struck me as great players. I think their decline was terribly sad. They had always been hard to beat. Their decline was tragic for world rugby. I think the game needs Wales at a higher level than they've been at for the last 10 years or so.

"England have improved now because they finally have their administrative act together. Back in our days, the more robust, rugged type of players just weren't considered for England selection because it wasn't considered to be part of the game to be aggressive. But that's completely changed now. Scotland used to give us as hard a time as any other country back in my day too."

Of the individual locks he faced, Meads has always rated his old Springbok rival Johan Claassen as the best he ever encountered. "I always respected Claassen," he says. "He was hard to put off his game, he was always going forward, he was a great lineout forward and a true international lock. Then there were the clashes we had with Willie-John McBride over the years. I had a lot of respect for him. And Walter

Spanghero from France was another whom I rated as one of the greats.

"Among the All Blacks, early in my career, Nev MacEwan was the lock we all respected. We came in after a great era of locks, the likes of the Tiny Whites, Bob Duffs and company. While I played with them as a youngster at trials, I never played with them at All Black level. But Nev MacEwan was a colossal man. He had a tremendous physique and was a huge jumper. But overall Stan (Meads) had to be the one. We played that much together that we had a real affinity. I felt we complemented each other. It was just the way it happened.

"Andy Haden always impressed me. I played against him when I was an old man and he was still a youngster. But Haden developed into a tremendous lock for New Zealand. He did New Zealand proud. Gary Whetton was very similar. The whole game has changed now of course. When Gary Whetton first came on the scene, he was considered a big, big lock. Now he's just a run-of-the-mill lock size-wise. He might not even be considered big enough now for some test teams."

Meads has some misgivings about the modern lineout. He detests the mass of arms and legs everywhere but doesn't agree with the common remedy offered of legalising lifting. "I don't think we want to get into lifting," he says. "I know a lot of people have advocated it but I think lineout jumping is a skill we should try to maintain. It's individual skill. Introduce lifting and it becomes a matter of who the strongest lifter is. I would like to see them back close together again. In our day, we stood right up against one another and we still got clean ball. Nowadays they're standing a yard apart and it's a real lottery. Everybody moves before the ball is thrown and there's a crunch and a crash. That's why the big, tall men have come into it, because of their extra height."

Meads also believes it was a backward move by administrators to make use of the outside arm illegal. "Everyone is either right-handed or left-handed," he says. "If you're right-handed, it's your outside hand and it's difficult to use only your left. I mean, if coaches wanted to get really technical about it, you would have one left-handed lock and one right-handed lock to maximise your chances."

Meads' appointment as All Black manager has kept him before a still adoring New Zealand rugby public. That same public richly honoured Meads in the final big game of his career which was to prove the catalyst of staggering scenes one Saturday afternoon in 1973 at

A legend still serving rugby...as an NZRFU councillor and as the current All Black manager.

Athletic Park. Following the postponement of the Springbok tour that year, the NZRFU hastily arranged an internal tour for the All Blacks. As a gesture to his great career, Meads was asked to lead a New Zealand Invitation XV against the All Blacks. The match was quickly seen as a final tribute to Meads.

With the help of an inspirational Sid Going, the scratch XV toppled the All Blacks. To this day, Meads genuinely regrets the result. Chaotic scenes followed the final whistle as Meads was brought to an elevated official dias in the stand. The cheering from the thousands of fans was overwhelming for Meads. They wanted to pay tribute to the great man. The goodwill was palpable. They were paying homage to Pinetree.

More than two decades later – as the scenes at Twickenham before the World Cup opener graphically illustrated – the respect still remains for Colin Meads, the greatest of All Black greats.

DENNIS WILLIAMS
'Legend'

The Poms had started well, quickly gaining the measure of the anxious Kiwis. They led 7-0 and New Zealand risked being overwhelmed. Dennis Williams, who had celebrated his 18th birthday the night before, hadn't been able to get into the game. He decided it was time to go looking for the ball. The Kiwis found themselves about 35 yards out from the Great Britain line when the leather finally fell in to Williams' hands for the first time. He ghosted crossfield, drawing the Pommie defence with him. Great Britain's legendary halfback Roger "The Dodger" Millward, then at the peak of his powers, shadowed him. Suddenly Williams, stopped, propped and sidestepped brilliantly through a half-gap between Millward and his inside centre. Up came the fullback. Bang! Another brilliant sidestep and he was over the line before the Poms realised what had happened. Dennis Williams had scored in his test debut with his first touch of the ball.

The car spun wildly on the dark highway before careering off the road. The passenger barely had time to register what was going on. When they arrived, the ambulance attendants found him lying dazed outside the wrecked vehicle. He was in severe shock. And although his only visible outward injury was a shattered and bloody elbow, he was obviously concussed. And who knows what sort of internal injuries he'd suffered. Dennis Williams was about to begin a battle requiring far more courage and tenacity than any he ever faced on the rugby league field.

IT boggles the mind to imagine what Dennis Williams would have been worth on the open football market had he been born 20 years later than he was.

Think about it for a moment. Consider a youngster so talented he played senior club football in Auckland at 15, was offered a full contract by Australian club Eastern Suburbs when he was just 16, was the Auckland representative team's leading tryscorer at 17, scored a try with his first touch of the ball in test football at 18 and was then offered a 10-year – yes, 10 years! – contract by glamour English club Wigan on the very same tour. Just what would John Monie and his Auckland Warriors be prepared to pay for a pedigree like that?

Former *Auckland Star* sports journalist Brian Doherty remembers the boy wonder Williams vividly. "In 1972, the Australians invited New Zealand on a three-match tour and the first test was played at the Sydney Cricket Ground," recalled Doherty. "Dennis was marking Bobby Fulton, who really was the golden-haired boy of the Australian scene by then. They thought he could do no wrong. Dennis was never the most graceful of joggers and I remember being in the SCG press box this day when he ran out. He had a sore calf muscle and so he had this small bandage on it.

"Combined with his jogging style, he looked a little ungainly. Anyhow, an Aussie writer next to me immediately began scoffing and saying: 'Jesus, have a look at the cripple marking 'Bozo' [Fulton]'. The game had been going about five minutes and, bang, Dennis went straight past Fulton with that magic step he had. So I piped up: 'Hell, the cripple's just beaten Bozo'. I didn't hear a word out of the bloke the rest of the game."

Dennis Williams was arguably the finest teenage prodigy New Zealand rugby league has ever seen. He remains the youngest player to wear the black jersey in a test, breaking into the team on the 1971 tour of Great Britain, going on to become vice-captain and then the captain before finally standing down from the international game in 1978, confirming his standing as one of the New Zealand game's greats without argument.

As early as 1969, the Auckland league grapevine was humming with talk of a brilliant young stand-off out Te Atatu way. At only 15 he was playing for Te Atatu's senior team in a rugged competition which, along with the aspiring stars in their 20s, featured battle-scarred freezing workers in their mid-to-late 30s who loved nothing more than throwing their considerable weight around the football field.

Dennis Williams scorches in for another try for Auckland in 1971, the year he broke into the Kiwis.

"The best player I every played with" – Mark Graham on Dennis Williams, pictured here against a French Selection in 1975.

But here was this kid not only surviving, but thriving. When he was only 16, Williams was selected in the Auckland Maori. He didn't tell them he had about as much Maori blood in him as Waka Nathan has Polish. His father was actually Samoan. But what the selectors didn't know wouldn't hurt them.

Dennis Williams was already an ambitious kid. "I was never a good sleeper as a kid and even as young as 13, I'd lie awake thinking about the day I was going to play for the Kiwis," he laughs. "Even back then I was plotting how I would get certain players out of the team. I was always a cocky, aggressive bugger." Indeed. But more importantly, Williams could back up his on-field swagger with footballing deeds. He so impressed the Auckland selectors that, despite his youth, they included him in an Auckland senior side to play the Kiwis who wanted a couple of warm-up games before heading off to the World Cup tournament in England and France that year. Still only 16, Williams crossed for two tries and kicked five goals as the Auckland seniors ran the Kiwis embarrassingly close.

Even though the Sydney club competition was a world away in those pre-Tina Turner days, word of this prodigious teenage talent in Auckland quickly filtered across the Tasman. Eastern Suburbs, later to play host to such rich Kiwi talents as Kurt Sorensen, Dean Bell, Gary Prohm, Kurt Sherlock and Gary Freeman, were quick to move. "Out of the blue, my parents got a phone call from Easts asking if we wanted to come over to have a look at their set-up," explained Williams. "They were very keen to sign me. They were prepared to pay me $20,000 over three years plus $200 a win, which in 1970 was a lot of money." Especially for a 16-year-old.

Williams was flattered, but never even got on the plane. "Things were a lot different back then," he explained. "Very few New Zealand players played professionally in Australia. Nobody here even knew what went on in the competition over there. Plus if you did accept a contract to play professionally in England or Australia, that was it as far as playing for New Zealand went. You were forgotten about. You couldn't play for your country. And at that stage of my life, I still wanted to play for New Zealand." Williams didn't have to wait long.

In 1971 Te Atatu had graduated to the Auckland premier competition and Williams quickly broke into the Auckland representative team. Australia toured the same year and Williams got two chances to show his wares against a formidable Kangaroo touring squad including some of the game's greats such as Fulton, Artie Beetson, Graeme Langlands, Bobby McCarthy and Ron Coote. The first came when he was selected in a New Zealand XIII to play the tourists in Huntly. Williams made an impression with a slick try. His second joust with the Australians came in Auckland colours. The Aussies had been beaten by New Zealand in the one-off test 24-3 and faced up to Auckland the following Tuesday night at Carlaw Park. Williams marked Fulton and was instrumental in helping Auckland to a famous one-point win.

The national selectors took immediate note. Thirteen tries in seven appearances for Auckland was more than enough to convince them they had a rare talent on their hands. Williams was elated when he was selected for the end-of-season tour to Great Britain and France. Gary Willard was the incumbent test stand-off, but Williams immediately had him under pressure with strong performances in four of the opening six tour games. He was named in the test reserves for the first international with Willard being retained. But then fate intervened. Willard was carrying an injury and failed a fitness test on the eve of the game. Kiwi coach Laurie Blanchard interrupted Williams'

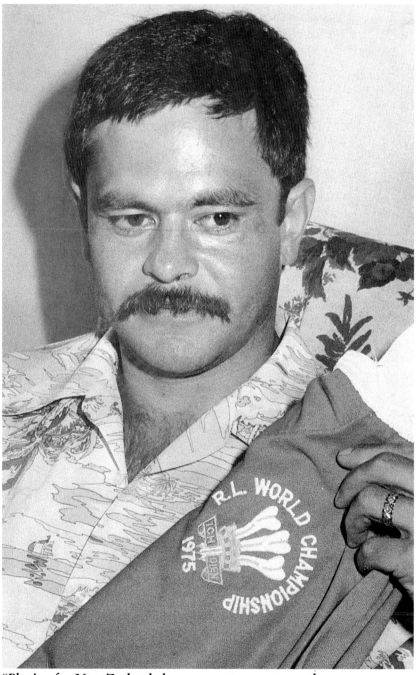

"Playing for New Zealand always meant more to me than overseas offers," says Dennis Williams.

18th birthday celebrations with three words that electrified the young-ster – "Kid, you're in."

It was the day Williams had dreamed about since he was 13. But now it was finally here, he was daunted. His knees were playing cym-bals in the dressing room before the game. "I spewed three times be-fore we even got on the field," he recalled. "They basically had to push me out there. It wasn't so much that I was scared. It was just the nerves. I was just *soooo* nervous." You would never have known it.

The Pommie halves of Roger Millward and Alex Murphy were considered the best in the game. Williams was a rookie and inside him was another youngster named Ken Stirling, set to also go on and be-come a legend, but at that time only in his second year in the Kiwis. But Williams' superb individual try stunned the Poms and New Zea-land went on to win 18-13. Williams' position in the side was sealed. The Kiwis went on to triumph 2-1 in the test series, which remains the only time New Zealand has won a series on British soil. Williams played all three tests and the three against France, dazzling the oppo-sition wherever he played.

Although he played many brilliant games in the following years, there is almost unanimous agreement that Williams played the finest football of his life on that '71 tour. Glamour English club Wigan cer-tainly agreed. They staggered Williams near the end of the tour when they offered him a 10-year contract. "I was amazed," said Williams. "When I turned them down, they must have wanted me pretty badly because they came back to me with a five-year offer." Once again, Williams turned them down. He had a sweetheart back in Auckland and the thought of being away from her for 10 years was too much. Dennis eventually married Sheryl. Little did Williams realise at the time just how astute his decision had been. "My other motivation was playing for New Zealand," said Williams. "I'd only just broken into the Kiwis and I didn't want to throw it all away after just one tour."

The thought of any youngster being offered lucrative contracts by the likes of Easts and Wigan and turning them down is staggering to most league observers. Williams admits he has often wondered about what might have been. "I guess I could have made myself some good money. But it was so much more difficult back then. There was no high-powered television coverage of the Winfield Cup like you have now. You left everybody behind, your family, everybody. And you couldn't play for New Zealand anymore. I would have liked to have made more money out of the game, but I'll never regret it because I got to play for my country and that meant more to me."

In 1972, Williams toured Australia with the Kiwis and went back to England and France again for the World Cup. It was in Paris that Williams was involved in what he believes was the most courageous Kiwi performance. "We played Australia at the Parc de Princes and there was hardly anybody there," he said. "It was one of the most totally committed Kiwi performances I've ever seen. We weren't rated at that World Cup because we'd fallen apart a bit after the great season in '71. A lot of players had retired and we were rebuilding. We had been wiped out by Australia on the tour there earlier in the year and nobody rated us. There were only about a thousand people in this massive stadium but the actual game of football was phenomenal."

New Zealand defied the tipsters to hold the Aussies to a pulsating 17-all draw. "My greatest memory of that game was being totally physically shattered after the match, the most shattered I'd ever been after any game of football. We gave it everything we could give."

Williams continued to shine for the Kiwis over the next few years. In 1975, he enjoyed a particularly inspiring season. While still possessing his bewitching sidestep and lightning speed off the mark, Williams had added a Wally Lewis-like ability to read a game while also perfecting his kicking game. The bomb had become a new tactical weapon in the game and Williams was the finest exponent in New Zealand. "We really began to use it as a tactic that year in the World Cup tournament," he explained. Indeed, Williams scored two tries off his own kicks and New Zealand got another off a towering bomb in their 17-all draw with England in Christchurch.

Many observers believe the English game was Williams' most impressive individual performance during his Kiwi career. And against France, he teased the opposition mercilessly in New Zealand's 27-0 triumph. Then there was a spectacular runaway try against Wales. "Yeah, I remember that one because John Bevan was chasing me," said Williams. "The year before he'd scored a try against us where he had run about 60 or 70 yards with his hand up in the air. We thought he was a bit of a smart arse so when he was chasing me and once I'd made sure I was going to get there, I put my hand up in the air and gave him a taste of his own."

Williams…"People used to drive miles to watch him play," says
Graham Lowe.

New Zealand were handily placed after the Down Under leg of the World Cup but it remains one of Williams' regrets that the Kiwis failed to fire when they got to England and France for the second half of the tournament. Williams remained a permanent fixture in the Kiwi test team through to the 1978 season, when New Zealand toured Australia and Papua-New Guinea under Ron Ackland, then in his second year in charge of the side. Ackland was a strict disciplinarian and Williams didn't really thrive under him. He found himself dropped towards the end of the tour.

Ces Mountford took over from Ackland and he clearly felt Williams still had something to offer. He was recalled for single tests in 1980 and 1981, but a serious knee injury against the French conspired to end his international career. Williams then moved into more of a player-coaching role, continuing to succeed and never failing to amaze onlookers with his prowess.

Graham Lowe, just beginning to make his mark as a coach with Otahuhu, was one of those spectators. "Back in the mid to late 70s, Dennis used to have these phenomenal battles with Olsen Filipaina," said Lowe. "People used to come for miles whenever Te Atatu played Mangere East. The pair of them were sensational. But in his early days, I remember him as this incredible matchwinner. His step was unbelievable. He would just glide across the field, putting the defence in two minds. Then suddenly he'd just straighten up, sidestep and he was gone. He was a freak."

Brian Doherty also remembers Williams as a teenage progidy but admires the way he turned himself into a complete footballer. "He could come up with a match-winning drop goal off his left foot, he could run, he could pass, he could tackle, he could kick. He had everything. As he matured, he lost some of that snap in his step so then instead of being the guy who made all the big breaks and finished them off, he became the architect inside."

Mark Graham, a man not given to delivering praise unless it is warranted, delivers the ultimate compliment to Williams. "He is the best player I have ever played with," wrote Graham in his book *Mark My Words*. Stop and think about that compliment for a moment. Mark Graham played with countless legends. He was one himself. Yet he is unequivocal in his statement about Williams. "The talent of the man was awe-inspiring," says Graham, who made his Kiwi debut in 1977. "He was a football genius who would have been a sensation had he

In the latter years of his Kiwi career, Williams became a canny playmaker rather than the explosive runner he had been in his early days.

decided to come and play in the Sydney competition. He was a real legend in my early days. I played with him in the Auckland Amco Cup sides and with him in 1975 when we beat Australia and Wales. He was superb that year. I remember the coach would say: 'Our long kicking game isn't good enough. Dennis, do you want to take it over?' And Dennis would just nonchalantly say: 'Yeah, no worries'. Next thing you know he'd be producing these 50 to 60 metre touchfinders."

Graham recalls a vivid example of Williams' innate skills which came on the training field. "I remember he was called back into the test team around '81 for a game and during training we decided to try a new move," he says. "I called Dennis over along with Mark Broadhurst and said: 'I'll pass the ball to you, you make out you're going to pass it to 'Broadie' but then run past him, across field and flick it back inside for him to accelerate on to'. Anyhow Dennis just said: 'Yep, sounds good mate' and started to walk away. I yelled out and asked where he was going and he said he thought training was over. I said we had to try the move first. So we did it and of course Dennis pulled it off perfectly. And once he'd made the pass to Broadie he just kept on running towards the dressing room! I could only stand there and marvel. I remember we were all saying: 'How good is this guy!'"

Mark Graham believes Williams' career was cut short by authoritative coaches who didn't appreciate his genius. "He was a player you had to cut some slack too," he says. "He was an instinctive player and once you start denying him the ability to try something out of the ordinary, you hobbled him. I remember when he came back into the side for that 1981 game, which was when Ces Mountford had taken over. We were playing charades one night and then one time at training we had an egg and spoon race. Dennis was rapt. I remember him saying to me: 'Mate, this is how it should be. This is what football is all about'."

Not suprisingly, Graham named Williams in his 'Greatest Ever New Zealand Team' in a special chapter in his book. But what was intriguing was that he selected him at inside centre rather than stand-off. "I thought he was best suited there," says Graham. "He was a great stand-off but he had the pace to play centre as well. And the little extra time and space he had there often brought out the best in him. If he had gained that extra experience playing overseas he would have been the best player in the world."

In his book, Graham goes on to describe a fictional 'Dream Test' between the best New Zealanders he ever played with and the best Australian stars he ever came up with. In the fantasy match, New Zealand wins 26-20 with the Kiwis scoring the match-sealing try with 30 seconds left on the clock. Guess who scores it? I'll leave it to Graham to commentate...'[Clayton] Friend at dummy half shapes for the pass to field goal specialist [Nicky] Wright. [Peter] Sterling and [Wally] Lewis rush through intent on cutting down Wright. Friend flicks to Williams who crosses under the posts after standing up a stunned [Brett] Kenny. Wright converts. Australia 20-New Zealand 26. The New Zealanders walk elatedly off the ground; Dennis Williams is named man of the match; [Graham] Lowe is hoisted high on Broadhurst and Tamati's shoulders.'

It's not as if any further endorsement is needed of Williams' brilliance following Graham Lowe and Mark Graham. But Kevin Tamati is another full of praise. "I got to play with Dennis only a couple of times, but I'll never forget it," says Tamati. "He was very, very gifted. If I had to liken him to somebody in the modern game so New Zealanders who follow Australian league could get an idea of how good he was, the bloke I can best compare him to is Allan Langer. That's how good he was."

Williams toyed with coaching towards the end of his career. He was player-coach at Te Atatu for several years and was into the second year of a coaching role for Northern Districts when his life was turned upside down. "It happened in October, 1983," said Williams. "I'd just re-signed for another year to coach Northern Districts and I was getting a lift home that night. We were going home via the Greenhithe highway in Auckland when we came around a corner. That's the last thing I remember."

The vehicle left the road, careering crazily as it flipped. Williams was found by ambulance attendants in a drain some distance from the car. He hadn't been thrown out, yet he has no recollection of climbing out of the shattered wreck. Outwardly, the damage to the league star looked disarmingly minor. His left elbow had smashed through the window upon impact. But other than the blood from the wound, Williams looked as if he wasn't seriously hurt. But if ever looks were deceiving, this was to be a classic example.

Sheryl raced to the hospital. And while Dennis's elbow was attended to, doctors advised her not to worry. Her husband would be out of hospital within a few days. But by the next morning Sheryl was worried. Dennis was babbling and was often incoherent. She wanted a brain scan. The doctors said one wasn't necessary; that her husband just had concussion and would be fine in a couple of days.

Within days of bringing Dennis home, Sheryl's fears intensified. "She had to do everything for me," said Dennis. "She had to show me where the shower was, how to operate it, turn it on and off for me. In fact, she would have to come in and tell me when to get out. If she didn't, I'd just stay there. I didn't know when it was time to get out." Complicating an already difficult situation was that Sheryl was in the last days of her third pregnancy. "Brooke was born the day I came out of hospital," said Dennis. "Sheryl came home with a newborn. We already had two children under six and here was her husband and he couldn't even remember his name. I don't know how she got through it all, I really don't. The only help we had at that time was from our immediate family."

Williams was taken to a specialist who determined what had become rather obvious to his family. Dennis had suffered brain damage in the accident. But there had been a second major setback. He had also suffered a stroke, undoubtedly brought on by the trauma of the accident. Both his speech and his ability to walk had been dramatically affected. "Basically, I had to learn to walk and talk all over again," Williams explained.

It was to prove a tougher war than any one ever fought with his football boots on. Williams had suffered major memory loss. Before his accident, the rumpus room in his Te Atatu home had been a shrine to his footballing prowess. On the walls were team photos of the great sides he'd played for while individual spoils such as trophies also had pride of place. But for Williams, the room was a mystery. He had no memory of any of the great feats he had achieved. With that went an unbearable sense of frustration. "I used to go down there and stare at the photos, trying to figure what they were all about. I'd look at pictures of me on the Eiffel Tower or meeting the Queen. Yet none of it meant anything to me," he says. "Quite often I'd be down there for 10 hours at a time, just staring at the wall."

Unable to sleep, Williams would pitifully shuffle through the house in the early hours of the morning. "Sheryl would often find me crying on the stairs," he says. There were to be further setbacks. ACC paid 80 per cent of Williams' wage as a forkhoist operator for the

Auckland Harbour Board while he received treatment. But that lasted for just a year, after which the Harbour Board let him go. "That was another kick in the guts," Williams admits.

It was while plunged into these depressive troughs that Williams momentarily contemplated suicide. "Yeah, I hate to admit it now but I did think about it," he says. "OK, now that obviously sounds ridiculous. The fight was there in me but it was just the frustration. I couldn't handle it." On a couple of occasions, the frustration almost completely overwhelmed Williams. "A few times Sheryl had to call my father over to settle me down," he says. "One time, I was trying to start the car. It was just as well I couldn't even get it going. God knows what would have happened if I had. I probably would have driven through the rumpus room."

Williams' battle back began as realistically as it could – with the smallest of victories. He regularly attended the Auckland Concussion Clinic and willed himself back to walking properly again by pushing Brooke in her pram from Dennis's home to his parents' a mile away each day. "It was often humiliating because I'd be pushing her down the street and I could see the looks in the faces of the people driving past. I could see them thinking: 'Is this guy drunk or what?' because I was shambling all over the place."

But Williams kept at it, every day recording the most minute of improvements. "I used to time myself. Walking that pushchair was very, very hard, but whenever I turned off the stopwatch and I'd have beaten my best time by 20 seconds, it was really rewarding." Not that Sheryl always appreciated the contests. "She'd say: 'It's not a race. Slow down, take your time'. But to me it was a race. I used to have my secret little battles that I wouldn't tell Sheryl about. That was the way I believed I had to do it. I also believed that because I had got myself into this, I had to get myself out."

Along the way, Williams also found himself reaching out to alternative medicines. He had acupuncture for his speech and memory loss. "I went and saw this guy who had a reputation for quite extreme approaches. I'd get 20 needles stuck in me once a week. They would go into my joints, fingers, elbows, toes, back and even my upper lip. At one stage, I had this little magnet in my ear that I had to turn three times a day. It was designed to help my memory. I had a year of acupuncture. People scoff at it but I'm certain it helped. I'm a lot more open to alternative medicines now."

Dennis Williams has all but won his battle now. He began driving again two and a half years after the accident. In early 1989, he began working again as a passenger assistant for Air New Zealand at Auckland International Airport. There are still minor battles to be won – and many regrets. "My oldest daughter Liana is a very good representative netballer. I want to train her but I can't. I wanted to show her how to do shuttle runs to help improve her reflexes, anticipation and general fitness. But I can't. I move too slowly for that. Every now and then that gets to me a little bit and I have to go away, be alone, sit myself down and deal with it."

Despite his own courage shown in battling back, Williams has no doubts what the most important factor in "becoming normal" again was. "Love," he says. "The love of my wife and the love of my family. I still don't know how Sheryl got through it all. It wasn't just the lack of money at the time, having to contend with a baby and two small kids. It was wondering if we would ever be a normal family again. That was hardly surprising. I wouldn't touch the baby for five or six months when Sheryl first brought her home. It took me months to know who I was, let alone my family."

Williams has come a long way since that traumatic evening in 1982. To look at him now, there is little evidence of the ramifications of that twisted car wreck. And much of his memory has been restored. "I can go into the rumpus room now and remember most of what it's all about," he says with a grin.

The many league fans whom Williams brought so much excitement and pleasure to will be pleased to hear it.

FRANK OLIVER
'Filth'

"I was playing for Wellington against Manawatu and Frank led that bloody awesome forward pack they had. I always used to make sure I never got caught in a ruck when we played Manawatu but you know Murphy's Law. I got pinned underneath this one ruck on the wrong side. There I was on the ground with my tiny little head poking out the back and I saw Frank rolling into the ruck last among the forwards. He saw me too. And he smiled. I thought: 'Well, here we go, Stewie. You've blown it now son". Anyhow, Frank put the big size 14 down right next to my ear, looked down and grinned: 'Silly boy, Stu. A flash back like you should know better than to get caught in a ruck like this'. Then I heard this sadistic chuckle as he stepped over me and left me unscathed. My only thought was: 'Thank God. And, please, never let me get caught in one of these things ever again!'" – Stu Wilson.

IT was the day after Munster's finest effort. The proud men from Ireland were still dining out on the feats of the previous day. And why not? The mighty All Blacks had been humbled, overwhelmed by the sheer commitment and tenacity from the men of Munster. By the end of the 1978 All Black tour of the United Kingdom, they would be able to claim something the English, Welsh, Irish and Scottish sides of that year would never be able to: They had beaten the mighty Grand Slam All Black tourists.

The All Blacks didn't begrudge Munster their victory. But the loss had created tension within the camp with the test against Ireland just four days away. Coach Jack Gleeson called a team meeting. The players were invited to contribute to what had gone wrong and what needed to be done to get the tour back on the rails. "Frank stood up to have his say," recalls Andy Haden. "Most of us expected him to talk about our tactics. Instead, he ripped into us. In the game against Munster, he'd seen one of the forwards deliberately kick one of their players in the head. Well, he stood up and let everybody know in no uncertain terms what he thought about it. He ended by declaring: 'If I ever see one of our blokes do that again, I'll never play in the same side with him'. There was stunned silence. Frank had made his point."

Oliver remembers the meeting....and the stunned silence that followed. Anybody who played in Oliver's era feared the Southland, Otago, Manawatu and All Black lock. He was not averse to "get-evens", either on behalf of a wronged team-mate or to right the ledger after copping a cheap shot himself. He was also unashamedly rugged if a rival player attempted to impede a ball coming back in a ruck. And while there was the odd occasion where his retribution often out-did the initial act, I could not find a single player prepared to criticise Oliver or tag him a dirty player.

Explaining his stand over the Munster incident, Oliver says: "I've always regarded the head as sancrosanct. I won't tolerate anybody kicking anyone in the head. I don't give a **** if they punch them, rake the shit out of them or whatever. But I can't cop head-kicking. I'd seen this bloke kick one of the Munster players and I almost jobbed him myself there and then. In fact, after that incident that's what I started doing. If I saw anybody from my side kick somebody in the head, I'd turn around and whack them myself. I probably should have done that at Munster."

So the incident had been well off-the-ball? "It wouldn't have mattered if it was on-the-ball," he replies. "You just don't go near the head. You can kill somebody doing that."

Oliver's uncompromising attitude towards rugby was instilled in young Frank while growing up in the rural central Otago township of Lawrence where he competed with five brothers and three sisters for the attention of his parents. Father was a rugby fan whose own career had been cut short by World War II during which he spent time in a prisoner-of-war camp. And Mrs Oliver provided the bulk of the sporting genes handed down to young Frank. A skilled netballer who represented Otago, South Canterbury and Canterbury, she also came from a strong rugby family with brothers who had turned out

Few All Blacks gave it more than Frank Oliver.

for Canterbury.

A promising junior career as a second-five-eighth(!) ended when Oliver literally outgrew the position. "I just got too big and I was shifted to lock," he shrugs. With a strong police background within his mother's family, Oliver headed to Wellington as a teenager to attend Trentham Police College. At 19, he was sent to Invercagill as a constable. "I began playing for the Marist club down there. Sport and coppers. That was the deal in my family," he said. He made an immediate impression, breaking into Southland's rugged pack of forwards that same year.

In 1970, he gained an unexpected surprise when he was selected for the All Black trials. Indeed, he was a regular trialist from '70 through to '76, when he made his international debut. Yet during those years, he never seriously considered he was good enough to become an All Black. "I saw them as consolidation years where I was learning the trade," he says. "But becoming an All Black? Nah, I didn't think that would happen."

But Oliver was starting to make his mark. He wasn't a domineering lineout jumper. In fact, he freely admits he never was during his career. He always got ball thrown to him, though, and he was forging a well-earned reputation as a powerful scrummager and mauler. Along the way, the word was getting out about the young gamecock from Invercargill who didn't lie down for anybody.

"Rugby was bloody hard back in those days," he recalled. "It was a completely different scene then. There were no judiciaries back then, or television cameras capturing every possible action. It was a battle-field and as a young fella you had to prove yourself. Every game you had to start from scratch again. You couldn't take a backwards step. There were a lot of hard bastards about and if you held back, basi-cally you were stuffed. And if the referee wasn't looking after you and penalising guys for infringing in the lineout you had to deal with the situation yourself, otherwise you didn't get any ball and your reputation suffered. Even later in my career, there was always some hungry young bastard coming through and looking to make a mark at your expense. You couldn't give them an inch. Basically, you had worked to hard to get the jersey and weren't going to give it away to some young Turk."

But at that stage of his career Oliver was the 'hungry young bas-tard', and now and then, that meant taking the occasional poke at some men with a lofty stature within the game. "In one Southland game against Canterbury, one of our centres chopped through and Grizz Wyllie stiff-armed him. So I flattened Grizz. There was a lot of yelling and carrying on straight afterwards and the referee was a gut-less bastard. Yeah, Grizz was a legend, but stiff shit. Legends are hu-man, aren't they? My attitude was that it didn't matter who it was. If you've gotta do it, you've gotta do it."

Oliver remembers being grateful he didn't have to "do it" the only time in his career he played against Colin Meads. "Pinetree was near-ing the end of his playing days then and we squared up in a charity game. Thankfully, Piney's mob won easily and I didn't have to hang one on him. I was pleased about that because I knew of his reputa-tion. Basically, if you hung one on Pinetree, it had to be a bloody ripper because you sure as hell were going to get a decent one back!" he laughed.

Oliver's All Black breakthrough came in 1976 at age 27, following a cleanout of the All Blacks under JJ Stewart. He was chosen for the tour of South Africa, joining as a second string lock behind the test pairing of Peter Whiting and Hamish Macdonald. Many of Oliver's

**Oliver watches team-mate Bill Bush mete out some jungle justice on
British Lions prop Graham Price.**

peers believe he played his best rugby for the All Blacks on the famed
Grand Slam tour of the UK in '78. But Oliver himself considers his
best displays in the black jumper were in South Africa. "Admittedly,
I was playing in the midweek team and we weren't facing the same
calibre of opposition as the test boys were, but I felt I played some
good football on that tour."

Oliver relished the physical challenge of taking on the Afrikaaner
on his home turf. "I really enjoyed that tour. The South Africans were
big, hard bastards but you knew where you stood with them. Their
referees were a problem but we always knew that. But I loved living
on a diet of rugby and training."

Given Oliver's approach to rugby, it was inevitable he would
quickly clash with some of the South African forwards on tour. He
has no hesitation in branding South Africans as the most competitive
rugby players in the world. "We had a lot of skirmishes on that tour,"
he recalled. "They're a strange lot, the Afrikaaner. If ever there's a
race you can't afford to take a backward step to, it's them. If you do,
they lose all respect for you. They always try to intimidate the opposition and then sit back to see what your reaction is. Back in '76, they
had a couple of dirty bastards too. We had to stand our ground a few
times."

Oliver's powerful midweek displays didn't go unnoticed. The All Blacks had levelled the series by winning the second test 15-9 at Bloemfontein after losing the opener 7-16 in Durban. But then they lost the third test at Newlands 15-10. Coach JJ Stewart had been unhappy with Hamish Macdonald's game and Oliver was called up to make his test debut partnering Peter Whiting. "I knew I was in with a bit of a chance," he recalls. "I felt like I was knocking on the door and churning out honest sorts of games. I felt I was getting more mature in my play."

Oliver has unhappy memories of his test debut, however. "We got ****ing robbed," he says of New Zealand's 15-14 loss at Ellis Park. "We played some good rugby that day but the bloody ref dealt to us." Indeed, Bruce Robertson was blatantly obstructed by his Springbok opposite Ian Robertson when he chipped ahead into the South African in-goal. Bryan Williams landed the penalty but many felt a penalty try was the more appropriate punishment.

Oliver found himself involved in several skirmishes in South Africa. "I got into a decent blue with Jimmy Young at Kimberly and he got sent off," he recalls. "He wasn't a bad guy to have a beer with but, shit, was he a ****ing stroppy bastard! He and I had a bust-up over something. He'd whacked one of our blokes so I gave him one back. The referee issued a general warning and told us all that the next bloke who threw one would be marched. At the next lineout there was another skirmish and I was about to hang a beauty on Jimmy when, out of the corner of my eye I saw the referee. I held back but Jimmy didn't. He let one go at me, the ref saw it and he got sent off! We had a good laugh about that one later."

On another occasion, Oliver found himself full of righteous indignation over a nasty incident in a midweek match where the opposing hooker kicked Kent Lambert in the head. "This bastard booted 'Lambo' and I remember telling Andy Leslie 'I'm going to get this prick'. Andy told me to wait until we were 20 or 30 points up first. So with about 10 minutes to go, Andy gave me the nod. I'd been talking to this prick all day. I told him how I was going to nail him and every scrum I'd say: 'this is the one where you're getting it'. The guy was shitting himself for about 50 minutes. He wouldn't come into a ruck. Anyhow I said to Billy Bush: 'Get your arse ready Bill, she's coming through'. As the scrum packed, I came through and whacked this bloke a beauty. He went tumbling out of the scrum and collapsed.

The referee didn't see a thing. I think I broke his nose in three places and after the game he came over to me. He could hardly see and he said: 'You hit me'. I said: 'Yes, and you know why I bloody well did too, don't you?' He nodded and told me that he had got away with things like that in the past. I told him: 'Well, you didn't ****ing get away with it this time'. He just said: 'I have no complaints', and we had a beer together. He got caught, he paid the price and he understood that."

The promise shown at Ellis Park led to Oliver becoming a test regular the following year when the British Lions toured. In the opening Test at Athletic Park, Oliver found himself paired alongside a promising Aucklander named Andy Haden. It was the beginning of an unusual friendship and highly successful on-field partnership. Even back then, Haden was already the quintessential Aucklander. On the surface, he and Oliver hardly appeared likely soulmates. Oliver the tough and teak southerner with rugged fists and tongue and Haden, the finicky lineout athlete who was always working the angle both on and off the field. But the pair immediately clicked.

"He's a mighty fella," says Oliver unprompted. "I always got on super well with Andy. We've always been good mates. I think the secret was that we respected each other's ability and we complemented each other as a duo. Andy was a big bastard and the principal ball-winner come lineout time. I was never as good a leaper as he was. I was probably a bit bloody short, but I just got away with it in my era. I wouldn't survive now, height-wise. I had to use a lot of guile to get my ball. Andy got most of our ball but I did other things. I was known for other strengths like my rucking and mauling power and my scrummaging. In a lot of ways, that carried me through. But I was also fortunate Andy was there because he was so dominant in the lineout they could still use me. Plus we found we were very similar off-the-field as well. We both liked a beer and a giggle. In 1979, we both spent an off-season playing in Italy, took our wives over. We had a bloody great time."

The Lions series represented a great chance for Oliver to firmly establish himself as a test All Black. He didn't let it slip by. The Tane Norton-led New Zealanders sent the Lions packing 4-0 in a series that was much closer than that scoreline indicates. Oliver remembers being mortified when the Lions pack rocked the All Black scrum in the opening test. "Shit, we got taught to scrum that day," he says.

Always in the thick of things. Oliver launches a raid against the 1977 British Lions.

"The Lions just absolutely bathed us come scrummaging time. That was difficult for us to come to grips with. In those days, most of us were farmers or foresty workers and thought of ourselves as reasonably bloody hard physical specimens. And here were these bloody schoolteachers, big fat Poms with pants up around their arses, pushing us around. It was ****ing embarrassing! It was like a slight on our manhood. It was a bloody shock to the system but we learned fast, I can tell you. It didn't take us too bloody long to redress that. We had a couple of think-tanks, got back on track and in '78 on the Grand Slam tour, we shoved the pricks all over the paddock."

Oliver went on to play both tests against France on the end of season tour the same year before gearing up for the challenge of the Australians the following season. He was unimpressed with the approach of the Frenchmen. "They were dirty, kicking bastards," he says. "Cholley, their loosehead prop who was apparently the national heavyweight boxing champ at the time, eye-gouged Gary Knight. It

Feeling the pinch...Oliver captained the All Blacks against Tony Shaw's Wallabies in 1978 and still regrets the heavy third test loss.

was a shocker. But they were bloody good players too. We didn't try to out-fight or out-muscle them, we just out-thought them. They bathed us in the first test (18-13 in Toulouse) but in the second test (won 15-3 by New Zealand in Paris) we used short lineouts and per-petual motion rugby to stuff them up."

Upon his return to New Zealand, Oliver moved to Otago when offered a job as a forestry contractor. "I moved there solely for work. Rugby didn't come into it. I'd made the All Blacks from Southland and Otago didn't even feature in my thinking."

The tour by the Australians featured an unexpected surprise for Oliver. In only his eighth test, he found himself named as All Black captain after Graham Mourie, who had led the team to France, was forced out of the series with a serious back injury. "Otago had beaten the Aussies early on in the tour but the captaincy was a bolt from the blue for me," he recalls. "It didn't worry me, though. I'd captained Southland. In fact, I'd captained most of the teams I'd played for. I never used to let it worry me."

The All Blacks, traditional slow starters in a home series, just squeaked to victory in the first test 13-12 at Athletic Park but were back to their dominating best in the second at Lancaster Park where they racked up an emphatic 22-6 winning scoreline. But the third test was to be Oliver's heaviest ever loss when wearing the black jersey. "Strange test, that third one," he grumbles. "Their coach, Daryl Haberecht, had a heart attack the week before the game. The Aussies were bloody crying over it. They were desperate to win the game for him and they just went apeshit when they got onto Eden Park. That was the test where Greg Cornelsen scored four tries."

Indeed, Australia won 30-16, a humiliating loss for the All Blacks. Oliver still kicks himself over the memory. "We didn't help ourselves that day," he declares. "The tour to the UK was coming up, we'd already won the series and our minds were on what was coming up rather than what we were facing there and then. I was bloody disappointed. I felt that as the captain, I'd let everybody down. We still bloody near got back into that game, though. I gave the guys a helluva bollicking at halftime [several of Oliver's charges that day confirm it was indeed hot oratory!] and we were nearly right back in there. But then we stuffed up a lineout on our line and "Corny" got over for another try."

The tour was relatively incident-free. "The Aussies are generally pretty good," says Oliver. "They did have a couple of silly frontrowers on that tour, though. I think I broke my thumb whacking one of them."

Oliver's career as an All Black captain proved short-lived. Mourie returned for the tour at the end of the year. Not that it worried Oliver who played strong rugby despite carrying a knee injury through what was to become known as "The Grand Slam Tour". "I enjoyed that tour. I was thrilled that we had got our scrummaging together."

The '78 Grand Slam All Blacks hold a special place among the lofty achivements of New Zealand rugby teams, being the first to achieve the Holy Grail of defeating England, Ireland, Scotland and Wales on the same tour. Yet Oliver is not entirely convinced that particular All Black side was, in his own inimitable words, 'that ****ing good'. "You analyse the team and you'll see that yourself," he dares. "But we were very efficient, we were well organised and we played some bloody good football at times. Basically, we were a side that made the most of what we had. We were well coached by Jack Gleeson, and Russ Thomas was a bloody good manager. Everybody got on well together and it reflected on the team."

After the infamous 1972-'73 tour of the UK with its self-styled mafia and the poorly-handled Keith Murdoch saga, the Fleet Street hawks drew a bead on the All Blacks the moment they arrived at Heathrow. "We never gave the bastards a thing to write about," smiles Oliver. "The boys were very good. There were no incidents. In fact, the worst thing that happened was one day when Jack [Gleeson] broke a potplant in a hotel when he leaned over to pick something up!"

In 1979, Oliver again remained an automatic test selection. But in the first international of the year, against the touring Frenchmen at Lancaster Park, he was forced off the field with injury for the first and only time of his All Black career. "I got kicked at the top of my spine," he explained. It was to be the first blow in what was quickly to become a frustrating season for the rugged lock. The All Blacks comfortably won the first test 23-9 and Oliver was selected for the second international at Eden Park. It was one of the few times he was to regret playing. "I still wasn't quite right but Eric [Eric Watson, the new All Black coach] talked me into playing. I got dropped after that."

The way Oliver spits out the words gives the distinct impression he wasn't overly enamoured with Watson, who had been the Otago coach before winning the coveted national job. A little further goading confirms the fact. "I wasn't expecting to get dropped. I felt like I was playing pretty good football at the time. It was probably to do with things other than rugby that I got dropped." Oliver's marriage had just broken up. He wanted to get out of Otago because of his personal situation. He suspects Watson didn't approve of his personal circumstances.

Wairarapa-Bush lock Mike McCool gained Oliver's jersey for the one-off test against Australia at the Sydney Cricket Ground where the Mark Loane-led Wallabies won back the Bledisloe Cup 12-6. Oliver still wasn't wanted for the end-of-season tour to Scotland and England, however. Instead, he played a season of club rugby in Italy, thoroughly enjoying the experience.

The 1980 season also saw Oliver on the All Black outer, with Wellington's John Fleming being preferred as Haden's locking partner. But Oliver compensated with a fresh challenge. He'd moved to Manawatu, adding an ever stronger edge to an already feared green and white forward pack. Oliver looks back on his first season of rep football in Palmerston North with unconcealed relish. Manawatu, boasting Gary Knight, Mark Shaw, Geoff Old and Oliver in the forwards and with Mark Donaldson calling the shots at halfback, were unstoppable, romping to the national championship. "We just absolutely murdered every team we played," he said.

Oliver's own part in the Manawatu juggernaut didn't go unnoticed. He was among six Manawatu players selected to visit Wales as part of the Welsh Rugby Union's centennial. "I didn't get to play the test [won 23-3 by the All Blacks]. They picked Graeme Higginson. Not that that worried me. He deserved his spot. He was playing bloody good football." But ironically it was an injury to Higginson which opened a door to Oliver he had come to believe had been firmly shut.

Scotland had visited for two tests early in the 1981 season and been ruthlessly dispatched. But the real challenge of the season was the Springboks, back on New Zealand soil for the first time in 16 years. The All Blacks grafted out a hard-fought 14-9 win in the opening test at Lancaster Park after the rookie 'Cowboy' Shaw dealt to South Africa's most obstructive forward Eben Jansen. Higginson then broke his ankle at training in the lead-up to the next test and Oliver got an unexpected chance to wear the All Black jersey once again. The selectors tracked him down in Australia, where he was playing a charity match for a paralysed player. "I think I got back to New Zealand the night before the game," recalls Oliver. "Hardly great preparation."

Oliver gave his all but the Springboks levelled the series with a 24-12 triumph. It came as no surprise to him when he was dumped for the deciding third test for the latest new kid on the block, a fresh-faced Aucklander named Gary Whetton. Frank Oliver's All Black career was over: 17 tests, 11 wins, six losses. "My time had gone and to be honest, I felt quite relaxed about it," he says. "I was realistic enough to accept that I'd only been brought in for the second test because I could slot straight back in."

His time in the black jersey might have come to an end but there was still plenty of rugby left in Oliver. He continued to play outstandingly for Manawatu whose forward pack consistently instilled fear and loathing among their opponents. "Did they ever!" says Stu Wilson, rolling his eyes for impact. "Their scrum was unbelievable. They used to have this move called the 'Corkscrew'. It was Frank's

The latter years of Oliver's career were spent welding Manawatu into a formidable force.

call and he used to do it only every now and then because it was such a tough call on "Axle" [prop Gary Knight]. Whenever Frank wanted the Corkscrew, he'd come through with the big underhanded grip and rip Axle's nuts. That was the signal for the Corkscrew, which was this massive power scrum. Axle would bore off his man onto the opposition hooker and the other prop would do the same. And together it would twist the hooker. All the weight of the scrum would just shift onto this one guy. The hooker's ribcage would just start popping because of the way he was being twisted and because he had nowhere to go. They reckon you'd hear this 'pop, pop, pop' of rib cartilages. It was just unbelievable. One year they went through five hookers."

Cowboy Shaw sheepishly confirms this statistic. Oliver just smiles and offers no comment. "I'm on record as saying the Manawatu pack of that era was probably superior to the All Black forward pack of the time. It was bloody awesome, especially come scrummaging time. There was a big emphasis on scrummaging back then. We used to pack down a hundred scrums some nights at training. It was bloody good. I reckon I played the best rugby of my career in those years with Manawatu."

There was to be one last controversy in Oliver's rugby career, though. When the '83 British Lions toured, by the time they reached Palmerston North a week out from the first test, the visitors were looking somewhat shaky. Led by an uninspirational captain in Ciaran Fitzgerald and managed by Willie-John McBride, who was managing to wreck the high esteem he'd won among New Zealanders as a player by consistently moaning and whinging his way through the country, the Manawatu match was crucial to the Lions.

The incident is covered at length and in great detail by *New Zealand Herald* journalist Don Cameron in his book *On the Lions' Trail*. Cameron recalls how after the game, won 25-18 by the Lions, McBride lashed Manawatu's approach, claiming four of his players had been deliberately stomped. Lions coach Jim Telfer joined in on the unsolicited verbal attack, declaring some things never changed in New Zealand rugby and that anyone lying on the ground in this country risked being kicked. Fitzgerald then waded in, claiming that anyone who kicked a defenceless player on the ground was "a coward".

The Lions' venom was mostly directed at Oliver over an incident where both the tourists and their ever-vigilant [but not always accurate] press claim he deliberately stomped Fitzgerald. The allegation was a mystery to Cameron and the other New Zealand scribes. They hadn't seen anything untoward. Oliver was also flummoxed. "We were on attack under their goalposts and you know what the bloody Poms are like in holding onto the ball on the ground," Oliver recalls. "Fitzgerald had it [the ball] tucked up in here [Oliver motions between his shoulder and chest]. I was about fourth or fifth to the ruck and he wouldn't let it go. We were going forward and I just blew over the bloody top of him. I remember looking back and he was still holding onto the ball, so I gave him three or four bloody good rakes. We got the ball back. The referee was right there and he penalised him for hanging onto the ball. We kicked a goal from that. TV picked it up and I think I might have scraped the side of his hair or something. But I never bloody jumped on him, which is what McBride tried to say I did. I knew what I'd done and what my intention was. Shit, if I'd gone for his head, he wouldn't have got up."

Several British pressmen went after Oliver. In his book *Two Sides To The Argument*, former Scottish international Ian Robertson wrote: "For such a great and distinguished player to stoop to such a dreadful act was, for me, one of the saddest moments of the whole tour. The scene in the Lions dressing room afterwards was a horrifying one, which the team doctor, Donald McLeod, viewed with revulsion."

Oliver was not amused. The controversy surprised Oliver, whose stand on foul play still remains unshakeable. He was upset over the Richard Loe affair and believes there are now more cheap shots in the game than in his day. "There was no kicking in my day," he declares. "If you were caught at the bottom of the ruck but you weren't making any attempt to stop the ball coming back, no bastard booted you...oh, maybe the odd Frenchman would. But that's all. There was a code of honour. Against the Lions in that match, we were going forward at a hundred miles per hour and he [Fitzgerald] copped one down the side of his ear. But it was nothing like the rubbish [British Lion] Dean Richards handed out against North Harbour [in the 1993 tour match] or Loe's carry-on. I don't think I've ever taken a cheap shot at any bastard. There might have been a couple of times where I've been a bit hard on a young fella and thought: 'Shit, I shouldn't have done that'. But you don't think that at the time. You never give a sucker an even break.

"The rules have changed the game now anyway, and removed much of the scope for the cheap shot merchants to have a go. There's a lot more movement in the game now and there's not so many static ruck and maul situations. So a lot of the opportunities are gone for that sort of shit. Plus there's a lot of younger blokes about now. You just have to look at the All Black trials each year to see that. They're all about 23 or 24 now. Most of us were a lot older in my era and we weren't prepared to take any crap. If anyone gave you any bloody aggro, you just donged them. But it all started to change in '83, round the time of that Lions incident. TV started to rear its head."

Oliver gave away first class rugby in 1984 and had a complete break from the game for two years. He was then convinced to coach his Marist club's under 19 team, then the Under-21s and finally the seniors in 1990. In his first year, he took the team from mid-table the previous year to runners-up in the Manawatu club competition. The next year they won the final under Oliver's tutelage.

At the same time, he was also doing work for the New Zealand Rugby Football Union as a staff coach. In 1992, he was asked to become a national under 19 selector. In '93, he became the national convenor of selectors, taking the New Zealand team on a three-match tour of Australia which was captained by his son Anton, a hooker with the Marlborough province and a player regarded as one of the most exciting emerging prospects on the national scene.

"It just happened, I didn't chase after it," Oliver says of his sure but steady rise through the coaching ranks. "I'm enjoying it and I like to think I've got something to offer. I didn't play under the new rules but I've coached teams under the changed laws. I understand what's happening and what people are trying to do."

Oliver could have had the Manawatu rep coaching post in 1993. After being assistant coach to Mark Donaldson for two years, he was asked to put his name forward but declined because he wanted a break from coaching senior players and was relishing the chance to work with the under 19s. "The young kids are a breath of fresh air," he says. "Their skill level is high, they're keen and you only have to tell them once and they do it!"

Then during the '93 season, he was approached to spend a season coaching in Ireland in control of second division club Galwegians. He enjoyed the experience and wants to continue his coaching apprenticeship. 'I like to think I still have something to offer rugby," he says.

MARK BROADHURST
'Broadie'

He could be an arrogant sort of bloke, Craig Young. And in the lead-up to the first test at Carlaw Park, the big Australian front rower had made it abundantly clear he didn't rate his Kiwi opposite. Throughout the game, Young had taken a few cheap shots at his rival. A scrum was set under the Australian posts and when the visitors were penalised, Young let fly with a punch he clearly expected to have an almighty impact. It did. Mark Broadhurst's patience snapped. Young, known in the game as 'Fat Albert', got one back. The Australian journalists sitting in the press box were stunned. Here was the man they had painted as one of the toughest hardmen in their game. And there was Fat Albert flat on his large-sized backside.

MARK Broadhurst was never one for worrying about reputations. While his fellow Kiwi prop Kevin Tamati deliberately went out to thump Les Boyd in his test debut to prove he was as tough as the legendary Australian, Broadhurst had to be told who Boyd was. When he joined glamour Australian club Manly in the early 1980s, he didn't even know what colour its jerseys were!

"I've never been one to read all the league magazines and that sort of stuff," he explains sheepishly. "To me, league was just a game where you didn't worry about the opposition. You just got out there and did the job." Broadhurst got "out there and did the job" in 17 tests for New Zealand between 1979 and 1983, not to mention the Papanui club in Christchurch, Canterbury, Manly, Illawarra and Hull Kingston Rovers in England.

There's always been a no-nonsense attitude about Broadhurst. It's

Mark Broadhurst..."reputations never meant anything to me."

reflected in his rugged face of which his latern jaw is his most distinguishing feature. During a brief flirtation with amateur boxing (where he won four out of four bouts, three of them knockouts), onlookers joked about his jaw being too easy a target for his rivals. Yet none was able to lay a clean shot on it.

League always appealed to Broadhurst. His father Ray had been a Kiwi trialist (scoring three tries in the match yet still missing out on selection) and although he had to play rugby for Papanui High's First XV, he pulled on his first Papanui league jersey at the age of seven. "I guess I began to really take the game seriously when I was around 15," he says. "I got chosen in a Kiwi schoolboy side that went to Australia. I played in both 'tests' over there but I actually got knocked cold in my first game there against the Christian Brothers. That was a hell of a introduction to Australian league!"

It was several years before Broadhurst wore a black jumper again. He quickly made his mark as a rugged but skilful second rower, adding a hard edge to Canterbury's often fruitless bids to unseat Auckland as the chief power in provincial league. His Canterbury debut came in 1975 as a raw-boned freezing worker. A fragmented World Cup competition was being played the same year and Canterbury hosted a fixture against Wales who were in New Zealand for key matches.

"That Welsh side was probably the dirtiest team I've ever played," recalls Broadhurst. "They were running up with the ball in one hand and their elbows out in front with the other. We were a pretty young side too. They were all professionals but bloody dirty." Several skirmishes broke out during the game. Late in the match, Wales sent on Jim Mills. Even though Broadhurst wasn't a man to scan the newspapers and read league magazines, Mills' reputation preceded him. "Wales had had a game against the West Coast and apparently Mills had thumped one of their forwards and he'd swallowed his tongue," he explained. "They had really got riled over there about that."

Mills had barely been on the field when another brawl broke out. For no other reason than the fact Broadhurst was the closest Canterbury forward to him, the burly Welsh prop felled the youngster from behind with a wicked karate chop. "All I remember is driving out of Hagley Park looking out the windows at the trees as they were taking me to hospital," says Broadhurst. Mills wasn't sent off, although several spectators almost took to him after the final whistle as he sauntered off. Mills was marched 19 times in his career. The same year he thumped Broadhurst from behind, he stomped on the face of Canterbury's Kiwi prop John Greengrass after the New Zealander had scored a try in his side's World Cup clash with the Welsh at Swansea. For that dastardly deed, he was banned from ever returning to New Zealand in any league capacity.

In 1978, with a tour to Australia beckoning, Broadhurst was named for the Kiwi trial in Auckland. He had been playing impressively as an occasionally wide-ranging second rower and his combination with Papanui's former Kiwi loose forward Ron Walker was assuming legendary proportions in the south. The Kiwi coach at the time was Ron Ackland, a strict disciplinarian. Broadhurst ultimately failed to win selection for the tour and there are plenty of people who will tell you he most certainly deserved to go. In his typically blunt fashion, Broadhurst disagrees.

"I arrived in Auckland and we were immediately put on this bus to go up to Waipu Cove for a training camp. When we got there, Ron goes, 'Righto, you've got five minutes to get into your training gear' and he then proceeded to thrash us around the paddock for two hours. I'd never had training like it. Then the very next morning, he had us up at 6am to go for a six mile run down the beach. I could hardly run and Gerry Gillman, another bloke from Canterbury, and I had only gone a mile when we flagged it away and went and sat up in the sandhills. Anyhow Ron came steaming up and gave us a mouthful. He yelled at us: 'You don't come up here for a trial and sit around'. He was pretty arrogant sort of a bloke, old Ron. But if I was in his position as a coach, there's no way I would have picked a guy who wasn't fit. That camp was a bit of a rude awakening for me. The Auckland guys were a bit more professional in their approach in those days. I was always a lazy trainer and you could get away with that in Canterbury. I never used to like the training but I seemed to be able to do it on the paddock when it counted. But my attitude towards training probably held me back for a while."

But come 1979, Ackland was no longer the Kiwi coach, replaced instead by Ces Mountford. Mountford, a no-nonsense West Coaster, appeared intent on a clean-out of the 'soft' Aucklanders. And perhaps because of his own tough ethic, he saw huge potential in Broadhurst. But he was also concerned about the tough Cantabrian's sloppy training habits. Only he decided to take a different tack. "Ces had come down to have a look at the Canterbury players and he held fitness tests out at QEII," said Broadhurst. "We'd done a time trial and I'd ended up having a big spew over by the dog track. Ces came over and said to me: 'I'll come back down in six weeks. If you can't get your fitness up to the level I want, you can forget about the Kiwis'. So that was make or break and I really knuckled down from there."

Mountford says he always knew Broadhurst would. "Mark's problem was that he could coast in the Canterbury club competition and get away with it," says Mountford, who now lives on Queensland's Gold Coast. "He simply had to get a lot fitter if he was going to foot it at international level. I could see he had a determination to play for his country and I took a punt that if I held that out in front of him, it would be enough to motivate him. In a way, it wasn't really a gamble. I knew he would train hard enough over those six weeks. When I saw him again he was in the sort of condition to finally do justice to his ability. Since then, he hasn't looked back."

Broadhurst was chosen to make his test debut against the Great Britain tourists that same year. But another big change was in the wind. He was still a second rower but had been pushed up into the front row when Canterbury played a Sydney metropolitan team. Mountford had noted his effectiveness in the new role. Broadhurst was chosen to make his first international appearance for New Zealand as a front rower alongside Dane Sorensen in a new-look side. "I probably didn't go that great in the first two tests [won by Great Britain] but Ces had decided that he was going to try and keep this side together. He was blooding new guys. Prior to that, the Kiwis weren't going that well and if you lost, you virtually got thrown out of the team and didn't get another chance. Ces was willing to spend a couple of years carrying the team until it all came together."

In fact, it all came together in the third test against the Poms when the Kiwis clicked and humbled the visitors 18-11. More than the odd observer has looked back on New Zealand's glory league days of the 1980s and pointed to the '79 test result as the beginning of a new era where the Kiwis regained international credibility.

Broadhurst held his position for the 1980 home series against Australia but was joined in the engine room by a new prop, a Maori warrior named Kevin Tamati. Together the pair were to become the most respected, and occasionally feared, Kiwi props of the 1980s. New Zealand still had a major inferiority complex in fronting up to the world's undisputed league champions. Not Broadhurst, though. Because he had never bothered to read league magazines, he didn't know his Australian opposite Craig Young was regarded as one of the toughest props going round.

"The first scrum, he sort of half-pie grabbed me," recalled Broadhurst. "I was doubtful about whether he really wanted to have a go or whether he was just trying a bit of gamesmanship. Not much more happened until later on when we packed a scrum and the Aussies got penalised right under their own posts. As we came up, he gave me one, so I let him have it. There wasn't much in it really."

Broadhurst has a habit of saying "there wasn't much in it really" when describing incidents in his career where he felt obliged to set a rival straight. Those who recall the punch that sat a stunned Young on his backside remember it differently. 'It was a beauty," says Kevin Tamati. "Young had respect for Mark when he got back up again, I can assure you."

The Aussies were obviously slow learners. On the same tour, Broadhurst turned out for the South Island against the tourists. The Aussies, expecting to win in a canter, were becoming increasingly frustrated that the southerners were proving so hard to shake. "In those days, the Aussies were renowned for jumping all over you in the play-the-ball, standing on your fingers, all that sort of rubbish. I was trying to get up to play the ball when one of their forwards, Graham Wynn, came past and jumped straight on the top of my leg. I grabbed his jersey as he was going past, pulled myself up and gave him one. There wasn't much in it really. The old Aussies have always been pretty arrogant. You give them a bit of their own back and they don't like it."

At the end of the year, the Kiwis made a tour of the United Kingdom that was significant in both Broadhurst's international career and the Kiwis' development as a force to be reckoned with during the early to mid-1980s. Broadhurst played strongly on tour, firmly establishing himself as a test regular. The tour bore fruit in other ways. Ken Arthurson, now the head of the Australian and International Rugby Leagues, was in England when the tour was on. In those days, Arthurson was secretary of the powerful Manly-Warringah club in Sydney. His cheque book was also rumoured to know no limit. A few weeks after Broadhurst returned to Christchurch, he was a few paddocks away on his farm when the phone rang. "I ran out to tell

Tough as teak, Broadhurst was far more than just a yardage prop. His ball skills were greatly admired.

him Ken Arthurson was on the phone and he didn't believe me," recalled wife Anne. "Eventually I convinced him I wasn't joking and he was over the fence as fast as he could go!"

Broadhurst explains his enthusiasm. "I was hoping the tour would get me some offers. In those days, everybody wanted to be a professional. I wanted to get into the money if I could." Broadhurst was now playing league for a living, achieving a life-long goal. But this was one time when he might have been better served reading a bit more about the Sydney premiership scene.

Broadhurst arrived in Sydney not even knowing what colours Manly wore. He was also blissfully unaware of the Sea Eagles' reputation as the greediest and most hated league club in Australia. Situated on a beautiful peninsula which is home to some of Sydney's richest residents, the Sea Eagles had always been loathed by rival supporters. But in the late 1970s and early 1980s, Manly intensified the antipathy towards them by going on a chequebook raid of other clubs, netting their most promising players. Derisively titled "The Silvertails", Manly's raids were mostly directed at the struggling Western Suburbs club. In one fell swoop, the ailing Magpies lost rugged second rower Les Boyd, hooker Ray Brown and exciting utility back John Dorahy.

Such was the feeling about the well-heeled Sea Eagles that when progress results from matches were relayed over the PA at matches around Sydney, both opposing groups of fans would cheer if Manly were being beaten. Broadhurst walked into this scenario without having any idea of how Manly were viewed. He may have been a freezing worker from Christchurch who relished the role of the underdog, but in the eyes of the Manly-hating Sydney league public, Broadhurst was a big-name Kiwi being paid good money to add even more lustre to an already star-studded line-up.

Broadhurst had another surprise to come after making his debut against Parramatta. Manly's second game of the season was away against Wests. Broadhurst still didn't understand the depth of feeling among the Magpies over their chequebook purge. He quickly found out. "We ran out and I was standing about 10 metres from halfway when the Wests guys came out. All of a sudden they started up at me, calling me a Kiwi mongrel and told me how I'd wish I'd never come over there!"

Despite a rugged introduction, Broadhurst made a bold start at Manly, scoring four tries in his first five matches. But even that early in his Sydney career, there were disconcerting signs for the big Kiwi. And not just the way rival clubs and supporters felt about Manly either. "During one of our first games, I remember saying to Les Boyd: 'Boydie, there's a big open blind here, come off my shoulder'. He just told me to get stuffed. The Australian internationals at the club were the ones who wanted to be the stars. They were the ones who wanted to run wide and score the tries. They'd say to me: 'Your job is just to take it up. That's all you have to do'. They didn't want anybody else to look good other than themselves. Quite often, I'd be looking for a player to off-load to and there would be nobody there. They wanted me to graft and nothing else."

The attitude grated on Broadhurst who had always believed props should be given free reign to use all their skills. He didn't want to just be a mobile battering ram. But Broadhurst was never a man to shirk his responsibilities. Manly were paying him to produce and, by God, he was going to produce. He was consistently a sterling performer for Manly, his pride overcoming his disdain for the way he was being used and growing uneasiness over the attitude of the Sea Eagles.

Manly reached the September play-offs and made the preliminary final, just one step away from the premiership decider. It was in that match that another chapter in Broadhurst's hardman reputation was written. Newton boasted a rugged prop named Steve Bowden. "We were into it from the first scrum," said Broadhurst. "Actually, he probably had the edge on me that day. Anyway there was a bit of a blue and he came in and knocked me half silly. He head-butted me and then had a go at me on the ground. The first one only knocked me, it was the second that did the damage."

In fact, Bowden had hit Broadhurst from behind and viciously head-butted the Kiwi. The referee had no hesitation in sending Bowden off. Most expected Broadhurst to be replaced. Bowden had smashed his cheekbone, closing the sinus vessel on one side of his face. In less than a minute, both of Broadhurst's eyes had puffed up. One was completely closed, the other blackened. Both cheeks were a swollen purple. His team-mates were mortified when Broadhurst refused to go off. "Just give me the ball and I'll take it up," Broadhurst growled. And he did. In the following weeks, he needed plastic surgery to rebuild his depressed left cheek.

Manly lost to Newtown but the following season went on to make the grand final. But Broadhurst didn't appear in the game's showpiece match. He had performed well for the Sea Eagles all season, consistently polling among the game's leading front rowers in media competitions. But he was becoming increasingly disgruntled with life in Sydney. "I hated it there. It was too much of a rat-race. And I used to hate the trainings. After playing on Sunday, I used to dread going to Brookvale on Tuesday night for training. It was tough adjusting. Nobody was going out of their way to help us either."

But playing for the Kiwis kept Broadhurst going. It was his loyalty to his country that was to cost him, though. He decided to go with the Kiwis to Papua-New Guinea midway through the 1982 season. "I got offside with Manly over that," he acknowledged. "At that stage, I'd told Ken Arthurson I didn't want to stay another year (Broadhurst was in the second year of a three-year contract). He said they wouldn't stand in my way but then they went dog on me and tried to kick me out of the squad straight away."

Indeed, Broadhurst had never played reserve grade from the day he arrived at Manly. But a week after telling the club he wanted out at the end of the season, he was dumped to the second-stringers for the weekend round against Eastern Suburbs. Then, in the greatest insult they could hand the proud Kiwi, Broadhurst was left out of the 26-man Manly squad to prepare for the grand final against Parramatta.

There was one further insult to come. Broadhurst had been among the leading props in the prestigious Dally M awards. He and Anne had received an invitation to the awards night and were delighted to discover they were going to be seated at a very prominent table, indicating Broadhurst was in with a good chance of winning the prop's trophy. "Then, out of the blue, we got a phone call saying our seats had been changed," explained Anne. "We were moved from the front to right at the back. Mark didn't win, of course. After all, that would have embarrassed Manly, with Mark having been dropped." The sarcasm in Anne Broadhurst's voice makes it clear how she feels about the incident.

Manly might not have rated, publicly anyway, Broadhurst but plenty of their rivals did. Easts, Cronulla, Penrith and Canberra all made him tempting offers to join them from 1983. The Broadhursts still planned to return to Christchurch, though. However, Manly teammate John Dorahy was another who had a high regard for the prop's abilities. Dorahy was joining the Illawarra Steelers, a new club based on the New South Wales south coast and was joining the competition

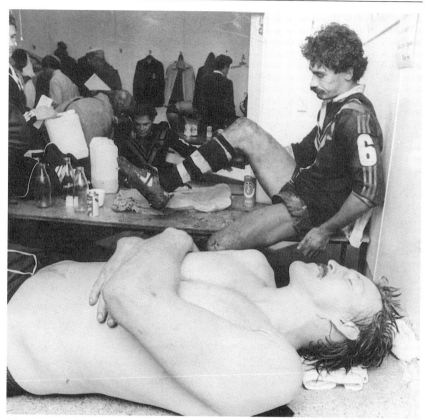

No-one could ever excuse Broadhurst of not giving his all.

along with the Canberra Raiders. Broadhurst liked Wollongong, the laid-back coastal city where the Steelers were based. He signed for two years.

They were largely productive seasons – he even kicked a field goal to give the Steelers a 12-11 win over North Sydney! But Australian league was rapidly becoming stereotyped and Illawarra used Broadhurst in much the same fashion as Manly had...as a battering ram.

The 1983 season was to contain an important triumph for Broadhurst, though. Graham Lowe had taken over the Kiwis who were preparing for a two-test series against Australia. New Zealand proved surprisingly competitive, despite losing the first match 16-4. The return international was set for Lang Park. Despite inspirational captain Mark Graham being on the sideline with an injury, the Kiwis carved out a historic 19-12 triumph in the famous Brisbane cauldron, setting the stage for some famous achievements to come in the following years.

For Broadhurst, it was a special match. For the first time in his test career, he had come off the ground a winner against Australia. "It was a pretty sweet win, one of the best I've had," he grins. "We'd got close to them in '82. This time we finished the job." Broadhurst remembers relishing the flight back to Sydney as the Australian and Kiwi players dispersed and returned to their clubs. In a delicious irony, the Kiwi found himself seated next to Australian and Manly captain Max Krilich. "Max had never played in a losing test as Australian captain and Lang Park was to be his international swansong. All I heard from him the whole flight back was how he had been injured before the game and shouldn't really have played," said Broadhurst with a wry grin.

Broadhurst didn't suspect it at the time but the against-the-odds Lang Park triumph was to be his last test. Mark Graham, Broadhurst's captain for so long, is effusive in his praise of his former team-mate. "Great man, thorough gentleman and a real hard bastard," is Graham's to-the-point assessment of his former team-mate. "He's an uncomplicated bloke. He always made the hard yards up the middle and if you wanted to have a fight, he'd beat the crapper out of you. He was one of those honest players who earned the Kiwis respect with the public because he always gave his all."

Kevin Tamati enthusiastically endorses Graham's assessment. "'Broadie' was one of the best open side props I ever played with," says Tamati. "He and I were so good together. I never saw him take a backward step. I have a great deal of respect for the man."

After seeing out his stint with Illawarra, Broadhurst received yet another unexpected offer; this time to take his family to the other side of the world to play for Hull Kingston Rovers in England's first division. It was a move that gave Broadhurst a new lease of life. It came at a cost, though. "The New Zealand Rugby League wanted the leading English-based contenders to return home six weeks before the end of the English season so the selectors could see them play. I couldn't be bothered with that so I decided to give away international football."

Broadhurst was an instant success at Hull KR. The lifestyle agreed with him and Anne. And the more open, crowd-orientated English game allowed him freer rein to use his skills rather than merely impersonating a human bludgeon as he had been forced so often to do in Australia. He helped Hull to the first division championship up the first two seasons he was there(1983-84 and 1984-85). "It was great. We lived in a little village just a few miles out of Hull. The training was nowhere near as severe as in Sydney. And if you made a mistake on the field, it wasn't the end of the world."

Content after two years of success, the Broadhursts then returned to Christchurch. But then, a season later, the phone went again. This time it was Wigan on the other end. Was he interested in a season at Central Park? Graham Lowe was soon to take over and it would be more than worth his while, said the voice on the other end. Broadhurst was tempted, but remembered a promise to Hull KR that if he ever returned to the English game, he would make his old club aware of the offer and give them an option to match or top it. Hull KR weren't about to let Broadhurst slip away. He went back for one more year, a season that featured a match against the touring Queensland team.

Queensland's attitude in the game irritated Broadhurst. "They were right over the top," he recalled. "They were just coming in with the knees the whole time and they put our hooker and one of our props out of the game." When Queensland hooker Shane Bernardin sunk his knees into Broadhurst in a tackle, that was the final straw. Broadhurst got up, played the ball... and decked Bernardin. Hull KR won the bitter match 8-6, inflicting Queensland's only defeat of the tour.

Later in the season, Broadhurst received news that his father had developed cancer. The family moved home again. Even though his professional career was over, Broadhurst continued to play in the Canterbury competition, taking the role of player-coach at Papanui for several years and still playing for the club right up to 1991 at the age of 36. In 1992, he became player-coach for Lincoln College, a young side playing senior league, one level below premier. The following year, he finally hung up his boots and now coaches the College side.

The game remains in his blood. With his five acres near the Christchurch airport, three young hockey-playing daughters and a couple of ponies to ride, Broadhurst is more than contented with his lot. The weekends are busy with he and Anne jostling between hockey and league coaching commitments. "I'm pretty happy," he smiles. "About my biggest problem now is keeping the students in my team off the grog on Friday nights."

KEVIN SKINNER
'The Bok Buster'

"When I got into camp in Christchurch, I couldn't believe what some of the guys were saying. I talked to Tiny White and Bob Duff and they said to me: 'Well, we're feeling a bit intimidated by the Boks, Kev'. Intimidated! I couldn't believe it. I said: 'C'mon you buggers, you're better than that.' See, you have to understand the Afrikaaner. Intimidation is part of their mentality. Let's face it, they've existed in the country since 1652 by kicking blacks' backsides round. That's their nature. I understood that. But a lot of the other guys in that '56 team didn't. By the time that third test rolled round, I knew it was time somebody stood up to the Boks."

IT takes a considerable amount to rile Kevin Skinner. Here's a man who is seemingly made for the cliché "gentle giant". His hands are huge, the size of the Argentine steaks the All Blacks relish whenever they tour the South American country. He even speaks gently. And a smile is never far from those genial features. All of which threw me a little when I first met Skinner. After all, this was the infamous "Bok Buster"; the man whom legend had it had single-handedly destroyed the 1956 touring Springboks in the crucial third test; the former heavy-weight boxing champion whom you tangled with at your peril. Such were the legends and aura surrounding Kevin Skinner, you almost expect to meet Hannibal Lecter in football boots!

But like so many legends, not all is what it seems. Skinner's rugby career is inexplicably tied to the 1956 Boks. It is one of the incongruities of rugby that certain All Blacks are remembered almost solely for one match. Mention the name Ron Elvidge and images of his epic performance in the third test against the 1950 Lions instantly spring to mind. And, even at this stage of his career, Zinzan Brooke is likely to be most remembered for his audacious tap penalty try against the Springboks at Ellis Park in 1992. So it goes with Skinner and the third test against the South Africans.

Yet so much of what happened that day at Lancaster Park has been steeped in myth and embellished. Unfortunately, the innocent victim is Kevin Skinner. So much so that when he stridently criticised Richard Loe for his behaviour of the 1992 season and declared he would send back his centennial tie to the New Zealand union if the Waikato prop was ever selected to play for the All Blacks again, the reaction from the misinformed was swift and vehement. How dare Skinner say that, wrote one irate Loe fan in *Rugby News*. Had we all forgotten that Skinner had been an absolute thug during the 56 series? The reality is different.

But first some background. Kevin Skinner grew up in Dunedin and Oamaru and by 16 was already such an impressive forward he was selected to play for Otago Town against Country. He was also a more than competent boxer and that same year of 1946 he became the Otago heavyweight champion. The following year he was to make his Otago debut under the man many regard as the father of New Zealand rugby, Vic Cavanagh. It was a memorable first match with Otago lifting the Ranfurly Shield from Southland 17-11.

His other major success that year came when Skinner added the New Zealand heavyweight title to his Otago belt. But despite his success in the ring, Skinner never seriously considered going on with his boxing. "In those days, there were only a handful of heavyweights going round and you simply didn't even think about going overseas," he recalls. "Basically, I felt like I'd gone as far as I could in boxing."

Skinner continued to pay his rugby dues for Otago in 1948, by this time moving into the front row from lock. His rise to prominence was quickly noted by the All Black selectors who named him in the touring squad to travel to South Africa. The 1949 series was to make an indelible impression on Skinner. The record-books mark the All Blacks of that year as, statistically, New Zealand's most unsuccessful national team in our proud 100-year-plus history. They lost all four tests and Fred Allen's distinguished playing career was tainted forever by the fact he led the team to the Dark Continent.

But the record books can be cruel. Skinner is emphatic the squad "wasn't that bad". "It's been well documented that we were very weak at halfback on that tour," he said. "But there were many other reasons. People talked about the refereeing we encountered but, to me, the travel was the most demanding factor. People simply have no conception of how vast that continent is. There was no air travel in those days. Everything was by train. It was incredibly draining."

Skinner was to emerge from the fateful tour as one of the few All Black successes. He was only 21 when the All Blacks left and was expected to play second-string tighthead prop to the tour vice-captain Ray Dalton. But Skinner was a young man in a hurry. Dalton didn't get a test on tour. Skinner made his debut in the first test, won 15-11 by the Boks, and never looked like surrendering it. In fact, the front row from that tour of Skinner, hooker Has Catley and strongarm man Johnny Simpson was to go on and become one of the most respected and feared in All Black history.

Skinner learnt much on the tour, including what went on between the ears of most Springbok forwards. The South Africans threw their weight round from the outset of the tour and some All Blacks buckled. Skinner quickly realised that intimidation was a big part of the South African rugby psyche.

Upon his return to New Zealand, Skinner quickly built on his growing reputation with powerful displays for the All Blacks in their series win over the 1950 British Lions. This was a series that featured a test considered to be the most dramatic in All Black history. The first test at Carisbrook had been drawn 9-all but New Zealand lifted their game to win the second 8-0. The third test was set for Athletic Park. The Lions led 3-0 early and not long after Skinner lost his inspirational front row partner Johnny Simpson with a serious knee injury. Then, just before halftime, a second blow. All Black captain Ron Elvidge clashed heads with a Lion rival and opened up a head gash that needed four stitches to close, while also badly injuring his collarbone.

But minutes into the second half, Elvidge came back on, his right eye covered in sticking plaster and his right arm limp by his side. The New Zealanders were forced to play with just six forwards, yet were still dominating the Lions at ruck and maul time. Then, out of nowhere, the All Blacks launched a telling raid and suddenly Elvidge popped up with the ball and dived over a mass of bodies for a match-winning try. The All Blacks prevailed 6-3 in a test regarded as one of

Kevin Skinner...his reputation began with the Pirates club side in Dunedin and quickly spread north.

the most dramatic in the game's history, before going on to take the fourth international as well.

In 1951, New Zealand toured Australia and Skinner scored his first – and only – test try against the Wallabies with a cheeky piece of gamesmanship. Fullback Maurice Cockerill had kicked ahead and Skinner was chief among the pursuers. A Wallaby ran the ball into touch. An alert Skinner yelled to winger Ron Jarden to take a quick throw-in and he then sprinted a handful of yards to touch down without a hand laid on him. There was only one problem. Jarden hadn't used the same ball which had gone into touch as the rules demanded. But even though the Australian crowd was going berserk, Skinner was jogging back to halfway with the referee seemingly oblivious to all that had happened. "I wasn't going to tell him, that's for sure," chuckles Skinner, obviously delighted to get one-up on our trans-Tasman rugby friends.

By this time, Skinner was being hailed as being ahead of his time as an international prop. Certainly, his aerobic fitness and ball skills were patently superior to his rival front rowers. "I think the boxing had helped," he said. "I enjoyed the training and it gave me superior fitness." In the era Skinner played, props rarely handled the football. "I went through whole test matches where I never got the thing in my hands. That was hardly a rarity," he says.

But when Skinner did get the ball between those two meaty slabs, he was a sight to behold. Extremely mobile and with a loose forward's ball skills, Skinner was very much the All Black prototype for the props of the 1980s and 1990s. His All Black career went from strength to strength. He captained the All Blacks when they drew the 1952 series against the touring Australians and played all five internationals on the 1953 tour to the United Kingdom and France led by Bob Stuart. Skinner played perhaps his best rugby on that tour.

In testimony to his ironman reputation, he played 27 of the 35 matches, captaining the side whenever Stuart didn't play. The All Blacks lost the internationals to Wales 13-8 and France 3-0 but beat Scotland 3-0 and England 5-0 with the Pommie front row being destroyed to such an extent that hooker Ron Hemi claimed eight tightheads!

Even though he was still at his prime, Skinner retired from All Black rugby in 1954 after 18 successive tests. The decision was forced on him by circumstances. "I was married by then and it was time for

Old scores...Australia's John Solomon and Skinner eye up the Bledisloe Cup, as eagerly sought in their days as it is today.

me to establish myself in business," he says. He spent the 1955 season playing club rugby in Dunedin but at the end of the year decided to move to Waiuku in rural south Auckland. Counties, just formed, was eager to make use of such a distinguished player and successfully talked Skinner into making himself available for provincial rugby.

But a bigger comeback was just around the corner. The 1956 Springbok tour captivated New Zealand. Never had there been such fervent anticipation surrounding a tour. New Zealand's rugby pride had been cruelly savaged by the 1949 rout. When the South Africans arrived, it was as if New Zealand had whipped itself into a frenzy. All that mattered was beating the Boks. And boy, did it matter!

Skinner was caught up as a passionate observer along with the rest of the nation. He was one man who certainly wanted to see the South Africans put in their place after the disappointments of '49. And lingering in the back of his mind was a regret that he wouldn't be getting the chance to balance the ledger. Little did he know...

Skinner listened intently on the radio as the All Blacks won a grim first test 10-6. The Bok tactics were already making an impression, though. "It was obvious the Springboks were up to their old tricks again," noted Skinner. "They open up with a bit of intimidation. They were pushing our guys around." Indeed. For the Boks, intimidation starts with the scrum. The Afrikaaner prides himself on physical dominance and the scrum represented the most obvious place to start. Rookie Otago prop Mark Irwin had a couple of ribs cracked after being knocked around, leaving the All Black selectors with a problem ahead of the second test.

New Zealand might have been 1-0 up in the series, but the selectors were worried. Realising they needed a harder mentality up front as well as a powerful scrummager, a discreet call was put through to Counties to enquire just what sort of nick Skinner was in. Tom Morrison, a selector at the time, then turned up at Pukekohe Stadium to watch Skinner and also North Auckland's Peter Jones go round. Both men were to have a marked effect on the ultimate outcome of the series. The selectors decided not to bring Skinner in for the second international, though. Their worst fears were quickly realised.

The Boks levelled the series with an 8-3 triumph at stormy Athletic Park where hundreds of fans had camped outside the ground overnight to get the best possible vantage spots. Frank McAtamney, brought in for Irwin, was given a torrid workover by the rugged South African props Chris Koch and the feared Jaap Bekker. The All Black scrum was in diabolical trouble. The public, obsessed with the series, were suddenly very worried. And adding to the anxiety was the feeling that the All Blacks were allowing themselves to be intimidated up front. Koch and Bekker were getting away with mayhem.

Bekker in particular seemed to have the New Zealand forwards' measure. The year before, the Boks had toured Australia and the story had filtered across the Tasman that Bekker, who was a real swaggering showman who delighted in drawing attention to himself, had scrummed against a set of goalposts during a practice session and broken the upright! But there was also a sinister side to the two South African powermen. Several New Zealand critics believed the Bok props were deliberately trying to work over the opposition front row. Frequently, the opposition was dangerously taken down. On other occasions, Bekker would bore in on his prop. Irwin's ribs had been cracked this way when Bekker wrenched him in the first test.

With the series teetering, the selectors went back to the prop who had served them so well in previous years. Skinner was recalled. He was ready. "Every Springbok side that has ever been picked is selected around their front row," Skinner explains. "That's their style.

Huge front rowers. And you've got to know what the next trick is that they're going to throw at you."

Skinner wasn't prepared for the mood in the All Black camp, though. The team was on a knife-edge. The pressure was enormous with the players constantly being told by their own officials, the media and the general public that they had to win for the sake of New Zealand rugby. "I had the feeling that some guys believed the world would end if we didn't beat the Boks. But some of the blokes were also saying they felt intimidated. I talked to Tiny White and Bob Duff and they said to me: 'Well, we're feeling a bit intimidated, Kevin'. I said: 'Come on, you fellas are better than that'. The thing was, I understood the Afrikaaner. They always try you on and you've got to let them know you're not going to stand for it. As soon as you do that, they knock it off and go back to playing football. I knew from that from '49. Intimidation is one of the things they live with over there. Let's face it, they've existed in the country since 1652 from kicking blacks' backsides around. That's their nature. I understood that, but a lot of the other guys from that '56 team didn't. Then there was the hype around them like Bekker supposedly snapping a set of goalposts in half. People believed that. Bekker was a good scrummager but not that good. If that happened, the bloody goalpost must have had woodworm."

Skinner is adamant he never went into the third test with the intention of hitting anybody. But he also wasn't going to stand for any rubbish from Koch and Bekker. "I wasn't going to be taken for a ride. They were cheating and if the referee wasn't going to do anything about it, I would," he declares. "I felt if there was going to be a problem it was going to come in the lineouts and not the scrums. The Boks had been coming through the entire series and our guys weren't doing a thing about it. In those days, if you got into the opposition's lineout, you got all hell. That's how it was. You stayed on your own side."

Indeed, Koch had thumped Tiny Hill in the match against Canterbury for exactly that reason. In the first lineout, Koch smashed through and monstered New Zealand's halfback. Skinner and Koch were actually friends. They'd made their debuts in the first test of the '49 series and Koch, upon arriving in New Zealand, had written to Skinner, said he would look up the New Zealander's mother while he was in Otago and added he hoped to 'catch up' to his old mate at some stage. He did catch up to Skinner. But not exactly how he planned.

When Koch burst through an early lineout, Skinner gave him an evil glare and said: "Chris, next time, there'll be trouble". Unfortunately for Koch, he didn't listen. On cue in the next lineout, he barged through. Skinner let fly with one of his specials. Koch never knew what had happened. The Bok forwards were stunned.

At halftime, Skinner swapped sides in the scrum with Waikato's Ian Clarke who, despite his impressive technique, was having trouble constantly countering Bekker who was also getting up to his old tricks. As the first scrum went down, it immediately broke up in a flurry of fists with Skinner and Bekker at the centre of it. "He was trying to pop me and I just turned it into a bit of a skirmish so the referee would notice what was going on and force him to deal with the situation," explained Skinner. Indeed, Bekker seemed stunned somebody had finally stood up to him. He immediately settled down and played rugby for the rest of the game. The All Blacks went on to win 17-10 before sealing a mighty series with an 11-5 win at Eden Park in a match famous for Peter Jones' gamebreaking try and "I'm buggered" quote over the PA system immediately after fulltime.

Rugby writers who covered the battles of '56 had no doubts Skinner's inclusion for the last two tests and his refusal to bow to South Africa's strongarm tactics swung the series New Zealand's way. But that did not stop the controversy that swirled around Skinner following the third test. This was a series that had created huge passion among both New Zealanders and South Africans. Emotions were running high. South Africans viewed Skinner's inclusion for the third test as highly provocative.

"South Africans were convinced that Skinner had been brought back into the All Black side primarily for the purpose of committing mayhem," wrote Graeme Barrow, a South African who has lived in New Zealand for many years, in his book *All Blacks versus Springboks: A Century of Rugby Rivalry*. "The circumstantial evidence was such that this conclusion seemed to be the only plausible one. The Springboks – in Jaap Bekker, Chris Koch, Harry Newton-Walker and Piet du Toit – had tremendously powerful props.....[when Skinner was called in] the South African reaction was immediate. Because New Zealand had been unable to find props capable of standing up to the Springboks props' greater strength and superior scrumming technique, Skinner had been brought back specifically to soften up first

Skinner and family. He quit All Black rugby in 1954 to spend more time with them.

Koch, and then Bekker, with illegitimate tactics. Once it was revealed that Skinner was a former New Zealand amateur heavyweight boxing champion, even the sceptical were convinced."

But Barrow was fair-minded enough to record that Skinner hardly had a reputation for thuggery. "Certainly he was recalled to add iron to a front row that had been outclassed, but recalled to punch two props into submission? He'd never done anything like it before – against South Africa, Australia, France or the Home Unions," wrote Barrow. "Besides, what was more logical than to recall, at a time when other props were shown to be inadequate, the country's strongest and most experienced prop – and one who had, moreover, experience of marking the Springbok props in South Africa?"

Team-mates of Skinner's confirm he warned Koch before decking him. And, to a man, endorsed their frontrower's actions. Yet immediately after the match and, indeed, in the 35 or more years that have followed, Skinner has had to regularly respond to charges of being a thug. Much of the reputation came from the colourful writing of the pressmen of the era, particularly the visiting South Africans. Fred Labuschagne wrote a book for South African readers titled *'Goodbye*

Newlands, Farewell Eden Park' where he penned the following about Skinner: "The All Black prop-forward's name will always be synonymous with the 1956 Springbok tour of New Zealand – at least as far as South Africans are concerned. Long after the kicking exploits of Don Clarke and the rhino-charges of Peter Jones are forgotten, South Africans will recall, as vividly as though they were in Christchurch themselves, the flying fists of the former amateur heavyweight boxing champion of New Zealand. He will always remain to Springbok supporters what Dr Danie Craven will be to New Zealanders – the most discussed and controversial figure of that unhappy series."

That was the South African perspective, of course. Here in New Zealand, several pressmen were equally determined to turn Skinner into an icon. He became lionised as 'The Bok Buster' and with every re-telling of the story, the punches became more dramatic and the action more brutal. It all became too much for Skinner who felt obliged to write a letter to the *Auckland Star* asking for the newspapers to knock off writing about the incidents. "It was beginning to get to me by that stage," he says. "For starters, I only hit Chris once. And I don't think I even got a solid hit in on Bekker. As I've always said, I just wanted to start a scuffle with him to get things sorted out. But the way the papers were going on it was getting right out of hand."

Indeed, one scribe wrote that Skinner had deliberately swapped sides with Ian Clarke so he could deal to Bekker. According to the reporter, Skinner had even said to Clarke after the deed: 'There you go, you'll be right now.' "Each guy who got a hold of the story would add something new. It became ridiculous," Skinner says.

Morrie Mackenzie, an esteemed rugby writer who covered every international tour of New Zealand by a major nation over a period spanning 50 years, offered a new twist in his book *Black, Black, Black*. Mackenzie believed Skinner's inclusion for the third test was almost providential. In his book, Mackenzie describes the illegal Springbok scrum technique: "In 1956, the Springboks showed that they had been experimenting with the possibilities of 'working' the opposing front row," he wrote. "At first it consisted of wrestling an opposing front rower off balance, dragging him downwards, screening his sight of the ball coming in or forcing him to either suddenly shoot up in the air or risk serious injury. An even more sinister aspect of these shenanigans occurred when the huge weight of an international 3-4-1 scrum was applied by suddenly straightening the legs, especially on an angled spearhead."

Mackenzie goes on to claim Irwin's injury was a direct result of one of these Springbok manoeuvres while also recalling how his replacement for the second test, McAtamney, was 'shot up in the air' in the first scrum. "The return of Kevin Skinner to the New Zealand team in the third test stopped all this from developing into something that could have rocked the game to its foundations," wrote Mackenzie. "Skinner was the strongest front row prop that ever lived, stronger even than Jaap Bekker, and he soon made it clear at Christchurch that these monkey tricks had to stop. It think it was providential they did, because I'm sure nobody in the Springbok camp realised the lethal possibilities of what they were experimenting with."

"I agree with that," Skinner says. "They were pulling guys down. I knew enough about the front row not to let them get me into that situation. But the likes of Frank McAtamney, well, I think he was led into it like a lamb to slaughter. He just wasn't ready for it."

Significantly, Skinner and Koch remained friends after the '56 series, the South African simply accepting the age-old rugby dictum that if you get up to no good on occasions on the field, you copped your medicine when it was dished out. And even Bekker said there were no hard feelings. At the third test dinner, he approached Skinner and joked to him that he should never have given up boxing. "You would have many medals," he teased his rival. Intriguingly, Bekker has even helped contribute to the embellishment of the Bok Buster stories. "See this tooth," he once told a New Zealand journalist while flashing the gold-capped subject of his conversation. "I was with Kevin Skinner and I told him to let me have a look at a gold ring he was wearing. He took it off and I put it in my pocket and I told him it would go in my front tooth when I got home to South Africa, the same tooth that he broke in the third test. Yes, the gold in my tooth came from Kevin's ring. Bekkers can't be choosers." Not quite. "No, that's rubbish," laughs Skinner. "Jaapie was always a showman."

Skinner played once more against the Boks on their '56 tour, turning out for a combined Bay of Plenty-Thames Valley-Counties side against the tourists after the third test. Some of the Boks were still angry over the Lancaster Park ructions and Jan Pickard declared loudly in a hotel bar that he was personally going to "fix" Skinner in this game. "He was laying bets round the countryside that he would have me off before five minutes were up," says Skinner. "Ned Barry, who was our coach, got a hold of me and said: 'Look, the whole town is seething about Pickard saying this, what are you going to do?' So I told Ned to let me mark the bugger in the lineouts because that way I'd know where he was if he did try anything. He put the boot into me once late in the game but other than that he never tried a thing." Wise move, Jan.

In his book *Old Heroes* Auckland journalist Warwick Roger relates just how fierce the feeling and the conflict was between the All Black and Springbok players. He relates a tale of an old newsreel film that was passed around in those pre-TV days. Test referee Bill Fright provides the commentary. At one point in the footage, Skinner goes down on the ball and Fright says: "Watch the Springbok forwards attempt to kick Skinner'. Apparently the incident is crystal clear in the film. Fright comments: "Skinner said in his slow drawl: 'You bastards can't even kick straight'."

Skinner retired again from international rugby after the '56 series, content in the knowledge he had finally redressed the biggest disappointment of his All Black career when the '49 side had been so summarily dealt with. "There have been greater games of rugby but the fever surrounding that series was special," he says. "The whole nation was just gripped with rugby and the atmosphere was unbelievable. The intensity of the series matched that. You would never have thought it was just a rugby game. At the time, it was like the greatest battle New Zealand had ever been involved in. But to get there and win it...well, I retired happily after that."

Indeed, Skinner played just two more years of club rugby, coached for one, moved to West Auckland and ran several successful businesses before retiring. He became president of the New Zealand Barbarians for several years and developed a passion for golf he still enjoys. He has even travelled to South Africa twice and admits surprise at the warm welcome he received. "Never once was any person discourteous to me," he says. "And even Danie Craven welcomed me. Now that was a surprise!"

Now and then, the myths of the '56 Bok Buster come back to haunt him. He was a vocal critic of Richard Loe's shenanigins during the 1992 season and, in a controversial article I wrote for Australian *Penthouse* magazine, declared he would send his All Black tie back to the New Zealand Rugby Football Union if Loe was ever picked to represent his country again following his six-month ban for eye-goug-ing Greg Cooper. Yet Skinner then had to endure newspaper letter writers and amateur critics branding him a hypocrite and claiming his antics of '56 were as bad as Loe's.

For Ian Clarke, Skinner's propping partner during the '56 series, those claims border on the sacrilegious. "Kevin was never a thug," says Clarke. "Loe's pretty good with blokes on the ground but I've never seen him take on a guy standing up. Kevin didn't go looking for trouble but he wouldn't tolerate anybody taking liberties with him or one of his team-mates. But when he did feel the need to straighten somebody out, it was never done with any fanfare. These big haymakers that travel two miles never hurt anybody. Kevin's used to travel about four inches and you wouldn't even see them. You didn't even know he had thrown one until the forwards had broken up and there's some bloke lying on the ground. But, I can guarantee you, everytime it happened, the guy deserved it."

KEVIN TAMATI
'KT'

Lang Park, Brisbane: It's the closest thing Australian sport has to a modern-day coliseum. And if you want to know how the Christians felt, just don the sky blue jumper of New South Wales or the black jersey of New Zealand.

Kevin Tamati could hear 40,000 Queenslanders baying for Kiwi blood. Australia had just been awarded a penalty in a great attacking position. Their momentum was building. Ten metres behind the tap kick, Australian second rower Rohan Hancock was twitching, readying himself for the impersonation of a charging rhino that he did so well. Hancock was a Queenslander too. They loved him up here. Tamati was also twitching...only, with anticipation. Hancock took the ball from hooker Max Krilich on the fly. The impact was frightening. Tamati had lined him up from 10 metres away and met the Australian with a full-blooded but legitimate shoulder charge. Hancock didn't just go backwards. He was propelled horizontally! He went down, and stayed down. Didn't move. A hush of silence came over the Coliseum. The television commentator remarked he'd never heard Lang Park so quiet. Tamati ran back to position with the hint of a smile on his face. If there was anything he really enjoyed, it was shutting up Australians.

TRY this word association test. Kevin Tamati? Hands up if you said Greg Dowling. Got you? Right! That's how it seems to be with Tamati, or "KT" as his closest mates refer to him.

Despite 22 Tests proudly played in the black jersey and a distinguished career for Warrington and Widnes in England, Tamati seemingly can't escape the Dowling curse. Everybody, and I mean everybody, inevitably asks him about *that* sideline brawl with the rugged Australian prop during the first Test in 1985. It is a yoke that hangs around Tamati's neck, an unfair burden that detracts from the qualities he brought to the black jersey between 1979 and 1986.

The true Tamati is reflected more in his massive hit on Rohan Hancock than in swapping meaty swings with Dowling. But, like it or not, the '85 brawl at Lang Park is part of the Tamati legend and cannot be ignored. In many ways, the incident was a microcosm of Tamati's career. Throughout his entire rugby league career, Kevin Tamati has had to overcome the odds.

The most fundamental was his size. Compared to most international props, he was giving the opposition a handy head start in weight. For most of his career, Tamati's optimum playing weight was only 95 kilograms (15 stone). Among forwards, let alone front rowers, that's sometimes not much more than pygmy status. When it comes to the rhino charges props must make to earn the hard yards on the field, every bit of extra bulk helps. Yet Tamati consistently played above his weight, his heart and an acute sense of timing more than compensating for any lack of body mass compared to his opposition.

Then there was his background. Raised in Hastings in a strictly working class family comprising four brothers and five sisters, Tamati's early working years were spent in a Wellington abattoir. He was a battler in every sense of the word. Indeed, when he first made the Kiwi team to face Australia, he suffered an acute identity crisis, struggling to believe that he had any right to even be on the same field as Australian superstars like Les Boyd and Craig Young. But eventually Tamati came to believe in himself. He soon realised that the Australians were not supermen, and that he was the equal of the game's top props. Yet he still often battled discrimination and lack of respect from some of his peers. It was arguably this latter fact that lit the fuse for the explosive Dowling incident.

The Kiwis went into the 1985 series against Australia convinced they had the talent, the skills and the coach to finally beat the world champions. With two tests to be played in New Zealand, their confidence was high that they could record the first series win over Australia since 1953. But the first test was to be played midweek under lights at infamous Lang Park, a seemingly innocuous suburban Brisbane football ground that transforms itself into a seething cauldron whenever Queensland or Australia plays there.

The first test was typically rugged and close until Australia skipped away during the second half. "As per usual in any encounter with Australia, it was a pretty niggly affair and there were quite a few square ups at different times," recalls Tamati. "Earlier on, Steve Roach had laid a ball on for Noel Cleal to score the first try just to the right of the sticks. Dowling took offence to Kurt (Sorensen) belting Roach after he'd laid the ball on. So it virtually started from there. All through the game there were little niggles going on. Then about five or six minutes from the end of the game, Dowling and I both found ourselves at the play-the-ball. We ended up having a go at each other and a bit of a fracas started and we both got sin-binned."

As the pair walked off the field towards the players' tunnel, an ugly brawl broke out and was vividly captured by television cameras. Egged on by rabid Lang Park fans, the pair slugged it out in a fierce confrontation. Footage of the incident shows Tamati walking off first with Dowling about a metre behind him. The Australian appears to say something to Tamati who then turned his head and fired back a few words of his own. Tamati continued to walk off but Dowling put his hand on the Kiwi's shoulder.

From there, all hell broke loose. Tamati threw the first punch and it was on. Tamati's explanation is typically to the point. "As we were walking off he was behind me and started saying: 'You ****ing black ****, that's all you're good for. You can't play football. You're nothing but a black ****'. I turned round and told him to let it go. But as we were about to walk through the gates he put his hand on my shoulder. As soon as he did, that was it, bang, I let him have it."

Tamati believes Dowling was being condescending. "The hand on the shoulder wasn't conciliatory as some people tried to tell me," he says. "Dowling was trying to belittle me. I don't mind taking verbal abuse...it's part and parcel of rugby league. It was my last series and I was quite happy just to head to the sin bin. But as soon as he touched me, that was it. I wasn't going to let him belittle me. Do you remember the English comedian Benny Hill and how he used to pat that little bald-headed guy on the head? It was like an attitude of "**** you". That was immediately how I felt and I just said to myself: 'I'm not taking this shit'. I don't regret it even now. I have never regretted it. The only thing I do regret is that it was shown on television in

FLASHPOINT!...Kevin Tamati responds with a few words of his own to Greg Dowling as the pair head for the sin bin at Lang Park in 1985.

IGNITION!...It's on as eager patrons cram for a better view.

THE AFTERMATH...A bloodied Dowling is escorted away with Australian team-mate Noel Cleal in tow.

front of impressionable kids."

What Tamati also regrets is the way the Dowling incident has followed him around, and the exaggerated rumours surrounding it. Scuttlebutt had it that the brawl continued down the players' tunnel. "Rubbish!" retorts Tamati. Another rumour had it that Tamati had taken exception to some disparaging comments Dowling had made about the Kiwis in *Rugby League Week* and had set out to get even. Tamati had never even read the article.

For years following the brawl, Tamati could barely go anywhere or hold a media interview without the Dowling subject coming up. "When I went back to New Zealand for the Kiwi Immortals dinner in Auckland around 1989 or 1990, they showed video clips of all the guys being honoured," he recalls. "They had Ken Stirling, Ron Ackland and Roger Bailey, guys like that. And all their footage was of the great tries they scored. I was sitting there really worried because I was thinking: 'What the hell are they going to show of me? It's sure to be the Dowling blue.' That was all I needed. To their credit, they didn't show it. Peter McLeod [the Auckland chairman at the time] said to me: 'We wouldn't do that to you, Kevin', and I was grateful for that. I like to think I played a lot of constructive rugby league and that I put a lot into the game and helped New Zealand gain some respect internationally. I don't want to be remembered solely for a one-off blue."

I contacted Dowling about the brawl. He was reluctant to speak about it, saying he preferred to put it behind him. Pressed for his thoughts on Kevin Tamati as a player, he replied: "Definitely a hard man. You would rather be playing alongside him than against him. That's about all I'd say." In some respects, that speaks volumes.

It's one of the ironies of Tamati's career that he entered the code entirely by accident. In the 1960s and early 70s, Hawke's Bay was anything but a league hotbed. Young Kevin grew up playing rugby and even remembers that while watching a game of league on television with one of his brothers, he declared: 'Anyone who plays that game has got to be bloody bananas!'

His greatest claim to fame as a schoolboy was playing for Hastings Boys High's First XV on the wing and at fullback. Around the age of 17, Tamati headed to Wellington to gain work in the abattoirs. "I was keen to play some football but most of the guys in the abattoir were tied up with the Petone league club," he says. "Eventually I found one of the guys played for the Petone rugby club and I told him I'd tag along to training with him. But he headed off before me. I thought I knew how to get there but when I turned up at the park, nobody was there. I knew where the league guys were so I went down there and trained with them instead. That was my first association with league."

Tamati made an immediate impact, scoring five or six 'tries' in the touch footy session, leading to the local coach doing his level best to hold on to his new discovery. He spent the 1970 season playing fullback for the third grade team. A few games later the side was short of a loose forward and Tamati volunteered to fill the vacancy. His forward career had begun. By 1972, he was a regular in the Petone first team forward pack while still a teenager.

That same season he was selected to play for the Junior Kiwis. It was a year that contained another pleasant surprise. Until then Kevin had no idea he had a league-playing cousin from Waitara in Taranaki named Howie. "I went to the Junior Kiwi trials and my father had come down from Hastings," says Kevin. "He brought Howie over and said, 'this is your cousin, son'. Until then, I didn't even know we had family over on the West Coast."

Both Tamatis made the Junior Kiwis that year, Howie (who is four months his senior) as hooker. Tamati's league career steadily grew in stature over the following years. He made the Wellington representative squad and the New Zealand Maoris in 1973. But in those early years, he never looked upon the game as a possible passport to a better life playing professional football. "I played the game purely for social reasons and friendship. As far as a career was concerned, that never ever entered my mind," he says.

One thing did, though. The more experienced he became, the fiercer the desire to play for New Zealand grew. "I was totally focused on playing for New Zealand," he says. "Even when I was a kid playing rugby union, all I wanted to do was become an All Black. I just had a burning desire to play for New Zealand and come hell or high water, that's what I was going to do."

The breakthrough came in 1979 at the ripe age of 26. Ron Ackland had lost the Kiwi coaching job and been replaced by Ces Mountford, a tough-minded West Coaster with more football intelligence than he was given credit for. Mountford believed New Zealand could become competitive if he selected a young and determined team and stuck with them through thick and thin. Out went some of the old timers. In came young lions like Mark Broadhurst, Mark Graham, Fred Ah Kuoi, James Leuluai, the Tamati cousins and others.

"Being a West Coaster, Ces didn't favour too many Aucklanders in his line-up and he opened the team up to blokes like Howie and I and Graeme West. He went for people south of the Bombay Hills," Tamati says. That season the Kiwis hosted Great Britain and Tamati played all three tests. His debut was in the second row and largely went by without incident. "We lost the game (16-8) but I was reasonably happy with my performance," he recalls. The Kiwis also lost the second test, although the 22-7 scoreline did not reflect the much-improved performance.

For the third international, Tamati was shifted to the front row to partner Mark Broadhurst. "Prior to that, all the feedback I'd been getting was that I was too small to be a loose forward," he explains. "The criteria then was to be around six feet two or four and around 17 or 18 stone. I was just too small so I decided to go after the hooker's position. I actually made the Wellington side as a hooker but then the team was short of a blindside prop for a couple of games and I found myself there. That 1979 season I played just about every position in the pack so when Ces put me there against the Poms, I wasn't daunted."

New Zealand won the test 18-11 in a performance more than one critic has referred to as the foundation stone of the great Kiwi era to follow through the early to mid-eighties. Tamati has no doubts about that theory. "We had played against each other for a long time, blokes like Mark Graham and Mark Broadhurst, myself, Alan Rushton, Tony Coll and Ray Baxendale. So we had that camaraderie among us. We also knew we had a bit of pace in the backs with Fred Ah Kuoi, James Leuluai and Dane O'Hara. All we needed was a bit of time to blend and gel. We knew there were a lot of us making our debuts in that first test and it was a good game in terms of us coming together. In the second test, we learned even more about each other. Then in the third test, everything just fell into place."

Tamati held his place for the 1980 tests against the touring Australians. This was to be the real litmus test of his abilities. Tamati had no problem getting himself up to face the Poms. But Australia was a different matter. He was intimidated by their reputations. "Back then everybody considered them supermen," he explains. "If you wore the green and gold you were invincible. I didn't even think I should be on the same field as them. I was an amateur who had to work for a living and they were fulltime professional footballers. I'd watch them and be mesmerised by their strength and skills. Now suddenly I was going to be playing them and I knew that if I was going to be effective I had to get over this belief that they were superhuman."

Australia's enforcer at the time was Les Boyd, a rugged second rower known as "The Baby Faced Killer". Boyd was a fine footballer but he had a disconcerting habit of allowing his brain to fuzz over whenever he stepped on to a football field. In his book *Inside League*, former coach turned league journalist Roy Masters describes Boyd's attitude towards the game as: "If you didn't punch about six blokes in a game and tread on a few hands and headbutt a few people, you weren't picked as a forward."

Towards the end of his career Boyd was ousted from the game for a year for viciously breaking the jaw of Queensland prop Darryl Brohman with an elbow jolt in a State of Origin match. It was inevitable Boyd and Tamati would tangle at some stage. "When I was leaving Wellington to join the test team, a mate of mine asked me which position I'd be playing," recalls Tamati. "I told him I expected to be in the second row and he said: 'You'll be marking Les Boyd then. And he's going to eat you up and spit you out'. Well, that really got under my skin. It was probably the kick in the pants I needed to make me determined to get over this inferiority complex I had about the Australians. I was determined to make my mark in that game. I was actually marking Rod Reddy but whenever I got the chance I went after Boyd as well."

Indeed, Tamati certainly made his mark. Boyd and he had several skirmishes. "I knocked seven bells of hell out of 'Boydie' with or without the ball," admits Tamati. "And when he started to bleed, that was all the self-belief I needed. The Superman mystique went out the door. I'd got over the stumbling block."

Maybe so. But there were some within the New Zealand Rugby League who were unimpressed with Tamati's methods. "The word got back to me that it wasn't the ideal way to play the game and that perhaps if I was serious about having a future in the New Zealand side I should play the game I was supposed to be playing. That was OK. By then I knew I had what it took," he says.

The Australians hadn't forgotten Tamati's first test antics, though.

VICTORY HAKA...Kevin (left) and cousin Howie lead the Kiwis in a powerful post-match haka following the 1985 shut-out of the Australians at Carlaw Park.

The get-square came in his old home town of Hastings playing for the Maoris against the tourists. Tamati wailed into an all-in brawl and got sat squarely on his backside by giant Queensland centre Chris Close, a man as wide as he was high. "One of the Aussie scribes wrote: 'Live by the sword, die by the sword'," smiles Tamati. "I felt that was fair too. If I was to gain respect in the game, if I was prepared to dish it out, I had to be prepared to take it. And I was prepared to do that. I like to think that's where I gained a great deal of respect. I didn't go out, have a swing here, have a swing there and go hibernating. I was there in offence and I was there in defence."

Tamati's feisty relationship with Boyd continued on for several years. There was history between them even before their 1980 altercations. It's one of life's ironies that they ended up team-mates at Warrington in England later in both men's careers. Asked about his off-field relationship with Boyd, Tamati tersely describes it as "manageable". Pressed to elaborate, he pauses for some time before saying: "I didn't like him because of some of the things he'd say. While I tried to work with him as best I could for the sake of the team, I didn't really like him. The first game I ever played in Australia was for Wellington in the old Amco Cup competition. He was playing for Illawarra and the first tackle I got into he started up. It was the Dowling stuff all over again. 'You ****ing black bastard this and you ****ing black bastard that'. It was unnecessary and it was vindictive. That was the nasty side of the guy that I couldn't stomach. As far as his playing ability goes, he was one of the best players to ever play the game. I can't take that away from him. But I don't have to take that other shit."

At the end of the 1980 season, the Kiwis toured England with Tamati playing all three tests. "It was a series we should have won," he says. "We were the young kids coming over to play the established and experienced professionals. But we learned from it. We were getting better all the time."

Tamati missed the 1981 tests against the touring Frenchmen because of a chronic hamstring injury but was back in the Kiwis for the tour of Australia the following year. By this time, he had forged a reputation as a determined, rock-hard player who never took a backward step. But a forward will never survive in the coliseum of international league if they don't have the skill to back up their aggression. Tamati did. Although not one of the classic ball-playing forwards, he was mobile and could back up a break. What's more, he always made his hard yards up the middle of the ruck.

But it was Tamati's uncanny ability to produce stirring defensive tackles that often caught the eye. He was blessed with an innate ability to read opposing teams' attacking patterns and brutally disrupt them with a shattering but perfectly legal tackle. The effect such an inspired "hit" can have on both teams is often staggering.

So it was with Tamati's awesome shoulder charge on Australia's Queensland forward Rohan Hancock in the first test under lights at Lang Park in 1982. But the shuddering body hit had as much to do with Tamati's intuitiveness and eye for detail as his commitment in putting his body on the line. Hancock hailed from the long-time league nursery of Towoomba, west of Brisbane, and was being promoted as the latest hardman to play his way into the Australian pack.

Tamati had had "a good look" at Hancock earlier in the tour when the Kiwis played Queensland and noted that while the stocky second rower was certainly tough, there was little subtlety in his game. "I noticed that whenever he stood way behind the ball, he always took it at pace and ran straight. That's OK but personally I feel it's good to have a little bit of a step, otherwise you leave yourself open," says Tamati. Hancock did that and more.

Tamati takes up the story. "Earlier in the game the Australians got a penalty and kicked for touch. As they were throwing the ball over to [Aussie hooker and captain] Max Krilich for the tap restart, I just knew Hancock was going to get the ball. As soon as Krilich took the tap, I was off charging and I knew I was going to level Hancock. In a way Krilich set him up because he tapped the ball and then held it for a second waiting for Hancock to come. By the time Hancock got to him, I had him lined up and I hit him up virtually at the same time with a shoulder charge. He was travelling at a hundred miles an hour and I knew he wasn't going to step. He didn't let me down either. I knew the moment I hit him that it was going to be a pearler. I went back a couple of yards myself but I knew he was going to be sick."

Indeed. Hancock hit the deck with a frightening thud and didn't move. Not one Australian tried to front Tamati, recognising he had made a fierce but perfectly legitimate body hit. Instead, their immediate concern was for Hancock who looked to have been knocked unconscious. The game was held up for several minutes before a groggy Hancock eventually got to his feet. He vainly played on for several minutes before having to bow to the stunning hit and leave the field.

Tamati has no hesitation in nominating the tackle as the best "hit" of his career but ruefully reflects on the irony that was to follow. Hancock was replaced by tall Parramatta backrower John Muggleton who went on to score a try in the dying minutes to give Australia a fortuitous 11-8 win. "If I hadn't have taken Hancock out, Muggleton would never have got on the field and scored that last try," notes Tamati. "But I also like to think that on the other side of the coin the Hancock hit really lifted our guys, shook the Australians and kept it close."

The narrow loss irked Tamati, who was beginning to wonder just what it was going to take to humble the Australians. "Back when they toured New Zealand in 1980, we couldn't even score a try against them. The only points we scored came from kicks," he recalls. "It was really frustrating. But eventually we started scoring tries against them. Then we began making more and more breaks. It was a gradual thing."

In the meantime, Tamati's frustration was bubbling over. It got the better of him when he publicly slated the Aussies as "cheats" in a newspaper article. "We'd taken a slating somewhere and out of frustration I lashed out and said that for us to be any good at this game we'd have to start learning how to cheat like the Aussies. See, at the end of the day being 'professional' is about cheating. You take things to the absolute limit. Back in those days my belief was that you got out there, you gave your best and you played the game fair and square. But that's the grounding and beliefs you develop as an amateur. When you enter the professional arena things change. The attitude there is that if you can get away with it you get away with it. Sure, I knew I was out of order at the time when I blasted them but it was what I felt at the time. Now I've been a professional for 12 years, I look at it differently. Now I see it for what it is – being professional."

Tamati was to tangle once again with Hancock before the series was out. The Queenslander obviously felt his reputation was at stake after the first test and the Australian press had also done its bit by building up the second international in Sydney as a 'title rematch' between the pair. "Rohan took the bait and started pulling on Kevin's face during the match," recalls Hugh McGahan – who made his test debut off the bench in the game – in his book. "After a while Kevin thought that enough was enough and pulled both Rohan and himself out of the scrum. Before Rohan knew what had happened Kevin had put half a dozen on him. By this stage a couple of other Australians and New Zealanders were looking interested, but KT was so fired up that no one dared intrude."

Australia won both the '82 Tests and at the end of the southern winter, Tamati decided it was time for him to "get professional". English clubs Wakefield Trinity and Carlisle had approached him about playing the 1982-83 season for them. While he was weighing up the offers, he received a phone call from the then Widnes boss Doug Laughton. The money was more than attractive and Tamati took the plunge, becoming a fulltime professional footballer.

The decision had one down side, however. Widnes wanted him on a two-year contract and Tamati felt that if he was going to do justice to his new sense of professionalism, he needed to have the 1983 New Zealand season off to ensure he remained fresh for the following English season. That meant making himself unavailable for the Kiwis in '83. It's history that the Kiwis, coached by Graham Lowe, downed Australia in the second test at Lang Park for New Zealand's first win

The last charge...Tamati rubs a bit of salt into the wound following the 1985 win over the Aussies.

over their arch-enemies since the famous 1971 victory.

Tamati admits to a pang of regret when he first heard the result but says that emotion was immediately overwhelmed by elation that New Zealand had finally put the world champions to the sword. "There was regret but there was also a lot of pride," he says. "It was another step in our evolvement."

In the meantime Tamati was making quite a mark in English league. His decision to take a break during the northern summer allowed him to overcome several niggling injuries. An outstanding season followed in the 1983-84 competition. Widnes won the Challenge Cup by defeating Wigan, who had Howie Tamati playing hooker for them. Playing at Wembley, a shrine of English sport, was an experience Kevin will never forget.

"That was my first and only experience at Wembley," he says. "It was a superb day. They've got amplifiers that pipe the crowd noise through into the dressing rooms as you're warming up. You can hear 80,000 people out there singing. It's a unique feeling. You walk out of the dressing rooms into the tunnel. It's a long walk up a slight incline and it's one of the greatest feelings in sport walking up there. The higher you get up the ramp, the louder the noise gets. It's awesome."

Tamati responded superbly to the occasion. He set up two tries for fullback Joe Lydon as Widnes took command. The first came as he broke clear and, when confronted by Wigan's fullback Shaun Edwards, sent a clever round-the-corner pass for Lydon to scamper away and score.

Lydon's second touchdown came late in the match with the game all but won. Again using his intuition, Tamati picked up on a Wigan set move. "Gary Stephens was the Wigan halfback and I knew his game quite well. Wigan often sent two runners inside for two tackles and then they would bring the ball back to the short side. I was on the short side and Stephens was on the open side. I was sure he was going to try the move and sure enough, he brought the ball back to the short side and I went straight in and cut him down. He lost the ball in the tackle, Joe Lydon scooped it up and he was gone."

Tamati was delighted to play his part in Lydon's second try but later had reason to partially regret his bone-jarring tackle on Stephens. Courtesy of his two tries, Lydon was named winner of the prestigious Lance Todd Medal for the man of the match. The Pommie pressmen told Tamati the medal was all but in the Kiwi's pocket until Lydon scampered 70 metres for his second try. "The bookies always put odds on who was going to win the Lance Todd and I was at about 45 to 1," recalls Tamati. "So I put 20 quid on myself while a few of the other lads had a 'tenner' each on me as well. We would have been rolling in it. As it was, Joe was slightly embarrassed about it too."

Tamati decided to make himself available for the Kiwis for the 1984 home series against Great Britain, and Graham Lowe had no hesitation in finding a place for the Maori Warrior in his front row . New Zealand crushed the Poms 3-0 to emerge as the undisputed No 2 power in international league. Many observers believe that Tamati played the finest football of his career over the 15 months encompassing the 1983-84 English season and home series against Great Britain. The man himself doesn't disagree. "I'd had the rest I needed and had gained two years experience of intense professional football in England," he says.

Certainly, he made a lasting impression on many emerging New Zealand stars during the 1984 season. Rather than playing a one-off season in Australia, he decided to play domestic football in New Zealand in a bid to show the national selectors his skills. Instead it was Tamati's professionalism and huge appetite for football that captured the most attention. Midweek he would play for Randwick in the Wellington competition and then every weekend he would fly north to Auckland to play for the Northcote Tigers.

At the time, the Tigers boasted a promising young halfback named Gary Freeman. Tamati was to have a profound impact on the man later to be tagged 'The Wizz' because of his all-action attacking game. "'KT' was simply amazing with his attitude," Freeman writes in his book *Tiger, Tiger, Kiwi, Rooster*. "He expected no special treatment either, even playing in reserve grade once. That's how all pros ought to behave, and there are plenty who could learn from the man known as 'The Warrior'...I never played with him in the Kiwis, but I couldn't help but be impressed with what I saw."

Tamati's professionalism also impressed Hugh McGahan in the formative years of the young loose forward's career. "He was exactly what his nickname [The Warrior] suggested and never bowed to anyone," said McGahan. "Although this was the case, he was somewhat unfairly tagged and it overshadowed his ability to play football. His competitiveness and desire to beat the man were things you couldn't help but admire and the thing I liked most about him was his way with the younger players. He would always see that they were looked after and taught them the dos and don'ts. This contrasted immensely with the image he had within the media."

Indeed, Tamati was often the player who drove the team minibus back from evening functions or celebrations. He would not drink so there was always somebody sober to ensure the team returned to the hotel safely.

Despite his fine season in 1984, one goal still eluded Tamati. He was desperate for a series win over Australia and the Dowling incident in the opening international in 1985 only hardened his resolve. More heartbreak was to follow, though. John Ribot's try in the last minute at Carlaw Park to give Australia a 10-6 second Test victory almost crushed the spirits of the Kiwis. After his Lang Park experience of 1982, Tamati couldn't believe lightning could strike twice. The intense disappointment of the narrow loss hit Tamati even harder since he had been in a position to win the game for the Kiwis. Ranging wide among the centres where he was often used as an effective shock attacking weapon, Tamati angled in when he saw Mark Graham take the ball up. "The inside defence went up to stop Mark but the outside defence hung off," said Tamati. "I hit the gap knowing Mark would make the ball available. He did and I went through with only [fullback] Gary Jack to beat. I turned to look for support and there was nobody there. I couldn't believe it. James [Leuluai] came up to me straight after the game and said: 'I knew I should have gone with you'. That could have been the series."

Indeed, it's history that New Zealand shut out the Australians 18-0 at Carlaw Park a week later. Had a Kiwi player backed up Tamati's break in the second test , the series may well have been New Zealand's. "That's the only regret of my career," notes Tamati. "I would dearly have loved a series win over all three league-playing nations. In the end, there wasn't much in it. But it still goes down in the record books against us. As 'Lowie' says, moral victories don't count for anything."

When Tamati returned to England for the 1985-86 season, it was to play for Warrington which he helped to victory over Halifax in the premiership final. Two further tests for the Kiwis on their end-of-year '85 tour of Great Britain rounded out Tamati's international career, giving him 22 proud appearances in the black jersey. An honest career at Warrington followed over the next four and a half years before Tamati was approached halfway through the 1988-89 season by the struggling Salford club to become their manager/coach.

At the age of 35 the time seemed appropriate to gracefully move into a coaching post, an area that had always interested Tamati.

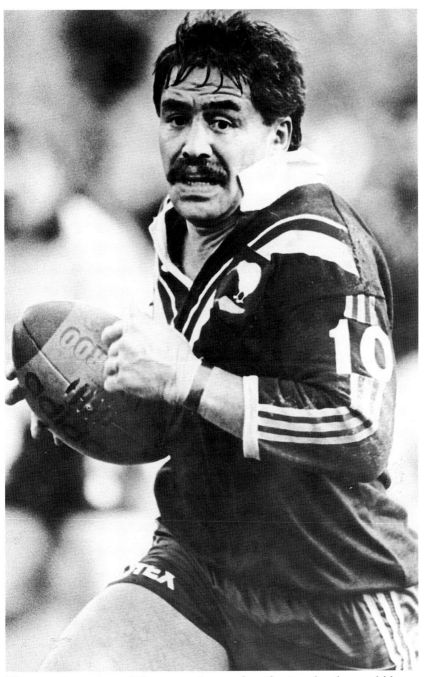

The Maori warrior…"There are plenty of professionals who could learn from his example," says Gary Freeman.

"Salford were struggling at the bottom of the first division and when I took on the job mid-season I pointed out we'd be lucky to avoid relegation and that it would take the following season before we could really begin to get our act together," says Tamati. Salford recognised that reality and although indeed relegated to the second division, Tamati made a swift impression.

In the 1990-91 season, Salford romped to the second division title, losing just one match. Back in the top grade for the '91-'92 season, Salford's success continued. Despite limited resources, Salford beat glamour club Wigan twice in the season and reached the semi-finals of the Regal Trophy. But a tougher season followed the next year and Tamati learned a harsh truth of coaching – that your days are numbered from the moment you accept the job.

"I was sacked, pure and simple," he says of the murkiness that surrounded his exit from Salford at the end of the 1992-93 season. "It hasn't affected my feelings about coaching. I'll go back to it when the time's right. It's just a matter of biding my time. I've said publicly several times that I intend to be the Kiwi coach one day. Nothing has changed. That will still happen."

Currently, Tamati earns his living as a rugby league development officer employed by the Warrington council. He enjoys the English lifestyle, although admits he often yearns for the simpler life in New Zealand. A frightening incident in 1992 also further shook the Tamati family. Kevin's then nine-year-old daughter Rkye was in downtown Warrington when an IRA bomb planted in a rubbish bin went off, killing two small children.

"She was just 150 yards away when it happened," says Kevin. "It was a frightening episode because we knew she was in town when we heard the news on the radio but we couldn't get in there because the police had closed all the streets off. It was 20 minutes before she could get to a phone and tell us she was OK. It stunned us but we've learned to live with it all. Whether it's a plane crash or a motorway accident, if it's fated, it'll happen."

I decided to give Tamati the final word on his career. Asked to describe himself as a player, he paused thoughtfully for some time. After several moments came the considered response..."very proud, very determined, a player not prepared to take a backward step, unruly but not necessarily ill-disciplined, and very physical. Above all else, I like to think I had the attitude of a winner."

FERGIE McCORMICK
'Fungus'

November 11, 1967. It was the pits of a day at Cardiff Arms Park. Cold, miserable and with a fair gale blowing as well. If you were a goalkicker, it was just about the worst possible conditions. It didn't stop Fergie McCormick, though. He'd already nailed conversions for Bill Davis and Bill Birtwistle's tries. The Davis touchdown was the turning point. McCormick had attempted a 40 metre penalty goal into the teeth of the howling wind. Few thought he'd even go remotely near the distance required. Yet the kick dropped just metres short, hanging in the ferocious wind. Welsh backrower John Jeffrey failed to clear it and the fast following Davis snapped up the precious leather and dived over the line to score. In the end, McCormick contributed seven points to New Zealand's 13-6 triumph over the bitter enemy. The All Black fullback had turned in his typically robust performance. Even in their wildest imagination, few in the sellout crowd could ever imagine that McCormick was playing with a torn rib cartilage and had been advised not to play for six weeks. McCormick compromised. He took two days off training.

IF ever a cartoonist wanted to caricature William Fergus McCormick by likening him to a particular animal, there would certainly be only one choice. If Terry Wright and John Gallagher were greyhounds, McCormick was a pit bull terrier....and one of those with a studded leather collar.

Strong, aggressive and always spoiling for a confrontation, not even age has wearied the former All Black fullback's pugnacious attitude towards life. Now 55, he remains feisty, opinionated and always ready to put forward his point of view. Some things not even age can change. It was like that even early in McCormick's life. His father Archie was a 1925 All Black and reasonably handy with his fists too. Good enough to become the New Zealand heavyweight boxing champion in 1922 and 1923, in fact. Mother Helen was no athletic slouch either. She made the New Zealand hockey team in the late 1920s.

But young Fergie was a slow developer physically. He was small for his age and battled to make an impact in age group rugby. The experience hardened him, though. All the club officials and school-teachers agreed. If ever a kid consistently played above his weight, it was young McCormick. By the mid-1950s, the teenage McCormick was beginning to make an impact in Christchurch rugby circles as a determined first-five-eighth. He made Canterbury age group rep teams and broke into the Linwood club's senior team.

In that same year of 1958, he played for the Canterbury Colts and Canterbury B. A promising career was gathering momentum. Then, as so often happens, a twist of fate really set him on his way. Linwood club stalwart Harry Davis has been an All Black selector. Not just any All Black selector, mind you. Old Harry had helped pick the 1924-25 All Blacks known to all as The Invincibles. Harry certainly knew his football. He liked the look of this young McCormick but sensed his true position was fullback rather than first-five. "It was pretty good advice," McCormick says, in somewhat of an understatement.

McCormick is a bit sheepish about the details but it was around this time that rugby began to have a significant impact on keeping him on the straight and narrow. He was a feisty teenager who enjoyed his partying and the odd beer. "Things could get pretty wild around Christchurch in those days," he says. "We used to get up to a bit, nothing too over the top, but put it this way, rugby helped me to get focused and stay out of trouble."

In 1959, McCormick got his big break when the Canterbury selectors picked him to face Wellington at Athletic Park. As he recalls, his first-class debut was "nothing flash" and Wellington won 20-17. There were two significant names in the Wellington squad, however. One was Mick Williment and the other was a rugged forward Ivan Vodanovich. McCormick hadn't seen the last of either man.

Even though he didn't think he'd gone particularly well, McCormick found himself retained for Canterbury's next match

Fergie McCormick smiles for Fleet Street upon arrival at Heathrow for the 1967 tour. Newspaper stories pointed out the 'smiling gentleman's job back home is a slaughterman.'

Fearless and always fully committed...two of McCormick's greatest qualities.

against the touring British Lions. When the Red and Blacks won 20-14 and McCormick shut down the dangerous Lions wingers Tony O'Reilly and John Young with a fearless display of tyro tackling, a star was born.

"We had a funny mix of a team that day," recalls McCormick. "There was a bit of experience but there was also a bit of inexperience too. We had Kel Tremain as a youngster, Bruce Watt at first-five-eighth and myself at fullback. But each guy in the Canterbury team played his role perfectly. We played as a team that day and that's why we beat the Lions." The local press enthused about the potential of their new No 15. With performances like that, he'd have a mortgage on the jersey, predicted the scribes. How right they were. It would be another 15 years before any other fullback would get a look in at Canterbury.

By the end of the '59 season, it wasn't just the fiercely parochial Lancaster Park fans who were raving about McCormick. Other critics around the country were also noting the fierce displays of the rising Canterbury star. In particular, his powerful tackling technique was creating attention. His front-on defence was devastating. He didn't just tackle the opposition, he broke them down for scrap!

Many feel McCormick pioneered the aggressive tackling that is now standard fare in the game. He explained his approach to Bob Howitt in the book *Rugby Greats*. "The first thing a fullback must have is good defence. Without that you're not sound. You work out the best way to succeed. For instance if a player is coming straight at you, you don't stand still and give him a choice of ways to run. You must work him towards the touchline, hanging back just enough so that he can't cut back. When he reaches that point of no-return, you charge at him and bring him down. Tackling has always been one of the easiest jobs for me."

Sounds simple, huh? McCormick's uncanny ability to put it into practice and his absolute refusal to play second to anybody on the field quickly made him an opponent to be both respected and feared.

The following season, McCormick's star continued to shine more brightly. He played in all 17 of Canterbury's rep matches and was chosen for the inter-island match where he scored 11 of the South Island's points in their 26-11 win. New Zealand XV honours came his way while he was also chosen in a Rest of New Zealand line-up to face the All Blacks upon their return from South Africa.

On that day, 21-year-old McCormick marked his hero, 'The Boot'. Don Clarke was considered immovable as the All Black fullback. McCormick might have been a kid with a big future but Clarke was going to take some shifting from the status he enjoyed as New Zealand's premier fullback. Clarke never looked like relinquishing his iron grip on a test jersey over the next few seasons. And while rugby fans mused over who was best suited to be his understudy, McCormick suddenly found himself battling a tough rival. Mick Williment had been gaining in stature since that Athletic Park clash in '59.

An elegant player with a reliable goalkicking boot, Williment quickly established a legion of fans in the capital who believed their man was infinitely superior to McCormick. But repeating those sentiments anywhere near Christchurch was like holding a pro-George Bush rally in Baghdad during the Gulf War. Adding further fuel to the argument was the wildly divergent personalities of the two rivals, on and off the field. The Wellington fans noted McCormick's ruthless streak and liked to portray McCormick as over-aggressive and uncouth. The Cantabrians saw the refined Williment, a university graduate, as being potentially weak in times of crisis. As far as they were concerned, when the going got tough, nobody did it better than Fergie.

But when Clarke was injured before the first test against Australia in 1964, the All Black selectors didn't agree. They opted for Williment instead. McCormick was to suffer further disappointment in 1965 when Clarke was forced into retirement with crook knees. Again the selectors plumped for the Wellington man even though he couldn't play in the All Black trial due to injury. McCormick consoled himself by working on his goalkicking. When he'd first broken into the Canterbury squad, Buddy Henderson had the duties. But now McCormick was furiously beavering away looking to add an extra string to his bow. If Wellington fans thought McCormick was readily going to surrender the fight to Williment, they had under-estimated him.

"All Mick's selection did was inspire me to battle harder. No way was I giving up," he said. Williment played the first three tests against the touring Springboks. Then McCormick got the break he was waiting for. Williment was concussed playing for New Zealand Universities against the South Africans and the All Black selectors didn't consider him. McCormick finally got the call up he had been waiting for. Curiously, McCormick doesn't believe Williment really was injured. The All Blacks had lost the third test 19-16 and McCormick believes the selectors were looking for a diplomatic way to get him into the test line-up.

Whether McCormick's theory was merely a reflection of the intense rivalry between the pair or Williment really was injured, the bottom line was that the Canterbury man now had his chance to prove his worth. And among the well-wishing telegrams he received before the match was one from his sparring partner – "Every good wish for a great game – Mick Williment". The rivalry may have been intense but the respect was mutual.

McCormick made a sound debut, though his goalkicking hardly set the world on fire with just one success from eight attempts. Fortunately it didn't matter. The All Blacks were a well-oiled machine by the mid-60s with the likes of Colin and Stan Meads and Brian Lochore backing up that formidable front row of Ken Gray, Bruce McLeod and Wilson Whineray. And inside him the likes of Chris Laidlaw and Mac Herewini helped soothe any first test nerves. The Boks were humbled 20-3 and the series won 3-1.

But while McCormick had finally got to wear the black jersey, his frustrations hadn't ended. Williment won back the test berth for the 1966 series against the British Lions and retained it for the only home test of the '67 season, the Jubilee international against Australia. McCormick admits he began to despair that he might become a one-test wonder. At 27, he was wondering if an international career had slipped past him. But the season was to hold a stunning surprise for the determined Cantabrian.

The All Black selection panel of convenor Fred Allen, Ivan Vodanovich and Les George dropped a bombshell when they named just one fullback in their squad to tour Great Britain and France. What's more the fullback was McCormick and not Williment. The selection process was bizarre. The selectors worked out their touring squad after the final All Black trial in early September and gave the names to the New Zealand Rugby Football Union chairman Tom Morrison. Morrison then did something that saved the selectors and the NZRFU considerable embarrassment. He counted the names. He discovered 31 instead of 30. Rushing back to the selectors, he pointed out their gaffe.

The full circumstances of what happened still seem to be guarded by the men involved. But Allen clearly wanted McCormick on the tour. He believed the Canterbury man would be more durable and his rugged qualities more suited to the UK and France than Williment. But, judging by the circumstances of 31 players being named, somebody else on the panel wanted Williment to tour. When the team was returned to the selectors with the orders to remove one name, it was the unfortunate Williment who drew the short straw.

Even though their rivalry was fierce, McCormick felt sorry for his old sparring partner. The pair sought each other out and offered both congratulations and condolences. The blunder of 31 names being writ-

Auckland's Lew Fell arrives too late to prevent McCormick clearing under pressure during Canterbury's Ranfurly Shield challenge in 1962.

ten down was kept secret for years but it's interesting that recent convenors confirm that chairmans now religiously count the names on the paper before publicly announcing any All Black team.

Enormous controversy raged over the decision. The Wellington press, who had never taken kindly to McCormick's robust play, railed long and hard over the omission. The niggly side of McCormick's game was ruthlessly ridiculed by the capital's scribes. But McCormick was to dramatically shut up his critics on the tour. Allen was more than vindicated when his fullback produced a string of outstanding performances.

"I think Fergie played his best rugby on that tour," Allen says today. "He did have an overly aggressive side to his game at the time but we sorted that out on the tour. Once that side of his game was brought under control, Fergie played some outstanding rugby. The Brits just couldn't handle him."

Williment never played another test. Interestingly, Williment was regarded as the superior goalkicker around the time, but Allen believed the All Blacks had to score tries in the UK if they were to win the internationals, not just kick goals.

McCormick, never one to fail to speak his mind, firmly believes he had earned his selection over Williment. "Mick was a very efficient fullback," he told Joseph Romanos in the book *Famous Fullbacks*. "He had a good press from Wellington. I didn't think he was ever better than me as a fullback. If he had to tackle someone he would, but he chased a lot of people to the corner flag." As for Williment on McCormick, he told Romanos: "I had a lot of respect for Fergie. He played a different type of game to me. His was built on a very, very combative, aggressive style. We weren't trying to do the same things. He was the strong man of the Canterbury team for many years and was so durable. Fergie was an exceptional competitor. He never regarded a situation as lost. He'd fight right to the end. I never used to sit down and wonder if I was a better player than him. In the years when I was getting picked, and later when he got in, I never considered the question of who should be there. Other people did that. I was happy enough to let the selectors make their choice. That's what they were there for."

Allen's belief in McCormick seemed to inspire the Cantabrian on the tour. Even the normally acerbic Pommie scribes praised his performances. In the first international of the tour against England, he converted all four All Black tries in New Zealand's 23-11 success despite playing with some discomfort from sore ribs. It was this injury, when aggravated, that led to the medical advice that he should have some six weeks off. McCormick ignored what he regarded as folly and played in New Zealand's 13-6 win over Wales, his seven-point contribution proving vital. His outstanding form continued against France two weeks later as the All Blacks produced a vibrant display of 15-man rugby to humble the Tricolores 21-15, this time booting eight points. Just one week later, the All Blacks added the Scottish scalp 14-3 in a test famous for the controversial sending off of Colin Meads.

By this time, McCormick was riding so high in confidence both with his boot and in general play that it seemed he could do little wrong. In four tests, he'd scored 32 valuable points. But pundits who followed the tour say McCormick scaled his greatest heights in the tour matches against East Wales and the Barbarians. East Wales had a coloured winger named F. H. Wilson who was renowned as a speedy try-poacher. Twice Wilson looked certain to score when McCormick came from nowhere to cut the Welshman's legs from underneath him with tremendous scything tackles. The tense match ended in a 3-all draw (the only blemish on the 15-match tour) with McCormick's impeccable defence proving the difference between All Black pride being trampled underfoot by the fired-up opposition.

Against the Barbarians in the tour finale at Twickenham, McCormick was equally devastating. Twice he ran Barbarians flyers Gerald Davies and Keri Jones down from behind to save certain tries to help the All Blacks score a magnificent 11-6 triumph, sealed when winger Tony Steele touched down in the last minute of play with McCormick nailing the conversion from the sideline. McCormick returned home a hero, his selection more than vindicated.

He retained his position for the 1968 tour of Australia, scoring 110 points in just eight matches. His boot was to prove vital in the second Test when New Zealand needed him to convert a controversial penalty try to secure a 19-18 victory at Ballymore. McCormick duly delivered. A tight home series against France followed the Australian tour and McCormick scored 28 out of New Zealand's 40 points as the All Blacks swept to a 3-0 clean sweep.

The 1969 season was to be another sweet year for McCormick, perhaps the sweetest. The lawmakers had made a significant change to the game, outlawing the antiquated rule that allowed the ball to be booted into touch on the full from anywhere on the ground. The idea was to encourage more running rugby, particularly from fullbacks. McCormick relished the change. "I was probably fortunate because Canterbury took to the style of using a running fullback far more readily than other provincial sides," he explains. "It suited me fine. Up to that time, the job of a fullback was basically regarded as simply the last line of defence but when they brought in that rule it provided the opportunity to turn defence into attack . That was the attitude we had in Canterbury. They say nowadays that you must have a running fullback. But who started the running game? It began with me at Canterbury." McCormick was never one for false modesty.

The Welsh found themselves hopelessly outclassed in the two tests in '69. The All Blacks won comfortably 19-0 at Lancaster Park in the opening international before thumping the hapless Welsh 33-12 in the second at Eden Park. It was in this match that McCormick established a new world record of 24 points courtesy of five penalties, three conversions and a phenomenal, long-range dropped goal. His general play was also faultless. The Welsh couldn't believe McCormick's fearless courage in repeatedly charging into the forwards and setting himself as a target for the thundering All Black forwards to charge

A walloping for Wales and a world record for McCormick. Alister Hopkinson souvenirs the ball McCormick used to nail 24 points in the 1969 clash.

over and set up second phase possession.

By the end of the '69 season, McCormick was averaging 11 points a match for the All Blacks. That may not seem as impressive along-side Grant Fox's phenomenal strike-rate but in those days it was considered one hell of a feat. By the end of the season, it seemed like McCormick had finally won over all of his critics. Even one Wellington newspaper tagged him "Our Fergie!" in one match report. The irony was that the beginning of the end for McCormick's All Black career was just around the corner.

The 1970 South African tour proved a difficult and frustrating one for McCormick. Even now McCormick becomes noticeably irritated when talking about it. Allen had departed as All Black coach and Ivan Vodanovich had taken over. McCormick wasn't a Vodanovich fan. He believes the former Wellington All Black unnecessarily ran the players into the ground in the republic with over-vigorous training sessions. Several other players support the claim. "Vodanovich was a bit of a fitness freak but he went overboard on that tour and took the edge off the team. The training was relentless and a lot of us lost our sting because of it," contends McCormick.

South Africa scored a convincing 17-6 win in the first test in Pretoria with McCormick having an unhappy day with his boot. But it was the second international at Newlands where the heat was really turned up on the New Zealand fullback. Springbok winger Sid Nomis got in the clear and kicked ahead when he was confronted by McCormick. What happened from there is dependent on whose version of the story you believe.

One thing can't be disputed. Nomis was knocked to the ground by McCormick. To the 55,000 spectators and every South African journalist at the ground, it appeared McCormick had deliberately stiff-armed Nomis and taken him out of play when it seemed certain he would score. It's a curious quirk of the Afrikaaner that while the Springboks have been guilty of some heinous deeds on the rugby field over the years, they have an incredible ability to adopt a holier-than-thou attitude when they believe one of their own has been hard done by. The way in which the crowd responded, you would have thought McCormick was Jack the Ripper in football boots.

To this day, McCormick contends he was the one harshly done by. "The ball was kicked through and I had to turn and chase," he explains. "I could sense Nomis was going to get the jump on me so as I turned I stuck out my arm to at least slightly slow his take-off if I could. As it turned out I copped him right across the face. It was the perfect stiff arm. It wasn't intentional, though. I wasn't even looking at him. But the crowd gave me hell about it."

So too did the South African newspapers. They were determined to turn McCormick into public enemy No 1. Adding to their motivation was the manner in which the second test had ended. Under immense pressure, McCormick successfully kicked a penalty in the dying minutes to give New Zealand a dramatic 9-8 victory. McCormick was expecting support from the All Black management as the South Africans continued to turn the heat up over "The Nomis Incident". He was stunned when it didn't come. "I just didn't get a fair go over there," he told Joseph Romanos in *Famous Fullbacks*. "Every player has times when he needs the support of the management. I needed it then. I hadn't done anything wrong, but instead [NZ manager] Ron Burk publicly admonished me. He condemned me to the papers about what he called a stiff-arm tackle, saying he didn't know why I did it. When some photographs were produced a few days later, showing it wasn't a stiff-arm after all, I asked him what he'd be doing in the way

Happier times on the troublesome 1970 South Africa tour. McCormick tries his hand at tennis.

of an apology. He said: 'For you, nothing'. It just put more and more pressure on me. Finally, my form slipped."

McCormick went into the third test at Port Elizabeth under tremendous pressure and with his greatest strength – his belief in his ability to perform at the highest level – savagely undermined. It was to be a test he would rather forget. Twice the South Africans scored tries when McCormick found himself caught up in mauls. He was strongly criticised for this fact, even though his detractors failed to note that New Zealand had taken the ball into the mauls only to have it ripped free by the Boks.

But for all that, McCormick did play poorly. The South African forwards appeared determined to extract revenge for Nomis and every time McCormick took the ball up, he was mercilessly thumped. With the vocal Port Elizabeth crowd also giving him a torrid time throughout, McCormick was a physical and emotional wreck by the time the whistle was blown for the last time with South Africa having won 14-3. With several stitches in his ear, a badly bruised back and a black eye, McCormick was a sorry sight in more ways than one. It wasn't a major surprise when he was dropped for the final test and replaced by Gerald Kember.

By the time he got back to New Zealand, McCormick had perked up a bit. The British Lions were coming in 1971 and he was determined to restore his battered reputation. At 31, he knew there were many critics ready to use his age against him. His confidence was partly restored late in the 1970 season when he landed a brilliant dropped goal against Wellington to give Canterbury a desperate 3-all draw and keep the prized Ranfurly Shield from travelling north. But while McCormick busied himself during the off-season in ensuring his fitness was up to scratch for the Lions tour, two men in the northern hemisphere were quietly plotting his demise.

Lions coach Carwyn James deliberately kept his trump card Barry John out of the key match against Canterbury a week before the first test. It is part of rugby folklore now that he told John to sit in the Lancaster Park grandstand and devote the entire match to studying McCormick's positional play. "I don't want to see McCormick again in the series after next Saturday," he told John. The Welsh first-five-eighth was an astute student. He absolutely tormented McCormick in the first test at Carisbrook. It was as if he could place the ball on a sixpence that day. No matter where McCormick positioned himself, John had him scrambling. It was a virtuoso tactical kicking performance which many old heads say still hasn't been matched by any other first five to this day.

Adding to McCormick's woes were two relatively easy penalties he missed which were to prove crucial towards the final outcome with the Lions winning 9-3. Ivan Vodanovich quickly rounded on McCormick. "You can't afford to miss goals like that," he lectured the fullback. "They cost us the test."

McCormick was dropped for the second test for current All Black coach Laurie Mains and never wore the silver fern again. After 43 games for New Zealand including 16 tests, he was no longer wanted. Even now, he grimaces when reminded of John's performance that day in Dunedin. "I don't think he ever played a game like that one again," McCormick says. "He just didn't seem to be able to put a foot wrong." Then with a trace of bitterness, he adds: "I didn't get much help from our loose forwards that day and the wingers didn't do much in defence either. John was a good player but he wasn't a world-beater. We made him look good that day."

McCormick had hoped his previous proud record as the All Black fullback would have earned him a second chance during the series but it wasn't to be. Several of his team-mates including Sid Going and Ian Kirkpatrick have since questioned the indecent haste with which McCormick was shoved aside. McCormick himself found the decision particularly frustrating because he personally believed he was at the peak of his career. "I reckon I played the best rugby of my career in the early 1970s but no matter what, I couldn't get back in there," he says. "I feel I could have gone on a little longer for New Zealand. They dumped me in '71 yet they still had me at the All Black trials in '74. What the hell were they doing? If I was dumped, I was dumped. If Trevor Morris was a good fullback, God we're in trouble. But selectors are human and every selector makes cock-ups."

Indeed, there was still some mighty fine rugby left in Fergie despite his advancing years. In 1972, he turned in a positively stunning performance when Canterbury defended the Ranfurly Shield against Otago. It was simply one of those days when he could do no wrong. Such was his impact on the game that his team-mates cheered him off Lancaster Park with him on their shoulders. In '74 he helped Canterbury to a famous victory over England, scored a sensational individual try against Scotland in '75 (good enough to win a national Pick the Best Try competition) and eclipsed the then New Zealand first-class points record which Don Clarke had held.

Midway through the '73 season, Clarke's mark of 1831 points was ready to fall to McCormick. He needed just 12 points in a match against West Coast in Greymouth but Canterbury captain Alex Wyllie cut him off at nine. 'Grizz' had decided the record had to fall at Lancaster Park. And few people argue with Grizz! Ironically, a rugby historian later discovered that a couple of matches McCormick had played against Tonga had been inadvertently overlooked. It meant he had actually broken the record the week before against Wellington. McCormick went on to rack up 2065 first class points which stood until Auckland's superboot Grant Fox eventually eclipsed the tally in 1988.

Controversy would still be McCormick's occasional bedmate, though. He hardly endeared himself to Wellington fans when he dropped Grant Batty with a coathanger tackle at Athletic Park. In 1975, McCormick's form dropped off so alarmingly that the Canterbury selectors had to do what had previously been regarded as sacrilege to even think about – drop Fergie. He'd played a staggering 222 matches for his beloved province.

Even though his first-class career was over, rugby continued to play a major role in McCormick's life. He coached the Canterbury Colts for a couple of years, doing extremely well with them, took the Cantabrians to England and Italy in 1979 and also coached Canterbury B and Christchurch club sides Albion and Lyttelton. It appeared McCormick was on the way to becoming the Red and Blacks' representative coach but it somehow eluded him, a strange fact given Canterbury's revolving door policy over the men in charge in recent years. He seemed likely to get the post in 1989 but lost out to Frank Jack. "I would have dearly loved to have coached the A team," he admits. "But who knows, I may have been no good. But all the sides I've had have gone well."

McCormick's business interests also limited time he could devote to coaching. At one stage he was running two pubs in Christchurch including the famed Cantabrian. Four years ago, the McCormick family bought a 100 acre farm at Greenparks just out of Christchurch and Fergie admits that's where his heart is nowadays. "We run cattle and sheep and even though I spend most of my time at the pub, I love my time out there," he says. "I enjoy animals. I enjoy seeing good stock grow. I enjoy that farming lifestyle."

McCormick has also continued to keep a weather eye on developing rugby trends through following the progress of his talented son,

Even in the twilight of his career, McCormick was still a handful. Here
he takes on the Auckland defence in 1975.

former All Black trialist Andrew who had a long Canterbury career before heading to Japan to finally make some money out of a code that puts extraordinary time demands on even its provincial representatives.

He readily admits several things worry him about where rugby is heading. McCormick firmly believes rugby is a physical game and that the All Blacks' long term success owes much to their aggressive style. In recent years, he feels the game has become overly sanitised. "It was pretty tough going out there back in my days," he explains. "You used to get a bit and you gave a bit back. They say we wouldn't get away with it these days but I always answer by saying you get away with what you can when you can. And if you've got to play with discipline where you can't jump on anyone or give someone a backhander, you discipline yourself. That's the way the Meads, Tremains, Lochores and others played, showing that discipline.

"Discipline can mean many things. How many backs do we see playing for the All Blacks who often don't get the basics right? How many drop-outs go out on the full? How many times do we get on attack and knock it on? You have to be disciplined. You take everything to the limit, of course. And if you've got to cut your limit back for the sake of your TV cameras, you do that."

Like many other subjects in this book, McCormick believes the day of the real rugby hardman is over. But curiously he doesn't subscribe to the popular theory that television is to blame. "I don't blame the probing TV camera eye. I blame the referees," he says. "Some referees tend to let the game slip out of their grasp by not putting their finger on the button to start with. It worries me when you see some of the reaction to big tackles nowadays. I used to make good head-on tackles in my day but now some of them would be ruled as dangerous. What the hell is happening to the game? You can't even retaliate now. And again I blame the referees. Some days the captain can't even talk to the referee and say: 'Look, that guy's infringing. What the hell are you going to do about it?' The refs need to realise that if they're not going to do something about it, the players are and the bloke is going to get whacked. But when that happens, the ref turns around and penalises that bloke.

"Some referees, and I mean only some, want to be No 1 on the field and they forget about the rugby. In some respects, the media has to take some of the blame too. I blame news media for isolating stupid little things in the game. Certain things are isolated and played over and over again. What's wrong with a big heavy tackle on a guy? He probably gets hurt in the tackle but it's fair."

McCormick is also one of the few former players around prepared to go to bat for Richard Loe. "I think Richard should have been disciplined, but not so harshly. Yes, he did pull at a guy's face and eye gouge [Greg Cooper] a bit but I don't think it warranted six months suspension."

Another trend McCormick finds disturbing is the growing influence of money in the game. "It was inevitable that money had to come into the game," he says. "The problem is that some players have got their hands out for the money. It's one of the things that worries me about modern rugby. Have our All Blacks got their eyes on the dollar or their eyes on the game? I don't blame the players for wanting their money. But they need to be careful. With this All Blacks Club, they're hitting Joe Public, who are their sponsors to begin with, a second time. The supporters pay to go to matches, we buy their Steinlager, who sponsor them. Now they're hitting Joe Public again for $100 to join their club. Right now I think some of our All Blacks have got their eye on the dollar instead of knuckling down and concentrating on the game alone."

On the subject of the fullback role he knows so well, McCormick also has very forthright views. He abhors the move to "create" fullbacks such as the current All Black panel's decision to switch John Timu from the wing to the No 15 jersey. "It's all a result of John Gallagher. Ever since he was lost to league, the selectors have been trying to create another Gallagher," he insists. "Gallagher was a brilliant runner of the ball and he had genuine pace. Modern day selectors are looking for genuine pace on the outside because other countries have it. We're now in a situation in New Zealand where specialist fullbacks are not getting a go. I think of the Cooper brothers. I think Matthew Cooper was the best fullback in the 1993 All Black trials by a street. Now, because of all this tinkering around, they're lacking pace on the wings which is where you need it most. If they can't find what they want in the current bunch of specialist fullbacks, they should go and find a youngster and start moulding him now for the World Cup."

And if that kid has half the courage, self-belief and tenacity of McCormick, he'll enjoy a lengthy career.

MARK SHAW
'Cowboy'

"It was 1986 and Cowboy and I had been selected in a Southern Hemisphere XV that took on a Northern Hemisphere team as part of the IRB's centenary celebrations. At the time there was a bit of bad blood still between the Australians and All Blacks but Brian Lochore, our coach for the festival matches, had worked hard to break that down. By the end of our time in the UK, we were all good mates so after the last game we decided to have a big night on the turps. We were all having a few beers when suddenly Cowboy thumped the bar with his fist. We got a bit of a shock and said: 'Cowboy, what's wrong mate?' He looked at us and scowled: 'I'm pissed off, that's what's wrong.' 'Why?' we asked. 'Because I'm getting to like you Australian bastards.' The whole lot of us fell about the place laughing. It was classic Cowboy." – Simon Poidevin, Wallaby flanker.

MARK Shaw was sitting in the grandstand, intensely focusing on the action unfolding in front of him as Manawatu battled Wairarapa-Bush. He was keeping a particularly close eye on the man wearing the green and white No 6 jersey which he would have been filling himself but for an untimely injury.

Shaw's position in the stands was close enough that he could occasionally hear the local Masterton radio commentator broadcasting the action on the field. Suddenly there was a minor skirmish. And just as quickly, Shaw heard his name bouncing about in the broadcasting box. He cocked an ear. "Aw...that bloody Shaw is at it again," he heard the commentator frothing into his microphone. "He's just decked one of our blokes and given away a penalty. When's this bloke finally going to learn!?" Shaw was dumbfounded. "Here I am sitting in the grandstand with a crook shoulder and this dickhead is saying I'm punching blokes on the field," he says. "I guess that pretty much sums up the way some people saw me. If there was a donnybrook on the field, people would say: 'Aw, Shaw's whacked some bastard again'."

If that was the perception of some rugby fans during Shaw's playing days, the critic will buy a huge argument with Shaw's team-mates at all levels. In interviewing many of those men who played alongside him, I was struck at the incredible affection they held for the man all and sundry referred to as "Cowboy". To a man, they were effusive in their praise. In an All Black side that featured individual geniuses like Stu Wilson and Bernie Fraser and dominating forwards like Andy Haden and Andy Dalton, Shaw was often referred to as the glue that welded the test team together.

Rugged, uncompromising, and yes, if necessary, ruthless, Shaw was prepared to lay everything on the line for his team-mates. If that meant pulling the odd rival into line, he was happy to oblige. In reality, the incidents where the infamous Cowboy short left was used were few and far between. Shaw's awesome commitment and pride influenced the outcome of more matches than his fists ever did. But when he did feel the need to straighten out an obstructive rival, the results were often devastating. Mark Shaw was one bloke with whom you didn't mess.

"My abiding memory of Cowboy remains the first test against the Springboks in 1981. Boy, did he fix up that Yarpie!" marvels Stu Wilson. "It won us the game. No doubt about it. He was huge, that bloke." That 'bloke' was South African flanker Eben Jansen who was throwing his considerable weight around the lineout in the opening test and creating mayhem in the process. Andy Haden was seeing virtually no ball and the big Lancaster Park crowd was starting to sense the All Blacks were in trouble.

"This Jansen guy was their best loose forward and he was probably around 6'4" or 6'5"," Wilson continues. "We were being outgunned at that stage. They were just too big and too mean for us and we were just slightly on the raw end of the game. We weren't looking too good. Cowboy had warned this fella in the previous lineout. He'd told him: 'Don't ever jump off my shoulder again, pal'. Cowboy called everybody 'pal'. But this guy was huge. I mean, he dwarfed Cowboy! But then came this lineout and Cowboy came out

Go ahead, make my day...Shaw lays down the law. But the flanker loathed his 'Dirty Harry' image.

with that left jab that only moves about a foot. It happened at number seven in the lineout and all you could hear was this mighty thump and here was this big South African log lying prone on the ground. I thought, 'Here we go, it's going to get messy now'. But then Cowboy stepped forward with his fist cocked and said: 'Now if anyone else wants a bit of this, step forward'. Guys like Mexted weren't too keen on that sort of stuff. No-one was really. But suddenly the South

Africans backed off and Cowboy had a few All Black mates along-side him, guys he probably hadn't expected to back him up. It changed the whole game and won us the match. I'm convinced of that."

Andy Haden remembers the same incident. "Funnily enough, I probably instigated it," says the former lineout kingpin. "The Boks had been giving us a pretty hard time for the first 20 or 30 minutes or so and we were back on our line about 15 or 20 metres out which is not usually the place where you scramble somebody. But they were jumping all over my back all the time and I said to Cowboy: 'Sort it out, I'm sick of it!' Next thing he hit Jansen with a punch that was so quick not even the television replay could pick it up. Jansen hit the deck and that was the end of him. He was the player they had the greatest hope for among their loosies yet he didn't play one more Saturday game on the tour after that. God, he hit him hard. It just literally took the knees out from underneath him. After that I always used to worry about telling Cowboy to sort a bloke out," laughs Haden.

As is his habit, Shaw dismisses the incident, considering it "not that important". He good-naturedly reflects on the notorious repu-tation such incidents earned him. "Let's be fair about it, I did get myself involved in the odd scuffle," he says a little sheepishly. "I'd always pick up the papers the day after a test and read: 'Haden was superb in the middle of the lineout, Mexted was devastating off the back of the lineout and did this and that. Oh, and Shaw was his nor-mal over-the-top self'. That was it. Haden used to walk off and get all the pats on the back and bouquets and I used to walk off with a bleed-ing nose and two black eyes because I'd done my job and made sure he got ball!"

If those remarks sound a bit catty, they are delivered in a tone anything but that. Shaw considered looking after his lineout jumpers was a crucial part of his job as a blindside flanker. And if that meant he had to engage in some pushing and shoving and put his body on the line, so be it. It was all part of the formula needed to win the match. "If you look back at all the scuffles I was involved in, nearly all of them started from lineouts," he says. "There were never any blues from rucks because I'd stomped somebody, gouged somebody's eyes or kneed some prick. They were all from lineouts. I might have ended up having the finger pointed at me afterwards but I had to make sure the boys got the ball come lineout time. Look, Haden and

Mexted were fantastic jumpers when they used to get a bit of room. I took all the shit on the ground, from the terraces and in the papers – but they got the ball. And if they got the ball, we won the test. End of story."

The media often dined out on Shaw's hardman image. With a nickname like Cowboy and incidents like the Jansen episode to fuel the notoriety, Shaw was readymade material for the headline writers. "Yeah, it used to cheese me off at times," he says. "Even the media used to call me by my nickname and it would conjure up all this Clint Eastwood-type bullshit. It seemed like I was the only bloke who always got called by his nickname. I mean, you'd never read 'Trapper' Loveridge or 'Frizz' Mexted."

Mark Shaw was born in Palmerston North in 1956 and grew up there until his parents moved to Waikanae to run the local hotel. Shaw finished his schooling at Kapiti College and at the age of 18, made his representative debut for Horowhenua at No 8 in 1976. But Shaw was a wandering spirit. He had travel-lust. "I headed off to Europe for a couple of years," he says. "I was out to sow my wild oats, you could say." He played social pub rugby in London and spent the summer trekking through North Africa and Spain before following Graham Mourie's All Black tourists around France in 1977, sleeping in a battered van he'd bought from his uncle and never once even imagining he would one day play alongside Mourie at international level.

He returned to New Zealand in 1978, this time heading to Palmerston North. After just a couple of club games, he found himself called into the Manawatu team at No 8 to deputise for Geoff Old who was away with the New Zealand Juniors in Australia. In those days, breaking into the Manawatu team was about as difficult as getting a start for Auckland in the late 80s. The feared Green and Whites were an awesome proposition, running roughshod over all opposition as they forged an iron grip on the Ranfurly Shield.

It is one of Shaw's few rugby regrets that he came along slightly too late to feature in Manawatu's great shield era. "I sat in the grandstand as a reserve for about six or seven shield defences," he says. "I'm a little disappointed I never got to play in a shield-holding game. But I'd just got off the boat from England, I'd been away for two years, was pretty skinny on it and my discipline wasn't what it should be. I couldn't just walk in and expect to replace a bloke of Geoff Old's calibre."

Shaw and a Bay of Plenty rival exchange pleasantries while a Zambuck tries a novel way of cooling tempers.

In 1979, Manawatu coach Graham Hamer suggested Shaw move to the blindside flank to help secure a permanent position. "I'd always been a No 8 up till then but back in those days there wasn't much difference between the two positions. It was nowhere near as sosphisticated as it became in the 1980s." Shaw took Hamer's advice and the reward was selection in the New Zealand Juniors that same season.

Given a taste of big-time rugby, Shaw began to knuckle down, believing higher honours could be within his reach if he was committed enough. His form was strong enough early in the 1980 season to earn his first All Black trial. But he had to contend with more than just a rookie's nerves. "I'd been tipped over in a club game the week before but I'd decided I was going to the trial no matter what," he says. "Perhaps in hindsight I shouldn't have gone but I had to have a crack. In the end I never saw it out." His painful back injury forced him off and Shaw believed he had little chance of being selected for the upcoming tour of Australia. He was wrong.

Mourie may have had a mortgage on the No 7 jersey but the other flanker's role was causing the selectors considerable heartburn with Lawrie Knight, Leicester Rutledge, Dick Myers, Barry Ashworth, Wayne Graham, Ash McGregor, Ken Stewart and Mike Burgoyne all used there at different stages since Ian Kirkpatrick's final series against the 1977 British Lions. In Shaw, new All Black coach Eric Watson saw something special. Certainly the raw-boned lad from Manawatu wasn't as naturally talented as many of the tight loosies who had gone before him; nor did he possess the footballing brain of a Mourie. But by God, was he committed! Shaw was named for the tour.

The tour was a troubled one. Mourie didn't want to go, nor did Andy Dalton. Incredibly, Bruce Robertson was left behind. So was Frank Oliver. Shaw was battling Waikato's Geoff Hines, also on his first tour, for a test jersey. When Hines performed poorly against Sydney, the door opened for Shaw and he didn't miss his chance.

His test debut, in terms of New Zealand's performance, was a forgettable one though. The Wallabies won the first test at the Sydney Cricket Ground 13-9 but the All Blacks squared the ledger at Ballymore 12-9 in a match that featured an absolutely stunning team try begun and finished by Hika Reid. But ultimately the series was lost when the Australians won the decider 26-10 with Shaw sitting on the bench after injuring knee ligaments against Queensland.

"We had a lot of problems on that tour," Shaw says. "Having a few senior guys pull out and leaving Frank [Oliver] and Bruce Robertson at home didn't help but the Aussies had a good side then. They had the Ellas, Michael Hawker, Brendan Moon and Roger Gould in a really class backline. Their forwards weren't that flash but they were very slick in the backs."

Even though the All Blacks failed to impress in Australia, Shaw made an impact in more ways than one. He developed an ironman reputation by playing in 13 of the 16 tour matches. Then there was the Steve Williams incident. The second test featured a desperate All Black team playing for their honour as much as squaring the series. Midway through the second half the tension erupted as both sets of forwards traded punches. Williams' second biggest mistake in the ensuing melée was to target Shaw as his opponent. The biggest? Missing with the haymaker he threw. Shaw let fly with the little short left jab. Unlike Jansen, Williams stayed on his feet...just. The Australian lock's jaw was shattered and he was doing a pretty good impersonation of a stunned mullet. Bravely, he soldiered on for a while until replaced.

"The short little left was the one that always did the damage," says Stu Wilson. Shaw introduces it to Wallaby Steve Williams in an infamous 1980 test.

The incident embellished Shaw's already growing "hitman" image and the Australian media tried their level best to make a meal of the episode. But interestingly Simon Poidevin, also playing in his first series for his country, says the Australian players had "no problems" about the incident. "There were a number of punches thrown by a whole group of players and it just so happened that 'Pal' [Shaw] landed the best one," said Poidevin. "Steve Williams is a pretty big guy, bigger than Cowboy anyway. So it wasn't as if he hit a halfback or anything. We could live with it. I never ever saw Cowboy as anything but a fiercely competitive player and never would I say he was a dirty player. He simply wasn't. There were people around at the time like [Australian prop] Steve Finnane who was more of a hitman than a player. I think it's unfortunate that many New Zealanders remember him more as a hitman than as the very good player he was. The impression that people had of him was nowhere near the reality."

Poidevin and Shaw went on to become fierce rivals on the field and firm friends off it, even if it took until the 1986 IRB centenary matches, where they played alongside each other for the first time, for Shaw to drop his natural defences towards Australians! "Cowboy and I were always running into each other in the early part of the '80s," recalls Poidevin. "New South Wales were frequently playing in New Zealand and we'd come up against Manawatu quite often. As I said, he was regarded as a hardman and very much the enforcer of New Zealand rugby, which immediately carries a certain implication that he was a dirty player. The way I saw it, if there were any problems during a game, the All Black forwards simply got together, identified the culprit and told 'Pal' to deal to him. Now when you consider there were some pretty tough customers in that All Black forward pack, such as John Ashworth and Gary Knight, it shows you just how hard Cowboy was. He was obviously held in very high esteem by his team-mates. Certainly, the Wallabies respected him for his footballing ability first and his uncompromising nature second."

Andy Haden confirms the "election" of Shaw as team troubleshooter. "Around that time, a lot of the American baseball jargon was gaining in popularity. We were in the middle of a team meeting when some of the guys started introducing the baseball jargon. Then someone piped up: 'Well, Cowboy, you can be our designated hitter'. Cowboy just grinned," laughed Haden.

After making the dramatic step from a provincial rep player to a test certainty within the space of one season, Shaw was more than looking forward to the All Blacks' end of year tour of Wales. The All Blacks played sublime rugby on the short tour, proving mammoth party-poopers for the Welsh Rugby Union's centenary celebrations when they romped to success in the Cardiff Arms international 23-3. "Everyone went to Wales and it was just a great tour," says Shaw. "We knew what we had to do and we just did it. A few of the guys like Billy Osborne, Frank Oliver and John Ashworth had been there in '78 and they had bad memories of the Welsh leg of the tour. Generally, they'd had a prick of a time in Wales and a lot of those guys were just so single-minded and focused about beating the Welsh that they just carried the rest of us along. I've never been in a team that has trained so hard yet enjoyed a tour so much socially. We would think nothing of going out and having a few beers on a Friday night before a game because we were so relaxed. We were playing well and nobody felt guilty about it."

Shaw saw the Welsh tour as an opportunity to cement a Test spot for the future. "It was a chance to cash in. The style of football suited me. I was always a bit short of a yard of pace and the tracks in Australia and South Africa didn't always suit me. But the Welsh grounds were a bit soft underfoot like here and I didn't mind that sort of stuff." Shaw played some outstanding rugby on the tour, his fearsome commitment often stunning even the most veteran of rugby scribes.

The Welsh tour was significant for another reason though. Many observers, Shaw included, pinpoint it as the emergence of the distinct and differing roles of a blindside and openside flanker. As Graham Mourie's career had developed, it had quickly become apparent that he had certain strengths. He would often stay out of the heavy physical exchanges early in a match, astutely pacing himself before often having a devastating effect in the second half of a game where his pace, ball skills and tactical vision made a major imprint on the opposition. Shaw preferred to rip into it from the opening whistle. He revelled in the physical confrontation and thrived on sorting out the troublemakers come lineout time. Yet by his own admission he was no speedster round the park.

"Mourie basically instigated the open and blindside situation on that Welsh tour," says Shaw. "We sat down and analysed our various strengths because we felt we needed to spend all day doing what we were very good at rather than trying to do a bit of everything. Mourie was good at running wide. He had great anticipation, ran beautiful angles and was a brilliant support player. That was his game. I was pretty good at smashing it up, playing the close game, making the hard tackles. 'Mex' [Murray Mexted] liked to float. He had a bit of gas and athleticism. So the entire back row combination developed from there and now it's standard fare. That combination of styles in the back row has become the strength of All Black rugby."

Shaw and Mourie were as effective a tight/loose back row duo as any coach could hope for. The irony was that they were very much rugby's version of *The Odd Couple*. "Mourie was very, very singleminded, aloof, which I guess you have to be to a certain extent as an All Black captain," says Shaw. "We weren't great mates, put it that way. But we weren't enemies either. I'm a pretty basic guy whereas he was more into mind games, psychology and all that shit. That's for the birds, mate. I mean, I'll truck along and do the best I can but don't send me some head-shrinker to tell me how to prepare for a game. But he was into that sort of stuff, you know, the John Hart approach. That might be all right for blokes like [John] Kirwan who have trouble getting their head right but I never had that problem. I couldn't relate to that crap. We were completely different, Graham and I. I was a freezing worker and he could have been a lecturer. Different strokes, I guess."

Indeed. The following season Mourie sensationally opted out of playing against the touring South Africans. Shaw ran the gauntlet of protestors to play. But living in a student-dominated city like Palmerston North meant he felt the heat more than many of his All Black team-mates. "There were a lot of those Roman sandal-wearing hippies riding round on 1920 pushbikes," he says with obvious disdain. "The bloody town was full of them. I got the abusive phone calls, the painted fences, rocks through the window, all that sort of rubbish."

It may be over-simpliflying the situation but Shaw just wanted to play rugby. He'd always wanted to pit himself against the Springboks, wanted to find out if they were as tough and indomitable as he'd been told they were.

Curiously, Shaw shared the same inherent mentality towards the Afrikaaner as Kevin Skinner and Frank Oliver before him. He understood them and therefore knew the importance of standing his ground in the this first test when Eben Jansen was seeking to intimidate the All Blacks. "The expression on the faces of the other South African forwards after I hit Jansen summed it all up," he recalls. "They were thinking: 'What's going on here?'. The Afrikaaner is like that. They treat you like a little black boy, they love giving orders. They've never had to take discipline themselves, nobody has ever told them what to do. So when you stand up to them and tell them, 'Do that again and I'll whack you', the penny suddenly drops and they start thinking about it."

Shaw had an outstanding series against the Boks, soured only by being forced out of the deciding third test after getting injured in a provincial match against Southland. In the first test at Lancaster Park, he scored the match-turning try – his first in an international – 12 minutes into the second half, emerging from a maul and crashing over the line for a crucial touchdown in New Zealand's 14-9 triumph. Shaw rates the 1981 Boks as the equal of any international opposition he faced during his lengthy career and believes the All Blacks' series victory in the midst of incredible chaos off the field contained much to admire. Shaw added to his growing tally of test caps when the All

Mark Shaw's commitment to the black jersey has never been questioned.

Blacks racked up tight wins over Romania and France on a tougher than expected end of year tour before the 1982 season which led to the renewing of acquaintances with the touring Wallabies. Once again, Shaw was a dominant personality with Wallaby coach Bob Dwyer nominating him as the player of the series after the All Blacks recovered from a 19-16 loss in the second test to thump the Australians 33-18 in the Eden Park decider after having won the opener 23-16 at Lancaster Park. The abrasive Manawatu forward scored tries in both the second and third tests and by this time was considered virtually indispensable as an All Black.

His dominating displays continued in 1983 when the hapless British Lions toured. Shaw's increasing strike-rate continued when he scored New Zealand's only try in the tight 16-12 win over the tourists in the first test in Christchurch, was central in a stirring second half performance in the second test when the All Blacks successfully protected a 9-0 lead into the teeth of a wicked Wellington gale and was again prominent in the third test 15-8 win at Carisbrook. And in the fourth test, New Zealand produced one of the all-time great All Black performances in wiping the floor 38-6 with the Lions before heading across the Tasman for a one-off Bledisloe Cup clash won comfortably 18-8.

"When I look back now, 1982 and 1983 were probably my best years as an All Black," says Shaw. "I was pretty happy with the '82 season. We had a good side and we played some bloody good football against the Aussies. I guess it was memorable too because after the 1980 series loss we really had to get square. The Aussies liked themselves a bit and they had to be sorted out. We had to make them realise they'd caught us under difficult circumstances in '80 and that wasn't going to happen every time."

Unfortunately for Shaw and the All Blacks, the wheels rather fell off the team on the end-of-season tour of Scotland and England which was plagued by the withdrawal of a host of key players including captain Andy Dalton and fellow front rowers, Gary Knight and John Ashworth. The New Zealanders were held to a 25-all draw against Scotland and lost 15-9 to England at Twickenham.

In 1984, the French toured and Shaw kept up his high standard. In the first test at Lancaster Park, he and Jock Hobbs caused merry hell among the classy French backs. New Zealand won a tight one 10-9 in a match where John Kirwan made his debut. In the second test at

Shaw may not have been a flashy flanker but he bagged his share of tries, this one coming in the first test against the 1983 Lions.

Eden Park, the All Blacks reproduced the sparkling form of the third Lions international the year before, walloping Philippe Dintrans' men 31-18.

Shaw put the disparity between the two performances to "first test blues".

"It was more pronounced in those days," he maintains. "They talk about being slow into a first test nowadays. That's crap as far as I'm concerned. In the old days, you went into a first test with half a dozen club games, maybe an All Black trial and a couple of shitty, friendly rep games against average opposition. And it was a bigger spread of players from all over the country too. You'd come together and after one and a half training runs you had to go out there and play an international side. We'd win...but they were scratchy wins. And everybody would be like they are now...'change this guy, change that guy, chop, chop, chop'. But by the time the boys got through the second and on to the third, they were just humming. These bastards today have got no excuse. Ten of them come from one province, they play

Super 10 football, two All Black trials, plenty of other big football. There's no excuses for those guys. Saying they're underdone, it's the first test and they're rusty, that's bull. I think we had a bit of an excuse in the old days."

The All Blacks also toured Australia in 1984 with the Wallabies looking to a new coach in Alan Jones for consistent success against New Zealand. The tour was to prove a frustrating one for Shaw. "They were playing a lot of five-man lineouts in the first test, basically so Steve Cutler had leap time and wouldn't get knocked around," he explained. "What it effectively meant was that the spare loosie was standing out in the backs all the time. That's not my game."

In the end, Shaw was forced off with injury and replaced by an emerging young Aucklander named Alan Whetton. "I remember coming off the ground and feeling like I hadn't done anything," he recalls. "I hadn't got to a ruck, hadn't made a tackle, hadn't got my hands on the nut, because I was standing out in the backs and by the time you get to the action, it's all over." To further aggravate Shaw, the Wallabies won 16-9 to go one up in the series.

Shaw missed out on playing the second and third tests with coach Bryce Rope preferring Bay of Plenty's Frank Shelford. Shaw had no problems with the decision given the lineout tactics of the Australians. "If they were going to continue those tactics, it made sense to have a tearaway rabbit out among the backs than somebody like me," he says. "But I'd probably also lost a bit of form and Frankie was going real good. That was a decision I could live with. In those sort of situations, you've just got to knuckle down and bear it."

So after 16 Tests in a row wearing the black No 6 jersey, Shaw watched from the sideline as, firstly, New Zealand levelled the series with a pulsating 19-15 win at Ballymore and then snuck home 25-24 in the decider at the Sydney Cricket Ground. Shaw may have been able to accept that Shelford had beaten him for his position on merit, along with some help from the hard Australian grounds and the Wallaby tactics. But if the Bay flanker – and Alan Whetton – had any thoughts of Shaw taking the hint and winding down his All Black career, they had forgotten just how deep the fires of commitment burned in the Manawatu man.

The All Blacks were due to tour South Africa in 1985. And more than anything, Shaw wanted to take on the old enemy in their backyard. "I saw it as the ultimate challenge – beating the Boks over there. I trained my backside off over summer, did heaps of work. The boys were going to Africa and there ain't no way they were going without me." Shaw had a powerful All Black trial and regained his test jersey for the two early season tests against England, won 18-13 and 42-15, with Shaw among five try-scorers in the latter match. He was delighted when his name was read out for the touring party to the republic.

But Shaw quickly plunged the depths of negative emotion when the tour was sabotaged by Auckland lawyers. He was crestfallen and admits that even now his hackles rise when the issue is broached. "I'll never forget it," he said of the tour cancellation announcement. "It was a Saturday afternoon and I was packing my bags when it came on television. At the time, I thought we'd still go. I believed it would still get sorted out quickly but of course as it turned out, it was all for nothing. I was devastated. We'd done so much training, got as far as packing our bags and it suddenly doesn't happen. It was pretty hard to motivate yourself to go back and play club games."

After a tight one-off Bledisloe Cup victory at Eden Park, the All Blacks left on a token tour of Argentina, hastily-arranged to atone for the disappointment of the cancelled visit to South Africa. But in the meantime, secret negotiations were being held for the rebel tour of the republic the following year. Shaw has no regrets about going on the Cavaliers tour. "The pressure we were under only intensified our will to win," he says. "I've never been involved with a team that's been so introverted, so single-minded, trained so hard and been as disciplined as that side was. There were all the distractions in the world while we were there but everybody was just so focused. We might not have been the All Blacks in name but we were the All Blacks in damn well every other sense. We knew that when we went on that tour, we virtually had to win the series to be able to go home proud."

They didn't, of course. And Shaw still remains bitter about some aspects of the tour. His anger at Welsh referee Ken Rowlands and his controversial handling of the 'fourth test' is still there. South Africa triumphed in the first clash at Cape Town 21-15 before the Cavaliers evened the score with a hard-fought 19-18 win in Durban. Naas Botha kicked 21 points as South African clearly won the third 'test' 33-18.

The ineffectual team performance was to cost Shaw, Kieran Crowley, John Ashworth and Grant Fox their positions for the fourth international. Shaw watched from the giant Ellis Park grandstand becoming increasingly frustrated with the enormous role Rowlands was playing in the match. The Welshman caned New Zealand 21-7 in the penalty count and the tourists were struggling to contain their resentment by the time Rowlands blew his whistle for the last time with the scoreboard reading 24-10 in South Africa's favour. Hooker Hika Reid was so angry he barged Rowlands as he left the field and Wayne Smith and Murray Mexted marched over and made their feelings known in no uncertain manner.

"I've never seen a dressing room like that one after a test," Shaw recalls, shaking his head to further convey his dismay. "Some of the boys broke down. That was the last shot for a lot of the guys, a lot of them never played for New Zealand again after that. They were just shattered. We had trained so hard and given everything. To have it all destroyed by Rowlands at the end when we knew we were a better team than the Boks, it was really tough to handle

Shaw didn't get as hard a time from tour protestors as he had received in 1981. "It was still pretty heated, though," he says. "They used to say that rugby was our national game and if you hurt rugby, you hurt New Zealand. Well yeah, maybe that's right but I'm a rugby player. I think of that Erin Baker sheila who runs triathlons. She's good at that, she's the world champion at that. We're good at playing rugby. Baker marched up and down the streets and got arrested for throwing eggs. So she's anti-South Africa, anti-rugby. And yet she thinks nothing about going over to Hawaii to run in that Ironman thing with about 20 South Africans in it. I was expected to sacrifice my footy but she was allowed to compete against the South Africans whenever she felt like it. It was the hypocrisy of the whole thing that used to piss me off."

The ramifications of the Cavaliers tour rumbled through the remainder of the New Zealand domestic season with those who had dared to travel to the republic earning a two-test suspension for defying the powers-that-be. With Jock Hobbs and Shaw among those sidelined, young Aucklander Mark Brooke-Cowden and Wairarapa-Bush's Brett Harvey were on the side of the scrum when New Zealand bravely dispatched the French 18-9 in the one-off test at Lancaster Park. "The Baby Blacks did bloody well, although it was about the time that the French started to slide down," says Shaw.

He was optimistic about a recall after the touring Australians won the first test 13-12 at Athletic Park. Instead, while the selectors swal-

Yes, even tough guys have a heart. There was a side to him a lot of people weren't aware of, say his team-mates.

lowed their pride and brought back 10 Cavaliers, Shaw was not among them. Alan Whetton was preferred for the No 6 jersey. "When that happened, I thought I'd played my last game for the All Blacks," Shaw admits. "I thought: 'Whetton's been waiting in the wings for a while, maybe his time has come'." Almost, but not quite.

The All Blacks won the second test by the same scoreline they'd lost the first. But Whetton was among three players dropped and Shaw got another crack at his old mate Simon Poidevin, becoming the fourth player to be used in the No 6 jersey that season. In an occasionally bizarre game in which New Zealand abandoned its traditional forward-based game for an often helter skelter approach, determined to match the Australians in backline brilliance, the All Blacks were soundly beaten 22-9. It was Shaw's 28th test – and his last.

He remains unimpressed at what he regards as tactical naivety in that last blast against the Australians. "We won enough ball that day to win three matches but all we did was spin it out, spin it out, get knocked over and get nowhere. We had the Aussies shot up front. David Kirk [captain for the day] should have given us a crack, run a bit, fed us, did a Loveridge and we would have fixed the Australians up. Kirk wasn't experienced enough at the time to be calling the shots. We lost and some of us had to go. I was one of them."

Shaw was still chosen for the end-of-year tour to France, though. He believed that he still had a chance of breaking back into the test line-up but says in hindsight he knew the selectors didn't really have him in mind for the top side. "Basically, Mexted had gone by then and Buck [Shelford] was cementing himself as the No 8. They could never play Buck and I in the same side because who would jump at the back of the lineout? They used Mike Brewer on the blindside and Jock Hobbs captained the team from the openside. Both of them missed the World Cup campaign in 1987 through injury. I believe they took me to France because they needed somebody to run the dirt-trackers. They knew some of the French midweek selection teams were going to be bloody hard and I was basically given the job as captain of the dirt-trackers."

Would he have still gone on the tour had he known he was un-likely to get a test? "Well, I'd like to say no but, yeah, I didn't mind looking after the dirt-trackers. I didn't have any problem with that. It was an enjoyable tour and I liked helping out the young blokes. There were blokes who did that for me when I first came in."

Even though the test line-up lost a furious second international at Nantes, significantly, the dirt-trackers went through the tour unbeaten. Shaw instilled a pride and commitment in the All Black newcomers that was to serve many of them well the following year – a season in which New Zealand established itself as the world's premier rugby nation.

Former All Black and Manawatu team-mate Frank Oliver remembers the early days of Shaw's captaincy career for Cowboy's less than subtle team talks. "He's changed them a bit now of course but I sat in on his team talk the very first time he captained Manawatu," says Oliver. "They were playing New Zealand Combined Services who had a pretty handy team back then with blokes like Buck Shelford running around for them. Manawatu had gone off the boil by then. We were always strong when we had forwards who were farmers, forestry workers and freezing workers while the backs were all the university students. It was the perfect mix. But by this time, the students were starting to infiltrate the forwards as well and Cowboy wasn't overly impressed with their commitment at times. This particular day, he began his team talk by saying: 'Righto boys, we haven't got much chance of winning this game today. You wanna know why? Because we're playing real men, that's why. We're playing men who crawl round on their bellies with guns in the middle of the night in winter in Waiouru. Not like you dope-smokin', roman sandal-wearing scarfies. But never mind, we'll give it our best, C'mon let's go'. And with that he walked out. I couldn't believe it. It was vintage Cowboy."

Given his sterling service to New Zealand rugby, it's a tragedy Shaw and so many top players from his era never got the chance to play in a World Cup. Typically, Shaw gave his utmost to beat his ageing legs and make the 1987 squad chasing the first William Webb Ellis Trophy. He got as far as the final trial in Whangarei before having to bow to the new zestful brigade of loose forwards headed by Michael Jones, Alan Whetton, Zinzan Brooke, Mark Brooke-Cowden and Buck Shelford.

"I had no beef about not making it," he says. "I was probably at the end of my time. Perhaps I could have hung in there, made the squad and sat in the grandstand for most of the games. But my attitude is that if you couldn't get on the track you might as well not be there. I would have loved to have played a World Cup, though," admits Shaw. "Haden was trying to get it off the ground three or four years before that first one. Some really great players missed out on the experience, some great teams too. Like your Frasers and Wilsons, your Mexteds and your Mouries. We had a good side in the early eighties and we would have liked to have played together in a World Cup."

Shaw was suitably impressed with the performances of the 1987 World Cup-winning All Blacks, but not overwhelmed. He acknowledges the fine football David Kirk's side played but puts forward his own theory that the rest of the rugby world had largely slipped in both form and imagination. "It's ironic because so many of the teams we used to find so difficult to beat in our day are now the minnows," he explains. "I'm talking about the likes of Wales, and, until 1984, even France. They were hard, good teams in the early 80s. The French had bloody good teams and we had to work bloody hard to beat them. Now, quite often, they're ordinary.

"Even the Aussies were the same. I know they came back and won the World Cup in 1991 but they went into a trough too between 1987 and 1989. I look back to the 1987 All Blacks now and find myself asking: 'Where they just so bloody good or had the opposition just deteriorated?' They were obviously a good side and they played an expansive game. But I felt the opposition had dropped a notch or two as well."

Even though his All Black career was over, Shaw still had an appetite for top rugby. By now he had established a reputation as an inspiring leader. Now living in Hawke's Bay, the once famous province was quick to benefit from his experience during the 1988 season. That same year the New Zealand Rugby Football Union created the Divisional XV concept. All Black selector Lane Penn was to coach the team, to be selected from second and third division players, on a six-match tour of the Pacific Islands. Remembering his feats in France, Shaw was named captain. The tour was a resounding success and Penn raved about Shaw's positive influence on the impressionable budding young stars.

Penn believes Shaw was the difference between a successful tour and a marginal one. "Mark would have made a great All Black captain had he been given that opportunity," says Penn. "I know he has this hardman image and all that but that all blurs the fact that he was very much a thinker of the game when he played. He knew how to relate to his team-mates, especially the younger, inexperienced ones. That's what made him so great on the South Pacific tour. His commitment was his other great strength. He seemed to inspire a will to win among the entire team. In a tight game, that can make all the difference."

With encouragement from Penn, Shaw began to toy with the idea of coaching. In 1989, he moved his young family to Paekakariki, a picturesque beachside town north of Wellington. Turning out for Hutt Old Boys in the Wellington club competition, he made a big impression in 1989 and 1990 before taking over as coach in 1991. In his first year as coach, Hutt dominated the Wellington club scene, winning the Jubilee Cup. Inbetween, Penn wooed him to help out as assistant coach of a New Zealand Development Squad which toured Canada at the same time the All Blacks were in France, further establishing his mana as a coach with a future.

Shaw continued his coaching association with Hutt Old Boys in '92 and '93. He confides that he could have had the Wellington representative coaching post in '93, a role taken by former team-mate David Kirk, but had to turn it down because of his work commitments with a Fletcher's subsidiary. While keen on furthering his coaching career, Shaw has his doubts that he can afford to look any further than controlling a club side. "I'd like to go further but you've got to have a job", he says. "To coach a top side, you've got to be self-employed nowadays. I've got a job for a company of Fletchers and times are tough, so the company has to perform. You get X amount of holidays and after that, that's it. You've got be be set up if you want to coach at the highest level and I just can't do it right now, not with a family of four young daughters."

He was surprised to find overseas interest in him early in 1994. The Northern Transvaal union approached him to spend three months in South Africa, working on the techniques of its leading forwards. Obviously he had made an impact in more ways than one in 1981.

Shaw's former All Black captain Andy Dalton, a skipper he greatly admired, probably best summed up the rugged blindside flanker's contribution to All Black rugby. "There's been more skilful loose forwards play for New Zealand but Cowboy's biggest strength was his commitment," says Dalton. "He was an earthy, down-home sort of bloke but everybody loved his company. He was a great tourist. What he lacked in pace and skill, he made up with in determination. He

Shaw, wife Mandy and two of his four daughters in the latter days of his playing career.

would give everything everytime he wore that black jersey, just literally run himself into the ground. About the biggest compliment that I can pay Cowboy is that if I had to pick a forward pack to go out and play for a Test for my life, he would be the blindside flanker. No risk."

It seems a lot of other people agree. When *Rugby News* asked a fleet of experts to pick their ultimate All Black team from every player who wore the silver fern during the 1980s, Shaw was named in the No 6 jersey he loved and wore with such distinction.

DEAN BELL
'Man of Steel'

The alarm goes off. It's 4am in the Kiwi team hotel, just 11 hours before the New Zealanders are due to take on the world champion Australians in the third test of the 1985 series at Carlaw Park. Dean Bell struggles out of his bed, gingerly putting weight on his injured knee. He heads for the door knowing Kiwi team physiotherapist Glenn Gallagher will have also been waken by an alarm. Two hours earlier the pair have gone through the same process. Under the instructions of coach Graham Lowe, Bell is receiving two-hourly physiotherapy through the night as well as the day in a desperate bid to get the Kiwi utility back on the field. Few give him any chance. As it was, the long-time injury had forced Bell off during the fateful second test a week earlier when the Australians had won with a try in the last minute of play. But Lowe believed he was needed for the third test. After a week of painful physio treatment and waking at 2am and 4am daily, Bell did indeed play. The Kiwis won 18-0 in one of New Zealand league's finest moments. Bell's reputation as a league ironman was enhanced yet again.

THOSE close to Dean Bell are not surprised at the lengths he went to in his bid to play in that third Carlaw Park test. He had always been fiercely determined, even as a kid playing for the Manukau club in Auckland where the entire Bell clan would line the sidelines supporting the young cousins. Some of the youngsters would be daunted by the presence of their elders, many of whom were leading luminaries within the Auckland league scene. Never Dean Bell. He simply always responded to a challenge.

Bell has forged a great career. He has been the consummate professional, perhaps matched only in his commitment and dedication among Kiwi players by Mark Graham and Hugh McGahan. In England he is held in awe, as recognised by his popular victory in the Man of Steel Award for the 1991-92 season. Significantly, the first thing John Monie did after agreeing to become the Auckland Warriors coach was to ring Bell and open negotiations with his Wigan captain to come home.

Bell's signing as Warriors skipper generated genuine excitement within New Zealand league circles. And justifiably so. Bell himself has been overwhelmed by the goodwill extended to him since the announcement he would play out the last year of his distinguished career with the Warriors in their maiden season in Australia's professional competition.

But recognition of his standing in the league world has been long coming within New Zealand, certainly among officialdom here anyway. Bell has had his share of run-ins with leading Kiwi league officials, although for the most part he has never picked a fight with them. He became their scapegoat after the 1988 World Cup final debacle and when he later put his Wigan ties ahead of his allegiances to his country, there were plenty of off-the-record murmurings in the ears of New Zealand league writers from administrators eager to have Bell painted as a money-hungry mercenary.

In fact, it's highly doubtful that Bell would have returned to Auckland had the Warriors been run by the New Zealand Rugby League. Monie's involvement and the savvy of Auckland's chief executive Ian Robson clearly swayed him to put aside the slings and arrows that have been fired at him by NZRL officialdom. Often it seems that Bell has paid the price for the perceived sins of other members of his family. Although he has only a sister among his immediate family, his father Cameron, a former Auckland representative coach who plotted Australia's only loss on their 1989 tour of New Zealand, comes from a family of 12. And most of that brood had families of five and six children. "I've lost count of how many cousins I've got," says Dean.

One of Bell's cousins is former Kiwi halfback Clayton Friend. One uncle, George, represented the New Zealand Maoris. Another uncle, Ian Bell, also played for New Zealand, captaining the Kiwis in 1978. It was in the company of Ian that Dean had his first serious run-in

Dean Bell...his first impact as a Kiwi came on the wing.

with New Zealand rugby league officialdom and its often narrow-minded attitudes. His footballing potential had already been evident for many years. His junior days were split between playing rugby at school and league from the age of four for the Manukau club where his father and many others among the Bell clan were staunch members. His early rugby skills were good enough to earn him representation in the South Auckland team to play in the annual Roller Mills tournament and later selection in a North Island side. But league was always his first love, despite his first XV status at Otara's Hillary College. He was a perennial performer in Auckland junior representative sides but occasionally seemed to inexplicably miss selection in certain teams.

As his teenage years progressed Bell began to suspect that he was encountering obstacles not of his own making. "I sometimes felt in some years that the Bell name wasn't helping me," he explains. "It seemed like in some circles higher up in the rugby league the family wasn't popular. The family was prominent in Auckland league and were always very vocal about things with which they didn't agree. There was never any reluctance to speak their mind. I felt that at times I was penalised because of that. I had no doubt that I was a far better player than some of those who took my place in certain rep sides. I remember once when I was left out of an important rep side and it really hurt. Then the winger got injured and I was called in. I ended up receiving the player of the tournament award. But I overcame that rubbish. All it did was make me more determined that my form would simply leave them no choice but to pick me."

If Dean had his suspicions about the stigma attached to the Bell name, they were all but confirmed a few years later in the 1982 Kiwi trial. In the meantime he had achieved his first major breakthrough, coming into the Auckland senior competition and representative squad the same season in 1979. His first senior game for Manukau, at the age of 17, was at Carlaw Park and he marked Dane O'Hara, the Kiwi try-scoring machine. "He was a real star and it was pretty daunting," recalls Bell. "But I went OK. I didn't set the world on fire but I didn't make a fool of myself either."

Don Hammond, the Auckland representative coach at the time, noted Bell's solid debut and several of his spectacular try-scoring feats in other grades. At the time Auckland were involved in the Amco Cup, a mid-week knockout competition across the Tasman. That same season Hammond included Bell in the Auckland rep squad as a reserve.

By early 1982 Bell was an Auckland regular and his star was shining brighter with every outing. Nobody was surprised when he was named to play in the Kiwi trial. One of the most pleased among the Bell family was his uncle Ian, also named to appear in the trial at Auckland's Ellerslie Domain. Dean was carrying a worrying and painful knee injury but the prospect of making the Kiwis was the best anaesthetic possible. His disappointment at the events that followed remain to this day.

"There were two teams named for the trial and like most football sides in those days everybody went out for a few drinks the night before," says Dean. "It's not like it was a wild night or anything and we all got back to the hotel at the same time. But for some reason, only myself and my uncle Ian got found out. Apparently nobody was supposed to go out. Ces Mountford was in charge at the time.

"The next day Ian and I got called up in front of the management and even though everybody had gone out, we were lectured about how they were very disappointed in our attitude. Then they told us that we would only be given half a game each in the trial. Straight away Ian told them where they could stick their trial. I told him that if he wasn't playing, I wasn't either. But he told me not to be silly, that I still had a career in front of me and that I had to play. I did play, although my knee bothered me throughout. I had major ligament damage but at the time I didn't know it. But even with one bung knee I still felt I out-played my opposite winger. But naturally enough, when the team was announced, they picked the guy I marked. I was disappointed but I had expected it. What really annoyed me was that everybody had gone out but we were the only ones who got hung out to dry."

Christchurch Press journalist John Coffey, the most experienced rugby league reporter in New Zealand, notes in *Rugby League Greats* that the omission of Bell from the 1982 tour of Australia was regarded as a minor scandal. Almost any coach of note at the time remarked on the folly of leaving the hottest young league prospect in the country at home.

Dismayed by the attitudes he was encountering, Bell decided to head to England. "I was like most young New Zealand guys at that age, I just wanted to see a bit of the world and gain some overseas experience," he says. "And if I could pick up some money playing for a club there, all the better." Along with Clayton Friend, he ended up with the Carlisle club in the deep north of England. The Kiwi half-back at the time, Shane Varley, had directed them towards Carlisle, a newly-created club looking to make its mark on the English scene.

"We weren't on much money, we were just after experience," says Bell. The two cousins made an impact in the first year. They were both named in the Cumbria rep team to play the touring Australians, nicknamed "The Invincibles" after trekking through the UK unbeaten. "We got rolled by 40 or so points but it was a great experience for me at 20 going up against guys like Mal Meninga and Steve Ella."

Bell returned to New Zealand at the end of the 1982-83 English season. Mountford had gone, replaced by Graham Lowe. Lowe already had a high opinion of Bell. And he was a coach with little time for administrators meddling in his business. Lowe wanted Bell in his team and the fledgling winger made his international debut against Australia in the first Test of the '83 series at Carlaw Park.

"It was pretty daunting," Bell says. "In years previous to that series Australia had been just so dominant over New Zealand. They were walloping us every time they played us in the late seventies. To play against them was a huge challenge. I guess some people saw Graham Lowe's selection of me as a gamble but he didn't think so. In many ways I felt fortunate to have `Lowie' as my coach that year because he helped me overcome that obstacle of being intimidated by the Australians. He put things into perspective for us. He taught us to look through the hype surrounding the Aussies. He made us realise that just because a bloke had a big glossy picture of himself on the front of *Rugby League Week* along with a write-up of what a great player he was, it wasn't always reality. The guy might have had a crap game but the Aussie media machine was simply hyping him. He was a great coach, Graham. That was his first game as New Zealand coach too, so I started my career with him."

Australia won the first test 16-4 but in the return clash at Brisbane's Lang Park both Lowe and Bell experienced the sensation of defeating the reigning world champions for the first time. "That was great, one of the biggest buzzes of my career without a doubt," Bell enthuses. "And I felt I had a good game which made it even more memorable. I was marking Kerry Boustead and he was regarded as the best winger in Australia at the time. I knew that I wasn't as fast as

Never lacking in commitment, Bell hits it up among the forwards in a Kiwi trial in 1987.

him but I also knew that if I closed down the room he had to move in he wouldn't be effective. So I made sure that every time he got the ball I was right on top of him."

Indeed, Bell's close-marking and physical approach seemed to fluster the normally unflappable Boustead, now chief executive of the North Queensland Cowboys club. The Queensland speed merchant was guilty of dropping several crucial passes under the suffocating pressure of Bell's defence and had probably the most forgettable match of a distinguished international career as Australia crashed 19-12.

Intimidating defence has always been a hallmark of Bell's game. His former Wigan and current Auckland Warriors coach John Monie describes Bell as the finest defensive centre he has coached. "He's unpassable," says Monie. Lowe echoes the claim. "Although he was sent off for a few head-high tackles during his career, Dean has always been a legitimate tackler," says Lowe. "His strength is that he often hits players with strong body checks. When I was at Wigan he was always forcing turnovers through his ball-and-all tackles."

Bell's determination to defeat Australia whenever he could was also fuelled by the arrogance of the world champions who always seem to find excuses on the occasion of rare defeats. "They typically came up with quite a few after losing that Lang Park match, but after that defeat they started taking New Zealand seriously," he says.

After the two tests against the Kangaroos, New Zealand made a quick tour of Papua-New Guinea where Bell got himself on the international try-scoring list for the first time. He crossed three times against the Kumuls but found himself overshadowed by the remarkable feats of Hugh McGahan who scored a world record six tries. "Hughie's effort was phenomenal and deserved all the accolades he received. Six tries in any game, especially from a forward, is outstanding," says Bell.

After the New Zealand season Bell returned to England, touring early in the northern season with the Maori. He had intended to return to Carlisle but first division giants Leeds had been impressed with what they had seen of him and offered a healthy contract which Bell accepted. But before moving to Headingley, Bell had some other important business to attend to in Carlisle. The previous year he had met a local lass named Jackie who had been dragged along to Carlisle matches by her sister. The pair immediately hit it off. Jackie travelled Down Under with Dean for the 1983 season and by the end of the year they were married.

Bell's first game for Leeds was a first round match in the knockout John Player Special competition against Hull Kingston Rovers. Leeds had been struggling up to that point but beat Hull KR and went on to defeat Widnes in the final. The club also reached the semi-finals of the Challenge Cup where a loss to Widnes ended 17 straight victories. "Seventeen games in a row is a big feat in England," notes Bell. "I didn't realise just how big a feat it was at the time."

Bell again returned to New Zealand in 1984, playing all three tests in the clean sweep of the touring Great Britain side. That meant he had six tests to his credit in just two seasons, thus making him eligible for a full international clearance under the NZRL's antiquated rules. At that time a New Zealander could only gain a clearance – and therefore the chance to pursue a professional career in Australia or England – once he had either six tests to his credit or had made two international tours with the Kiwis.

It was a demand that angered Bell who considers the NZRL robbed many promising New Zealand players of a moral right to make a living from what they did best. "I was fortunate to get my six tests up so quickly," he says. "But some players had to wait years. If they got injured, or they had a guy like Mark Graham or Kurt Sorensen playing in the same position as them, they just had no chance. It was a ludicrous system. I had plenty of overseas clubs interested in me from the first time I made the Kiwis but I was untouchable because of this ridiculous six-test rule. Balmain and Canterbury-Bankstown both wanted me. Canterbury had just won two premierships at the time and they were a huge force. But they heard about the restrictions, and also the transfer fee, and they immediately lost interest.

"I think it was grossly unfair of the NZRL to do that to players. They were basically stopping guys from making a living from something they were good at."

But once he was eligible for a full clearance, the overseas clubs swooped. Sydney club Eastern Suburbs made the most attractive offer and Bell headed for Bondi Junction in 1985 along with Hugh McGahan. He still has vivid memories of his debut for Easts against neighbouring South Sydney. "I wasn't aware that there was quite a history between Souths and Easts and that they didn't like each other," says Bell. "The intensity of feeling in the game shocked me. Souths were into Hugh and I from the start. The sledging was unbelievable.

It was 'we're going to get you, you ****ing Kiwi bastards'. I was staggered by it. I mean, I didn't expect them to roll out the welcome mat but I didn't expect that either. I remember thinking: 'Geez, I hope it's not like this every week'. It's since come out in Mario Fenech's book that several of the Souths players from those days were on drugs and I'd believe it too. That doesn't surprise me because, honestly, their eyes were just lit up."

Bell had a better than average first season and carried his form into New Zealand's exciting three-test series with Australia that year despite a worrying knee injury. The knee was a consistent concern for Bell and largely sabotaged his season with Easts in 1986. Bell admits to often playing in ignorance of the damage. "Back then footballers didn't know as much as they do now," he explains. "Nowadays you would be straight in for an operation but back then the attitude was: 'Oh, I'll be right'."

It wasn't right in the second test in '85, however. "I had major cartilage damage and with 20 minutes to go, the knee completely folded on me. I was stretchered off and Joe Ropati came on for me."

The injury meant Bell was the only New Zealander at Carlaw Park who didn't witness Australian winger John Ribot score in the last minute and deny the Kiwis a deserved victory. "I was in the dressing room and I felt sure we had the game," he recalls. "Then I heard a giant roar and I thought the game was over and we'd won. A few seconds later everybody started coming in and I could see some of them were crying. That was when the penny dropped and I knew we must have lost. I was shattered. I started weeping too. That was a feeling I'll never forget."

If ever a team deserved to win and didn't, it was that Kiwi team that day. But from the ashes of disappointment rose a fierce desire to gain retribution in the third test at the same venue a week later. Hence Bell's all-night physiotherapy sessions with Glenn Gallagher. "Realistically my knee was totally stuffed but I was determined to play in that test," he says. "Ordinarily, I would have given up earlier in the week but I just knew we were capable of something special in that third game. Because the guys were so shattered by the result of the second test, the public had got right in behind us and that had created a very strong resolve.

"Right up to the day before the game I was still saying: 'It's [the knee] no good, it's no good' and I was sure Mark Elia was going to take my place. Then I decided to have one last run to test it. Glenn and Lowie took me to this paddock somewhere near the hotel and I went through a few drills with the knee strapped. It wasn't 100 per cent but I knew I could handle a game. So I managed to get out there. I didn't do a lot in that test. I held my own but it wasn't a fit Dean Bell. But just to be a part of that – you know, 18-0 against Australia – it was huge. It was worth all that effort."

New Zealand's captain in that test, Mark Graham, says Bell didn't realise how much of an inspiration he was to his team-mates in just getting on the field. "I gave him no chance of playing that test," says Graham. "Lowie was giving him until the last possible moment but secretly we didn't believe he had a hope. But Dean is as tough as nails and we couldn't believe it when he played. With that sort of spirit, our morale soared. He contributed a hell of a lot just by being there. It inspired the other guys."

It's no surprise that Graham included Bell in the 'Dream New Zealand' team he selected in his book *Mark My Words*, describing him as a 'fierce competitor with an extraordinary will to win and ability to match'.

At the end of 1985 the Kiwis toured the United Kingdom, squaring the series against the Poms. The first test was particularly brutal and a portent for what was to become an acidic series. The Kiwis triumphed narrowly but were outclassed in the second test at Wigan's Central Park when a rampant Garry Schofield crossed for four touchdowns. Bell does not have fond memories of the drawn third test. It was one of the few games in his career where his temper got the better of him. The refereeing didn't help. The Kiwis were caned 22-7 in the penalty count and many of the New Zealanders had difficulty reconciling fairness with the referee's approach.

But it was the touch judges who really got under Bell's skin. "I've never been as wild in my life as I was in that game," he says. "The English touch judges just kept coming on. And every time they came on, the penalty inevitably went to Great Britain. I believe touch judges should stay out of it unless it's something really serious. But they kept coming on in this game and it was really frustrating."

The final straw for Bell came in the dying stages with the Kiwis desperately clinging to a 6-4 advantage. Suddenly an English touch judge was on the field again and, predictably, the Poms were awarded a penalty. Prop Lee Crooks kicked a goal from the sideline to square the game and the series. "I totally lost my cool," recalls Bell. "I went over and abused the touch judges and told them they'd cost us the bloody game. Fortunately, somebody cooled me down. Later on we'd had a few drinks and we were getting a taxi somewhere. This taxi driver made some smart arse comment and Jackie had to pull me off him! I was so wound up about the whole thing that I actually had my hands around his throat. That game left a hell of a bitter taste in my mouth."

The 1986 season was a frustrating one for Bell. As in the previous year when he was banned for eight weeks near the end of the season, he was outed on a lengthy suspension by the Australian judiciary while playing for Easts. The second ban of 10 weeks in '86 cost him tests against Australia and Papua-New Guinea. "The two incidents were both for high tackles and they were both against Canberra," he says. "I deserved to be sent off, let's get that right from the outset. But there was nothing malicious in either tackle. To me, malice is somebody standing on somebody's head or deliberately raising an elbow going into a tackle. Mine were attempted tackles that I got wrong. Rightly I was sent off. I have no argument with that. But it seemed to me that every time I came up in front of the judiciary they wanted to make an example of somebody and, being a Kiwi, I was an easy target. I think I got some of the biggest suspensions being handed out in Australia at that time. It was my fault at the end of the day but the severity of the sentence didn't match the circumstances."

Bell's knee was also causing him consistent grief. "Every Friday I'd be down at the leagues club at Bondi getting all the fluid drained from my knee and some cortisone injected into it so I could play on the Sunday," he says. "That went on for a couple of months. Under those circumstances it's very difficult to play well and I struggled all that year with injury."

Despite his injury problems, Easts were keen to re-sign Bell for 1987 but found themselves outbid by Leeds who had fond memories of their earlier ties with the Kiwi. Bell was all set to sign when he unexpectedly received a phone call from the then Wigan club chairman Maurice Lindsay. Lindsay told him how the club had just signed Graham Lowe as their coach and he was keen to have Bell on board with him at the Cherry Whites. Was Bell interested? "I certainly was," he says. "In the end I actually signed for Wigan for less money than I would have got at Leeds simply because Graham Lowe was there.

"A fierce competitor with an extraordinary will to win and ability to match" – Mark Graham on Dean Bell.

Looking at it now, it was the best decision I ever made."

Leeds fans didn't think so, though, and Bell got a torrid reception when he turned out against his old club. Not that he fully understood at the time. "Every time I got the ball the Leeds supporters started yelling out, 'Judas, Judas!' But I thought they were saying, `Genius, Genius!',," laughs Bell. "After the game I remarked to one of our guys about what good supporters the Leeds fans were. He just looked at me and said: 'You've gotta be kidding!' I took a fair bit of ribbing about that and immediately got nicknamed Judas. Even now, I'm still called it at times."

Lowe's arrival at Central Park coincided with Wigan's emergence as the most dominant league power on the English scene in years. In his first season, Wigan won every trophy available bar the Challenge Cup where they lost in the first round to Oldham. The following season, 1987-88, they were not to be denied, this time going to Wembley and defeating Halifax in the showpiece match of the English game.

It was Bell's first trip to Wembley – an annual pilgrimage he made seven years in succession, a testimony to the iron grip Wigan has held on the Challenge Cup. Not once has Bell played in the losing side at Wembley. Nothing will surpass the experience of his first appearance at the hallowed shrine of English sport, though. "It's an amazing place," he says. "I get goosebumps just talking about it. That first time at Wembley has to be the biggest day of my career. The size of the crowd is the best feeling for me at Wembley. The walk down the tunnel is incredible. You hear the noise from the moment you leave the dressing room but it doesn't hit you until you walk out of the tunnel itself. That's the real mind-blowing moment. Even now I get tingles just talking about it. You can never get enough of that feeling. To me, that's what playing the game is all about. That makes the cold training nights in Wigan and all the hill-running at Coromandel when I was a kid all seem worthwhile."

Bell's time at Wigan is dear to his heart. He loves the town as well as the club. Indeed, following his single season with the Auckland Warriors, he plans to return permanently to Wigan. It's an open secret within the famous club that he will ultimately become their coach. "It's a special club; it has to be to have achieved what it has," he says. "They demand excellence and that is why I have enjoyed it there. I can't think of another club in world sport that has dominated its code to the same extent as Wigan has British league. Nobody in soccer has, no country in world rugby has, no Winfield Cup club has. Nor have they bought their success either. Graham Lowe might have taken some New Zealanders there but he was instrumental in bringing on juniors like Dennis Betts. Sure, the club has bought developed players from other clubs like Martin Offiah and Gary Connolly but generally Wigan develops its own talent. You only have to look at the likes of Jason Robinson, Andy Farrell, Barrie-Jon Mather and Mick Cassidy as the most recent examples of that. Their scouting programme and their development schemes are very, very good."

After his first year at Wigan, Bell returned to play for New Zealand in the off-season and found himself rewarded by being named touring team vice-captain for the 1987 trek to Australia and Papua-New Guinea. Then Ron O'Regan was forced out through injury and Bell was elevated to touring team captain by new coach Tony Gordon. "It was totally unexpected," said Bell. "I hadn't captained any major senior teams. We played really well on that little tour. Hugh McGahan came into the team as captain for the Australian Test but I led them against PNG and a few other teams we played along the way."

The tour was also notable for the spectacular one-off 13-6 test win over Australia at Lang Park. With Mark Graham declaring himself unavailable because of the NZRL's treatment of Graham Lowe, and other experienced caps like Kurt Sorensen unavailable, few gave the new-look Kiwis any hope of humbling Wally Lewis's men. The headline in *The Australian* newspaper the next morning summed up the match perfectly. "Kiwis dance a haka on the Invincibles' Grave" screamed the banner headline in reference to the fearsome war dance the New Zealanders performed immediately after the fulltime whistle.

For Bell, the victory completed a unique feat. He is the only player to have been involved in all three of New Zealand's upset wins over Australia during the 1980s.

But the heroics of '87 at Lang Park seemed a distant memory about 15 months later when Bell suffered his greatest indignity in the black jersey. The pain remains even now. The 1988 World Cup final received unprecedented media build-up within New Zealand. It was meant to be the game where New Zealand rugby league finally came of age. It was even being played at Eden Park, the home of New Zealand rugby and venue where a year earlier David Kirk had lifted the World Cup for union.

The Australians had been beaten the last time they had faced New Zealand, Kiwi greats Mark Graham and Kurt Sorensen had made themselves available for the match and many of the Aussies had not played for several weeks because of the October scheduling of the game. Everything was in place.

Instead, the match turned out to be Dean Bell's worst nightmare. With Hugh McGahan unavailable because of a serious injury, coach Gordon named Bell as his captain, resisting the temptation to give Mark Graham leadership of the side. Some critics questioned the decision but Bell had certainly done well the year before. Unbeknown to New Zealanders eagerly awaiting the clash, the captaincy was to become a major issue within the Kiwi camp.

Mark Graham quickly found himself at odds with the approach Gordon took in coaching the Kiwis. He spoke up. Bell found himself in an invidious position. His respect for Graham was immense. "And I think that affected my input," he says. "I was thinking, 'How can I stand up here and talk about how we should go about things when I'm looking at Kurt Sorensen and Mark Graham, two of the best professionals in the game'. I felt very awkward. Knowing what I know now, I'd be able to deal with that situation but back then I couldn't because I didn't have the experience to cope with it."

Bell admits the entire World Cup exercise was frayed from the beginning. "There were things going on that should have been picked up on, like the amount of time we were spending on practising the haka. We were too worried about getting that right rather than getting on with the game."

It's history the Australians won comfortably 25-12 despite Wally Lewis breaking his arm. Bell considers the World Cup final a great opportunity lost to put league on the map in New Zealand. "But you have to put it in perspective," he argues. "We were playing the reigning world champions. In previous years, we might have achieved one-off wins against them but we still hadn't won a series over them. They were still the No 1 nation in the world and we were overawed by them. The occasion got to us. There was so much riding on it."

Bell was crushed afterwards but worse was to come. Several weeks after the match, the then NZRL chairman George Rainey released a report on the match which was particularly scathing of Bell's captaincy skills. Bell found out about the report via the media. Memories of six years earlier when he and his uncle Ian were unfairly castigated came flooding back. "OK, we'd lost the game but we didn't do it on purpose," protests Bell. "Nobody loses on purpose. I didn't expect what happened with that report. If I'd seen it coming, I might have been able to prepare myself for it."

The Rainey report hurt Bell more than any flak the team took from the disappointed public. "At that time we needed the support of the country's leading administrator, not him bagging us," he said. "I didn't think there was any need for a big witch-hunt. Surely that's not up to the league hierarchy anyway. It's up to the coach, management and players collectively. Once a team gets on the field it's got nothing to do with other people. It's out of their control."

Shortly after the report, an angry Bell threatened to make himself unavailable for the Kiwis because of Rainey's criticism. Indeed, the common perception is that Bell carried out his threat and hasn't worn the black jersey since the World Cup debacle. He did play for the Kiwis in all five tests on the 1989-90 tour of Great Britain before then retiring from international play at Wigan's request. "What I actually said after the World Cup was that if this was the attitude of the NZRL after a loss, I would have to seriously reconsider whether I wanted to play for New Zealand again," Bell explains. "I was about 27 at the time but I felt strongly about it. As the captain, I probably took it a bit more personally than some of the other players."

Bell has never hidden the fact that Wigan offered him extra money to make himself unavailable for New Zealand from 1990 onwards. Nor does he use what could be a convenient excuse of saying he was sick of administrators meddling in his career. "I was just thinking of the money," he says candidly. "I thought I could last a little bit longer in the game by doing it. It's a big upheaval to move your family over to New Zealand every year just to play a couple of test matches. I wanted a more settled lifestyle. The money Wigan were offering wasn't small bikkies either. It was worth doing it for."

Bell admitted he was worried about the reaction his stand would generate back in New Zealand but was encouraged when many friends and supporters said they backed him. The irony is that Bell has played the best football of his career since his decision. By then permanently playing in the centres, his form for Wigan over the past four seasons has been scintillating. He has consistently dominated the English game's best centres and his Man of Steel award was even lauded by British reporters as well overdue.

In his book, Gary Freeman wonders in print if Bell regrets his unavailability for the Kiwis given his outstanding form of recent years. Bell assures the 'Whiz' that, under the circumstances, he doesn't. And while the Kiwis had to make do without him, the Auckland Warriors were a side who were not prepared to follow suit.

Like Graham Lowe, John Monie has always been a coach who readily recognised Bell's stature in the game. And like Lowe, he was quickly on the phone to Bell after accepting the coaching post at Auckland. Initially, Bell wasn't really interested in becoming a Warrior. He is well settled in Wigan with Jackie and their two young children, Curtis and Chloe. And Jackie also has a thriving boutique in the Wigan township. Although flattered, Bell's first impression was that he would remain with Wigan.

That attitude changed when he returned to New Zealand for the first time in four years in the winter of 1993 to be a surprise guest at a *This Is Your Life* tribute for Lowe in Auckland. He stayed on to watch New Zealand's two tests against Australia and in moving through the country was overwhelmed with the interest being shown in the Warriors and the new found respect rugby league had garnered within New Zealand, courtesy of exposure to the Winfield Cup. "It opened my eyes and it got me excited about league in New Zealand again," he says. "Basically, it persuaded me to accept John Monie's offer to come home and captain the Warriors in their first year in the Winfield Cup."

Bell and his family arrived back in Auckland in August, 1993, and he will play just the single season for the Warriors before retiring as a player and returning to Wigan where he is widely tipped to inherit the coaching post with the Riversiders. Bell is eagerly anticipating the Warriors' debut in the rugged Australian professional competition. His intensity has been heightened by a personally frustrating last playing season with Wigan. He missed a large slice of the 1993-94 season with a serious groin injury which required an operation and at one stage threatened his future with the Warriors. Fortunately, he returned at the business end of the season and his influential captaincy steadied a suprisingly shaky Wigan outfit enough for the Cherry Whites to win their fifth successive first division league championship (although this time on points difference) and their seventh consecutive Challenge Cup success, beating Leeds in the final.

Bell's steadying influence has convinced the Warriors of their de-

Dean Bell displays the sort of aggression for Wigan that earned him the 1991-92 Man of Steel Award in England.

cision to make him their skipper for the maiden year in the Australian competition. John Monie, although an Australian, neatly sums up the contribution Bell has made to New Zealand rugby league. "When we started tossing around names as potential captains of the Warriors, his name was the first to come up," says Monie.

ALEX WYLLIE
'Grizz'

Mark Stevens should have known better. The Wellington loose forward had had a flick at Alex Wyllie early in the match. Now it was time for the get square. Revenge came at a lineout. Stevens was dealt to. The Zambucks ran on to the field and an irate Wellington halfback, Dave Henderson, standing over the prone figure of Stevens, angrily demanded: "Who was the dirty bastard who did this?" Wyllie lifted his head from the Canterbury huddle and said: "It was me." Henderson gulped before replying: "Nice punch, Grizz."

LONG before he was bestowed the nickname of "Grizz", Alex Wyllie was known by a different tag among his schoolboy rugby mates. They referred to him as "The Tank".

At only 16, Wyllie's feats for the St Andrew's First XV and the Canterbury Under-20 rep team in Christchurch were already the stuff of legends. If there was a tougher or meaner forward playing the game at schoolboy level, nobody had his address. For some observers, he was perhaps too headstrong, too rugged. But he had potential. Few were surprised when he ultimately went on to become an All Black, playing 11 tests for his country. However, it's doubtful anyone ever imagined Wyllie would also progress to become one of the most successful provincial and All Black coaches in our history. But then, Alex Wyllie has made a habit of proving people wrong.

Wyllie's rugby career is squarely split into two categories – his achievements as a player and his successes as a coach. That he would do something in rugby was never doubted. The game was the life-blood of the Wyllie family of six children. Born in 1944 and fifth in line, young Alex relished his father Joe's role as a coach for the Glenmark club. Growing up in the Omihi Valley in north Canterbury, Wyllie soon learnt that the small rugby club was the focal point of the tight-knit community and that to make a mark, the locals looked to sport.

It was always destined that Wyllie would be a forward. He'd relished physical confrontation and the challenge of psychologically dominating an opponent. As a loose forward or No 8, he was virtually unstoppable at schoolboy level. When he was selected in the Canterbury team for the first time as a 19-year-old in 1963, the honour had been tipped for some time.

It didn't take long for Wyllie to make his mark either. In just his third game for the Red and Blacks, Wyllie travelled to Eden Park for a clash with Auckland. He had to mark a cagey Auckland loose forward named Lew Fell who was famous in Queen City rugby circles for his full-blooded commitment and determination to make the lives of inside backs merry hell. Fell liked to try and psyche out his rival loosies early in the game. So, when the first opportunity arose, he ran directly at Wyllie. The young Cantabrian flattened him with a copybook tackle. A chagrined Fell leapt to his feet and began flailing his fists in Wyllie's direction. His surname was apt because that was exactly what happened again as Wyllie responded. As was the custom in those days, the rugby bush jungle quickly circulated the story around the country. Here was a young fellow not to be trifled with.

Bob Duff was the Canterbury coach at the time and admits Wyllie was a rugged customer. "His appearance in those days was a wee bit frightening to some backs," Duff told Wyllie's biographer, Phil Gifford, for the excellent book *Grizz: The Legend*. "He was physically hard, and very aggressive, and he had the ability to really give it a go, to break tackles." His captain that day was John Graham, the former All Black No 8 who is now assistant coach of Auckland. Graham was another who had seen Wyllie emerge swiftly. "I was coaching a Boy's High Second XV that played St Andrew's," Graham told Gifford of Wyllie's schoolboy days. "And in those days Alex was really the terror of secondary school rugby. He dominated the game. He was so hard physically, and a lot of the kids genuinely feared him. When he began for Canterbury, he was rawboned, largely untutored in the finer points of the game, but he had all the skills needed to be a top loose forward. He was quick and strong, with

Wyllie relished the physical confrontation of loose forward rugby, often saving his most dynamic performances for when he wore the much-loved red and black for Canterbury.

extremely good hands, and the natural sense of how play would develop that lifts naturals like Michael Jones and Graham Mourie from being good players to being outstanding."

It was during these formative years in Wyllie's career that the "Grizz" tag was first born. The nickname came from his prickly on-field demeanour. It quickly stuck. By 1965, Wyllie was a regular in a fearsome Canterbury forward pack. He had his first taste of international football that same year, playing in the Red and Blacks' heroic 6-5 loss to the touring Springboks. By the time he stood down, Wyllie had played a staggering 214 matches for his beloved Canterbury and captained them for the last eight years of his career.

Along the way there were several lows but infinitely more highs as Wyllie helped, first as a player and later as a coach, to make Canterbury a byword for rugby might. His first real high was to come in 1969 when Canterbury lifted the Ranfurly Shield from Hawke's Bay. The Red and Blacks won 18-11, and Wyllie missed the plane back to Christchurch the next day after he and, among others, Alister Hopkinson, Ian Kirkpatrick and Kerry Tanner had slipped away for a few extra celebratory beers during a stopover in Wellington.

The Ranfurly Shield was to play a major role in Wyllie's career as both a player and coach. Here he holds aloft the log o' wood after Canterbury's successful challenge at Eden Park in 1972.

By this time, Wyllie was making a firm impression on the national scene. He had earned All Black trials in 1967, 1968 and 1969 but the New Zealand team of the late sixties was a formidable beast and difficult for any youngster to break into, especially with backrowers such as Lochore, Kirkpatrick and Tremain, not to mention Graham Williams and Tom Lister as well.

Wyllie probably didn't help himself with a moment of bravado that could be put down to youthful cockiness. Not long after he had broken into the Canterbury team, Wyllie had played well in an 11-3 win over Otago at Carisbrook. He had marked Don Clark who had just been named in the All Black team to face the Wallabies. Late in the night, Wyllie was asked how he rated Clark. The reply wasn't exactly flattering. A few minutes later Wyllie was making a pit-stop in the function room loos when he heard a harsh voice behind him, saying: "You want to learn to keep your bloody mouth shut about things, Snow." The voice belonged to All Black selector Fred Allen. Wyllie heeded the advice.

By 1970, he had finally broken through. Somebody in power had had a quiet word in his ear at the end of '69 season and told him he was in with a good chance of making the All Black tour to South Africa. Wyllie trained like never before over the summer. His New Zealand career got off to an inauspicious start, though. The All Blacks played two matches in Perth on their way to South Africa. Wyllie played flanker in the main game, wearing a pair of boots a size too small. The tourists thumped Western Australia but Wyllie was unhappy with his All Black debut.

The national selectors had targeted Wyllie for South Africa, believing his style was ideally suited to the hard grounds in the republic. Unlike Mark Shaw, who was to follow in Wyllie's footsteps not long after he retired, the Canterbury loosie always preferred a dry track. He immediately made an impression, excelling in the early tour matches.

Any rugby historian, with the considerable benefit of hindsight of course, can accurately put his finger on why the 1970 tour came unstuck. There was Colin Meads' broken arm, Brian Lochore's broken thumb, the antiquated training methods of coach Ivan Vodanovich and the high number of provincial matches the All Blacks had to play before the first test. But Wyllie believes the last-mentioned factor was the one most responsible for the loss of the series. He points out that Johan Claassen was the South African coach. "Claassen helped coached some of the teams we faced early on so he encouraged them to try different tactics against us to see what worked and what didn't," explained Wyllie. "They even filmed every game so they could study everything we did. Our mistake was in showing our hand before the first test. We should have kept something in reserve but we didn't. Worse than that, we didn't change our tactics. They knew exactly what we were going to do at any given time."

Couple that, says Wyllie, with the big forwards the Springboks played in the first test and their hard-tackling midfield backs and New Zealand had virtually handed the game to the South Africans on a plate. As Wyllie watched from the grandstand, the All Blacks were soundly beaten 17-6 by a largely unimaginative Springbok outfit.

The New Zealand press was not impressed with the meek All Black effort and in a celebrated column for the *Truth* newspaper, broadcaster Winston McCarthy called for several "meanies" to be included in the forward pack for the second test. Among those McCarthy recommended were Alan Sutherland and Wyllie. Vodanovich, Lochore and Meads, the trio who effectively picked the side, agreed and Wyllie was named for his All Black test debut.

There had been much discussion in the lead-up to the second international about the South Africans' spoiling offside tactics during the first test which had escaped the detection of the referee. It was decided that if the man in the middle wasn't going to pull the Boks into line, the All Blacks would have to do it themselves. Not surprisingly, the clash proved to be a rugged encounter with the All Blacks squeezing out a 9-8 victory. Wyllie recalls the match as a spiteful encounter. "There were quite a few cheap shots," he recalled. "I wouldn't rate it as one of the great advertisements for rugby."

Wyllie's debut was impressive, though. Ian Kirkpatrick remembers him making South African first-five Piet Visagie's life a nightmare. "Grizz was in bloody good form off the back of the lineout," Kirkpatrick told Phil Gifford. "He certainly put a bit of fear into Visagie."

During the second test, All Black fullback Fergie McCormick had been involved in a nasty incident with Springbok winger Sid Nomis (see the chapter on McCormick for a full explanation). McCormick was largely the victim of circumstances and was unfairly maligned for his part in the role. But the South African players, press and public were determined to get even for the perceived crime. McCormick was battered from pillar to post in the third test. McCormick recalls that Wyllie desperately tried to help him during the game. "Alex came back and helped me on numerous occasions," Fergie says in *Grizz: The Legend*. "I admire him for that, that's the sort of man he is. I told him to leave me, but he wouldn't, and I believe that's why he lost his position for the fourth test. I'm not the only one who thinks that."

Indeed, most observers felt Wyllie played well in the third test, won 14-3 by the home team. Some suspect Wyllie was dropped for the fourth international because there were fears the All Blacks might lose their cool if they lost again. The South Africans didn't see it that way. Instead they were delighted. The local press struggled to contain its glee over Wyllie's omission. South Africa won 20-17.

Despite the 3-1 series loss, Wyllie enjoyed the tour and immediately felt an affinity with South Africa. He has always encouraged rugby ties with the republic and was delighted when the Springboks were welcomed back into the international fold in 1992. His only regret was that it came after he had stood down as All Black coach. One senses Wyllie would have relished the opportunity to lead New

Zealand to South Africa. Yet he was opposed to the 1986 Cavaliers tour. He believes the falsehoods and deceptions employed in putting the rebel tour together did neither the New Zealand players nor their South African hosts any credit. He is also convinced the Cavaliers tour indirectly kept the republic in isolation for much longer than necessary through the rugby world's anger at the recruitment of rebel visits.

Once South Africa was officially readmitted to world rugby, however, Wyllie was delighted to receive an offer to coach there. Eastern Province, recognising the negative effects years of isolation had imprinted on its players, approached Wyllie during 1992 in the hope he could help restore them to their former glory. The New Zealander has just completed his third successful season with Eastern Province.

Following the 1970 trek to South Africa, Wyllie was determined to forge a lengthy All Black career. But he missed out on the first test of the '71 season. Alan Sutherland, Ian Kirkpatrick and Allan McNaughton formed the All Black back row for the 9-3 first test loss against the British Lions. But then Sutherland broke his leg in a charity game and Wyllie found himself called up to play No 8 for the remaining three tests. Although he played well in New Zealand's 22-12 second test triumph, the test series was to ultimately mirror the disappointments of the previous year's clash with the Springboks. The Lions won the third test 13-3 and held the desperate All Blacks to 14-all in the fourth international. Two years in the All Blacks and Wyllie was yet to win a series.

Nor did he get a chance in the home series against a poor Australian side in 1972. Sutherland had made a successful return and claimed the No 8 jersey for the three-test clean sweep while Wyllie watched from the reserves bench. But his chance to break into the test team came when he was selected for the end of season tour to the United Kingdom and France.

History has judged the '72-'73 tour as one of the most troubled in the proud All Black record. The Keith Murdoch affair overshadowed the entire tour. Compared to the sublime play of the 1967 All Blacks, this New Zealand team wasn't in the same class. It dropped games it shouldn't have and generally struggled through the tour, although it must be said they did play well in the internationals. A large New Zealand press contingent on tour was also critical of the team's behaviour.

Wyllie, Alan Sutherland and Tane Norton in the 'mafia' black hats that drew so much criticism during the 1972-73 tour.

Experienced Auckland journalist Terry McLean was unimpressed by a section of the team, namely Wyllie, Sutherland, Tane Norton and Sid Going, who had taken to wearing black hats. Dubbed the back seat Black Hat gang, the players were seen as an All Black mafia. The suggestion was that discipline within the team was poor, to say the least, and that the older players were lording it over the young. Wyllie dismisses this as a gross over-reaction. He says the hats were bought in jest in Vancouver on the way to the UK and were worn as a joke at court sessions and on the bus. The younger players often tried to steal them while the owners were determined to hang on to them come hell or high water. Wyllie says it was a means of generating team spirit more than dismantling it.

New Zealand beat Wales 19-16, Scotland 14-9 and England 9-0 before drawing 10-all with Ireland, thus only just missing the Grand Slam. The final international of the tour was lost to France 13-6. Wyllie came on as a replacement for flanker Alister Scown in the Welsh test, played at No 8 against Scotland, moved back to the side of the scrum against England and held his position there for the draw against Ireland and the defeat to France.

The following season the Kirk government cancelled the planned tour by South Africa and the All Blacks were forced into an ad hoc season where they made a disastrous internal tour before facing England in a one-off international. They lost to the Junior All Blacks and an Invitation XV featuring Colin Meads and Sid Going. Meads and Going were later to express their horror that they had beaten the All Blacks. England arrived and promptly lost to Taranaki, Wellington and Canterbury. Then they defeated the All Blacks.

The match was to be Wyllie's last in the black jersey. The coach of the time, J.J. Stewart, dropped him for the more fleet-footed Ken Stewart. This led to a major irony in Wyllie's career. As a player – with five test wins, two draws and four losses – he did not feature in one of the great All Black teams. Yet, 15 years later, he was presiding over the most successful All Black side in our history, this time as coach.

It was no surprise to those close to Wyllie that he ended up in coaching. Such is his love for rugby that watching from the sidelines as a dispassionate observer was never a consideration. Wyllie stopped playing representative rugby in 1979 and was coaching Canterbury Country by 1981. His step into the coaching ring coincided with a poor season from the Canterbury representative squad by the Red and Blacks' lofty standards. Several union officials had noted the steel Wyllie had put into the Country side's backbone. It was suggested to him by one of the Canterbury union's major sponsors that he put forward his name for the major job in 1982. Wyllie was initially reluctant and even when he did put forward his nomination he was still wondering if he'd done the right thing. It took three ballots for the position to be decided but it went to Wyllie ahead of five other contenders, including his old mate Fergie McCormick.

Wyllie admits to being mortified over the early season fitness standards among the Canterbury team when he first assembled them for the '82 season. He couldn't believe the lack of fitness and the lackadaisical attitude of many players. "I was fitter myself than half the players," he says in his book. "We had some long and hard training runs to try to improve the fitness. We didn't do any moves for a start, because we couldn't pass the ball to the wings without dropping it anyway. So I said: 'Forget the moves until we can pass it out without dropping it'. Then we gradually brought in some simple moves, like bringing the fullback in and missing him with the pass. By the time we'd finished, we had some moves you knew could only be used in a game you were completely on top in."

It didn't take long for Wyllie to defy his image as a limited tactician. Those who played with Wyllie frequently noted that he was far more skilled than he was generally given credit for. While his reputation was made as a hard-charging, aggressive backrower, there was far more subtlety in his game. Certainly, the Canterbury players from '82 onwards were impressed by the depth of knowledge Wyllie possessed. Backs were not only surprised when Wyllie would pull them up and tell them why an elaborate move was breaking down but often flabbergasted when the former forward would show them the skills needed to successfully complete the manoeuvre.

His first captain Don Hayes remarks on Wyllie's thoroughness. Hayes said the coach honed basic forward skills, showing players how to jump more effectively in the lineout and improving moves off the back of the scrum. "He was able to get very technical," noted Hayes. Backline general Wayne Smith was another to blow the myth of Wyllie being one-dimensional in his coaching approach. "He really was the complete rugby thinker," said Smith. "He could tell the backs what to do. He could tell the forwards what to do. He was very intelligent." Robbie Deans is equally emphatic. "If you believed the media you would think he was just a rough oaf," Deans says in Wyllie's book. "His tactical appreciation of the game was so often underestimated. He's constantly thinking about the game, and areas that can be exploited."

In his first year of coaching Canterbury, Wyllie lifted the Ranfurly Shield. Despite being down 9-4 at halftime, Canterbury stormed back in the second spell to beat holders Wellington 16-12. But the Red and Blacks almost lost it in their very first defence, Robbie Deans nailing a pressure goal in the dying minutes to scramble a draw against Counties. Canterbury were then to go on and put together a sequence of 25 successful defences.

One of those defences was against Auckland in 1983. Under impressive new coach John Hart, Auckland seemed to be building towards a massive challenge for the log of wood. Instead they were repelled 31-9 in one of the great Canterbury performances of all time. There was an intriguing postscript to the result. As Canterbury were standing in the tunnel, ready to run out, Wyllie suddenly grabbed Wayne Smith's jersey and whispered into his ear: 'Run it from everywhere'. Smith was surprised but heeded the instructions, changing the game plan. "He (Wyllie) just had a feeling," Smith told Wyllie's biographer, Phil Gifford. "Maybe he'd seen something in the Aucklanders' eyes, maybe he knew we were at our peak, and we could tear them apart." His intuition was proved deadly accurate.

The '83 season was a spectacular success for Canterbury: 36 matches, 30 victories. The Red and Blacks collected the early season South Pacific Championship, held on to the Ranfurly Shield and won the national championship. The Shield was to remain in Christchurch for four years under Wyllie's tutelage before Auckland removed it in that epic 1985 encounter now steeped in New Zealand rugby folk-lore as "The Game of the Century". The Red and Blacks were behind 24-0 at halftime. During the break, Wyllie strode on to Lancaster Park, grabbed the ball and fixed his players in the eye. "This is the ball," he thundered. "If they can score 24 points with it, so can you." Then he walked off. Canterbury stormed back in the second spell. With two minutes to go, the scoreline read 28-23 with Auckland panicking. Hart's team held on for the narrowest of victories.

Wyllie was not too distraught. "I knew eventually we'd have to lose it [the Shield]. I just wanted us to go out blazing when we did. That second half ensured we did."

Wyllie had one more year with Canterbury after they lost the Shield. His record was sensational. Of 92 games at the helm of the Red and Blacks, he could claim 76 victories, four draws and just 12 losses.

By this time, Wyllie was hankering for a fresh challenge though. He had stood for the role of All Black convenor in 1985, more to signal his desire to the New Zealand Rugby Football Union council that he was interested in higher honours than anything else. The tur-moil of the 1986 season with the Cavaliers tour opened the door the following year. Wyllie succeeded another Cantabrian in Tiny Hill on the national panel. Joining him was his old adversary John Hart with the gentlemanly Brian Lochore appointed the convenor. In their first year, the trio plotted a successful highjacking of the inaugural World Cup. All was sweetness and light within New Zealand rugby. Or so it seemed.

In reality, the first schism was to develop on the end-of-season tour to Japan. Lochore had made it clear he wasn't going beyond 1987. Now the jockeying was on to establish his successor. Earlier in the year it had been agreed that Wyllie would handle the New Zea-land Colts while Hart took what was supposed to be a development

**With the help of his assistant coach, Doug Bruce, Wyllie turned Can-
terbury into the pre-eminent provincial team in the country during
the early eighties.**

team away to Japan with Wyllie as his assistant. What happened after
that is a matter of conjecture and where you happen to live.

The team that went to Japan turned out to have more established
All Blacks than first expected, a concession to the Japanese obsession
with New Zealand rugby. And with only 26 players on the tour, there
was little for Wyllie to do. Hart ran the whole show. Come the elec-
tions for the role of convenor for the 1988 season and opinion was
divided over which man would get the job, although Hart seemed
favoured. It's rugby history now that Wyllie won the convenor's job
and Hart, through Auckland councillor Malcolm Dick, advised coun-

cil he would not be available to stand purely as a selector because of work commitments.

Wyllie supporters saw Hart's move as a colossal dummy spit. Wyllie detractors saw the decision to appoint the Cantabrian as folly and an insult to the best coach in the country. Earle Kirton and Lane Penn were to be elected as fellow selectors and Wyllie's first year as All Black coach proved a spectacular success.

With Buck Shelford as his captain, Wales was thumped by record scores in two tests, 52-3 and 54-9. Then followed a tour of Australia. The Wallabies were blitzed 32-7 in the first test. Bob Dwyer's desperate men regrouped enough to draw the second international 19-all at Ballymore. It was to be the one blemish (if it can be described that way) on New Zealand's staggering record from 1987 to 1990. The Brisbane test proved to be just a hiccup for the all-conquering black machine. The third international was convincingly won 30-9.

The following year Hart was to return to the panel as a selector, at Kirton's expense. On the surface, things seemed to be humming along with little drama. Despite a few anxious moments in the first test at Lancaster Park, the French were repelled in two internationals, Argentina was sent packing and Australia stylishly defeated in a one-off Bledisloe Cup clash at Eden Park. At the end of the season, the All Blacks headed to the United Kingdom where they completed an unbeaten tour of Wales and Ireland before beating the Barbarians on Twickenham. Wyllie's record as All Black coach stood at 12 Tests, 11 wins, 1 draw.

It was during the 1990 season that the first cracks began to appear in the All Blacks. Scotland shocked New Zealand fans by coming uncomfortably close to humbling the All Blacks in the second test. Then Australia, after dropping the first two tests, ended New Zealand's four-season unbeaten record by winning the third international 21-9 in appalling conditions at Athletic Park.

It was during this season that the undermining of Wyllie's coaching ability began. The culprits, with the exception of vocal Aucklander Andy Haden, were to prove shadowy customers. Wyllie had never been overly articulate when a TV camera, radio microphone or reporter's tape recorder was poked in his face. Ridiculous as it was, some of his detractors leapt on his discomfort in an attempt to perpetuate the myth that Wyllie could not think on his feet. The inference was he wasn't capable of the lateral thinking an All Black coach needed. He was too slow to recognise problems, too inflexible to change tactics. Anybody who had played under Wyllie at Canterbury knew the folly of such claims.

There were also strong suggestions that Hart was "white-anting" Wyllie by deliberately creating doubts about the Cantabrian in the minds of influential players and council members. While some, ludicriously, tried to suggest there was not a problem between the pair, their respective biographies showed just how much they were poles apart. Phil Gifford makes it very clear in *Grizz: The Legend* that he believes Hart was secretly undermining Wyllie. In Hart's book, written by Paul Thomas, the charges are reversed. Hart maintains he was only trying to help Wyllie and ended up being shafted for it.

I can only speak from my perspective of the situation. I have covered every test played by the All Blacks in New Zealand since 1989 as well as the 1991 World Cup campaign. While Wyllie did have difficulty conveying his concepts to the media, I saw absolutely no evidence of charges he was out of his depth. With, admittedly, the considerable benefit of hindsight, the NZRFU were foolish to foist Hart on Wyllie for the defence of the World Cup. If a coach is appointed for a set term, he should be left alone to do it his way. The ultimate litmus test is his results. He lives or dies on the win-loss tally.

When Wyllie was left alone, he appeared to respond positively to any challenge. The 1990 French tour is a classic example. Two losses to invitational regional XVs had the Wyllie critics frothing back in New Zealand. Yet the All Blacks were masterful in the two internationals, sending the French – and Wyllie's detractors – packing. But the Cantabrians' critics were far more relentless than the French. They seized on sub-standard performances from the All Blacks on the short tour of Argentina in 1991, conveniently forgetting just what a difficult country it is to tour, and against Australia the same season to further knobble Wyllie.

What the anti-Grizz faction failed to take into account was the players' role in all of this. The All Black machine had sprung a leak, not so much because the coach was not up to it but more because a once great side was on a downhill slide without enough new players coming through to plug the gaps. Despite that, the All Blacks still very nearly won the World Cup. Had the speed of John Gallagher been available to capitalise on the many half-breaks John Kirwan made in the second half of the fateful Dublin semi-final against Australia, and had Michael Jones been able to play (it was a Sunday match), things could have been so different. As it was, it took Australia's finest performance since their 19-all draw with the 1988 All Blacks to ultimately deny Wyllie's men.

You wouldn't know it from the witch-hunt that followed in the aftermath of the failed Cup campaign, though. It was during this time that I personally feel Wyllie was very shabbily treated. Not long after the World Cup, an appalling rumour began circulating rugby circles that during the tournament Wyllie had been so hung over from a heavy drinking session that he was unable to take a training session the next day. As I was covering the tour for several New Zealand daily newspapers, I was required to be at every training session. Wyllie didn't miss one. True, Wyllie enjoyed a drink. But never did I see any evidence of it interfering with his coaching, and nor did I ever see him act in a manner that reflected poorly on his role in the game.

The slights on his character Wyllie often had to endure were grossly unfair to him, although not once did he complain publicly. The final straw came following the World Cup. In the wash-up following the tournament, Wyllie had been justifiably critical of the manner in which Hart was foisted on him for the World Cup campaign. NZRFU chairman Eddie Tonks, in a rare lapse of judgement, issued a memo to his fellow councillors which virtually instructed them not to vote for Wyllie during the coming election of selectors. The memo was leaked to the New Zealand Press Association by a councillor sympathetic to Wyllie. The All Black coach could see the writing on the wall and withdrew his nomination.

What must have been especially galling for Wyllie is the fact that Hart often made subtle criticisms of the coach through the media without being pulled into line by the NZRFU. Yet the moment Wyllie did the same, the wrath of officialdom descended upon him. But Wyllie is a proud man. Rather than wait for councillors to kneecap him, he went on his own terms.

So Wyllie stood down as All Black coach with a record from 29 tests of 25 victories, one draw and just three losses. Statistically, it makes him the most successful All Black coach in our history. Wyllie diplomatically points out he had a special team for much of his era. True enough. By the same token, even the greatest teams don't coach themselves.

Once he voluntarily vacated the All Black job, Wyllie was in limbo

Happier days…Wyllie and John Hart get their hands on the most prized silverware of all, the World Cup. But after 1987, the pair's relationship deteriorated.

for just a few short months. Then, while watching a match at Lancaster Park during cricket's World Cup, he was quietly approached by a South African. Would he be interested in coaching the Eastern Province union in the republic, he was asked. A group of influential businessmen in Port Elizabeth were concerned about the state of rugby within the Eastern Province and believed Wyllie was the answer to their problems. The offer was timely, the challenge stimulating. And if he needed an omen, Eastern Province's colours were red and black! Wyllie accepted.

Since then, he has done remarkably well, ridding Eastern Province of the easybeat status it had acquired and within a year helping the union qualify for the Super 10 series at the expense of Northern Transvaal. One needs to understand just how poorly rated Eastern Province is within South African rugby circles to appreciate Wyllie's achievements with the side. Eastern Province qualifying for the Super 10 series is not unlike King Country doing the same within New Zealand. We're talking about a province that has never won the Currie Cup, symbol of supremacy within South African rugby, or even remotely threatened to. A leper could count on one hand how many Springboks the province has. Time and again, Eastern Province finished the season with the wooden spoon. In sporting terms, the area was more famous for being home to the South African cricket captain Kepler Wessels.

Enter Wyllie. His reputation may have preceded him among the forward-thinking businessmen and rugby officials but the message hadn't yet got through to the players who, not surprisingly, had become accustomed to heavy losses. Wyllie knew he had some tough work ahead of him when he called his first training session for 5pm and the players didn't turn up until 5.45. That was the players' first mistake. Needless to say, players now arrive well before 5pm to ensure they don't invoke the wrath of the coach. But Wyllie still found his first two seasons with Eastern Province mind-numbingly frustrating.

Despite South Africa's reputation as the hardest and most uncompromising of rugby nations, Wyllie found too many players are not prepared to pay the price for success. He discovered many lazy trainers and too many players with poor attitudes. Nor does he believe the current South African rugby player is as hard-nosed and uncompromising as the men he faced in 1970. "If they get a bump or a bruise they'll shoot off to the doctor, tell him what's wrong and he'll say rest it, miss training and hopefully you'll be right by the weekend. In New Zealand, a player will take the knock, train and then see how it is. If it's no good, it's only then he'll go to a doctor to seek treatment."

Not surprisingly, Wyllie's no-nonsense approach often rubbed players the wrong way. Some left the province. Wyllie was unapologetic. "If they don't accept my methods, they needn't come back," he barks. Early in the 1994 season, a delightful story emerged that the Eastern Province players had performed so badly against Queensland in their debut Super 10 match because they were 'frightened' of Wyllie. The coach had been at a loss to get any explanation for the poor performance, so he sent the union president in to see if he could get any answers. Only then did the players own up that they had not been prepared to take any chances during the game because they were worried about Wyllie's reaction! The coach himself was stunned. Wyllie could be hard on players. But you only had to look at the style his Canterbury and All Black teams produced to know he was the last coach who would stymie a bold approach.

In his fine book *The Game The Goal*, Grant Fox, while recording his distress that John Hart was never given a chance to coach the All Blacks, pays homage to Wyllie. "I have strong views on the elimination of Hart from top level coaching," Fox said, "but I never regretted my All Black career with Wyllie. Here he was, we supposed, this rough, tough bugger with red-and-black eyeballs, straining at the leash to put us through his gut-busting training runs. Preconceptions are notoriously frail. Grizz was no charmer, just a gruff straight-shooter, basically shy till you were accepted, a man who needed the company of men for whom he had respect and who respected him. And, if I may extend the psycho-analysis into something more tangible: he was, in his singular way, a hell of a rugby coach."

But perhaps the final word should go the man whom many regard as the finest ever All Black coach, Fred "The Needle" Allen. During Wyllie's tenure as Canterbury coach, Allen felt compelled to send him a letter. "I told him I was enthralled with the way his team was going," Allen told Phil Gifford. "If you'd ever seen a side playing brilliant 15-man rugby it was that Canterbury side. His record really speaks for itself with Canterbury and the All Blacks. He gets results. That's what I say when people criticise him, I tell them to look at the bloody record. Look at the bloody record."

KURT SORENSEN
'Sumo'

The Australians had gone into the second test in 1983 supremely confident they would ride home on the power of a Queensland-dominated pack. That year's State of Origin series had proven their rugged forwards could handle anything. So the Aussies said, anyway. If Kurt Sorensen needed to be fired up anymore than usual, he already had the ammunition. A week earlier he'd made his test comeback after a five-year international exile and had been bagged for 'inactivity'. He'd prove them wrong this night. He was everywhere. But it was his bruising defence that most upset the Aussies, during and after the match. The Kiwis won 19-12 and the whinging from the Australians went on for weeks after. Sorensen had been unnecessarily rugged in his approach, the Aussies bleated. "Tough," said Sorensen. "It's not a game where you wear dresses, you know."

IN Australia in recent years, much has been made of the great career forged by Terry Lamb. Lamb has just completed his 14th season in Australia's professional competition. The Canterbury-Bankstown utility back is certainly one of the game's great survivors. But even his record pales alongside Kurt Sorensen's. The rugged former Aucklander made his debut for the Kiwis against Australia in 1975 when he was only 18. A staggering 17 years later he was not only still playing but scored a try for his Widnes team in English league's showpiece game, the Challenge Cup final, at Wembley in 1993.

Even now, Sorensen has only just stopped terrorising opponents. As player-coach of the Whitehaven club in the English second division, the man nicknamed "Sumo" by his team-mates lined up in the 1993-94 season for his 20th successive year of first class rugby league. Close friends and admirers are not surprised by Sorensen's staying power. Along with his older brother Dane, Kurt had always been fiercely determined, prodigiously talented and, most of all, never one to back away from a confrontation.

The Sorensens, born of parents of Scandinavian and Tongan descent, first made an impression as enormously talented teenagers on the Auckland club scene. The Sorensen name already carried considerable weight in New Zealand league circles. The brothers' uncle, Bill, had played for the Kiwis as a 19-year-old utility back on the 1951 tour of Great Britain and France. Bill Sorensen was later to become Auckland coach and a Kiwi selector. Dave Sorensen, another uncle, also toured the United Kingdom and France with the great 1971 Kiwi side. He didn't make the test team but did play an international against Australia the following year.

But while their two uncles naturally had a big impact on the Sorensen brothers as youngsters, the major influence came from their mentor, Tom Newton. A Maori who lived for league, Newton was the pair's coach from the first time they pulled on football jerseys as four-year-olds. "He took us through from then to when we played senior grade as teenagers," said Kurt. "I can't understate just how much influence he had on us. Tom really knew his football. He was a Maori coach, Maori selector and a New Zealand selector for a while. He taught us the basics well right from that early age and I believe that placed us in great stead for later on."

The young Sorensen brothers were quick learners as teenagers. Dane was a rugged performer, often intimidating rivals many years his senior. Kurt had the same ability but was blessed with more explosive power than his brother. He often placed himself strategically wide of the ruck where his bull-like charges would regularly shatter defences. Add in his ball skills and searing pace and Kurt Sorensen was one hell of a rugby league player.

Few were surprised when he made the Kiwis as a teenager. He and Dane had already represented the Junior Kiwis and Kurt first played premier football in 1973 as a centre for the Mt Wellington club when aged just 15. At 19 he was already stalking off with the major individual awards in the Auckland senior competition. Playing for the Mt Wellington club, he won the Auckland player-of-the-year award, scoring 18 tries in 22 games. But what was noticeable was his strong on-field relationship with Dane. The elder Sorensen sibling had spent the early part of the 1976 season in the United States. While Dane was away, Kurt scored four tries in 11 games. Upon Dane's return, he crossed 14 times in 11 games.

In those early days, Dane was an impressive ball player as well as a more than handy goalkicker (he landed six goals from seven attempts in atrocious conditions in his test debut against France). It was to be a part of his game that was gradually undermined by the yardage-obsessed Australian style of rugby league. Many consider it was a shame; that Dane was a far better footballer before being statically programmed by the Australians. "I felt the Sydney game did change Dane and detract from some of his other strengths," agrees Kurt. "I didn't change my game, but I know Dane felt pressured to." Certainly though, in the brothers' Auckland club days, theirs was a tandem act hard to beat. Dane would put Kurt through the gaps and the younger brother's pace and bulk would do the rest. Both brothers were selected in the squad for the World Cup match against Australia at Carlaw Park in 1975. Dane had already made his debut, starting against France while Kurt sat on the bench. He was retained for the game against Australia and was delighted when Kurt got on to the field late in the match as a replacement. It was to be the beginning of a lengthy and chequered career in New Zealand colours. Kurt was aged 18 years 323 days at the time. Nineteen years later he was to be named man of the match in Widnes' clash with the touring Australians.

Immediately after the Australian game in '75, the Sorensen brothers toured the United Kingdom with the New Zealand team for further World Cup matches. Kurt played his first full international against Wales at Swansea. It was to be an infamous encounter. Kurt was in the second row while Dane propped alongside Canterbury's John Greengrass. Among the other Kiwis was a goalkicking wing, Tony Gordon, who was later to become Kurt's Kiwi coach. The match featured a shocking incident where rugged the Welsh prop Jim Mills callously stomped on Greengrass's head after the New Zealander had scored a try under the posts. Mills was to be banned from ever playing in New Zealand again following the ugly incident. The Welsh prop was sent off 21 times in his career.

The clash, won 25-24 by Wales, certainly opened Sorensen's eyes

Kurt Sorensen was often seen at his blockbusting best when he scouted out wide among the centres.

As a prodigious teenager, Sorensen quickly fashioned a reputation as a prolific tryscorer.

to the more brutal side of international league. In a supreme irony, Sorensen and Mills later became firm friends and business partners. Mills became chairman of the powerful Widnes club when Sorensen was captain there and the pair went into a partnership running a nightclub. "Yeah, it's rather ironic how that turned out," Sorensen says. "I've seen video of the Greengrass incident and it's just shocking. Jim was a bloke who just used to see red on the field. He just didn't seem to be able to control himself. But off the field, he was a completely different bloke. Almost charming." Sorensen was to go on and play another 26 tests for New Zealand. He could easily have set a record for the most capped player in Kiwi league history but for antiquated international rules that rendered him ineligible for 18 tests between 1978 and 1982. After his explosive debut season in the black jersey, Sorensen had drawn major interest from English and Australian talent scouts. He spent a brief off-season with Wigan where legendary British loose forward Vince "Wild Bull" Karalius took special interest in the rising 20-year-old. "He had a profound effect on me," Sorensen said of the then Wigan coach. "His coaching techniques were ahead of their time. He played me out wide a lot but he also had me running off the second man. It didn't matter to him as long as I had a good workrate."

Sorensen made an immediate impact, winning five man of the match awards in just 16 appearances for the English club. It was no surprise when Wigan offered him a three-year contract. He was unable to take it up because of New Zealand's prohibitive transfer laws, however. The following southern hemisphere winter Sorensen turned out for the Kiwis in the 1977 World Cup tournament, the same season Mark Graham made his debut for New Zealand. It was to be another five seasons before arguably the two finest forwards in recent Kiwi history would be together again in a New Zealand test pack.

Sydney club Cronulla-Sutherland had approached Kurt to join them. A professional career was a huge carrot for the powerful forward but under the New Zealand Rugby League's prohibitive transfer laws, joining the club was going to prove very difficult. There was one way around it, though. If a player was prepared to stand down out of all football for a full year, he was entitled to a free transfer. Smug NZRL officials reasoned that no young promising footballer would be prepared to give up a year of his career and therefore felt comfortable about their stand. But in Dane and Kurt Sorensen, they had taken on two very determined players.

Dane was the first to willingly spend a season on the sidelines while working in Australia to establish residency. Kurt did the same during the '78 season so he too could pursue a professional career with the Sharks. He admits it was tough. "In the whole year, the only football I played was touch – it was very, very frustrating," he said. "I was already over in Sydney and of course Dane was already playing for Cronulla. I used to go down and watch Dane go round every weekend. There were a few times I was tempted to jump the fence, I can tell you. But in the long run, it was the right decision. The only way I could get to Cronulla was standing down for a year. It was hard at the time but it was the best thing I've ever done in my career."

As if making up for lost time, Sorensen was devastating in his first season in the Sydney competition, unleashing his pent-up energy from a year on the sidelines. Whereas the Australians did change Dane's style of game, turning him into a yardage prop and failing to exploit the ball skills he did possess, Cronulla didn't do the same with Kurt. In fact, Mark Graham, Kurt and, to a lesser degree, Hugh McGahan are arguably the only Kiwi forwards who have transferred to Sydney clubs and not had their natural game reprogrammed by the Australians. Not that Cronulla would have wanted to alter the way Kurt played for them in '79. He was unstoppable. Used wide of the ruck, defences simply couldn't contain him. It was no surprise when he took out the award for the individual "superstar" of the midweek Amco Cup competition, a knockout tournament similar to English soccer's FA Cup, that same year. Cronulla won the competition, the club's last major success, in fact. Current Australian coach Bob Fulton was so impressed with Sorensen that he lauded the rookie Kiwi as the best forward in the world. Writing a column in the high circulation Sydney *Daily Mirror*, the then Eastern Suburbs coach said that Sorensen would rate in a photo finish with Australian star Ray Price for the title. "He convinced me of this when he helped tear apart my club," Fulton wrote. "Sorensen plays so well that he would make New Zealand a chance in winning any test game."

Fulton's latter comment was laced with irony. The most ridiculous thing about Sorensen's impact in Sydney was that he wasn't able to play for the Kiwis. At that stage, the international laws had no teeth and once a New Zealand player signed fulltime for an English or Australian club, that club had complete control of him and wasn't

Dane Sorensen...Sydney clubs re-programmed him and took the
natural flair out of his game, says Kurt.

obliged to release him for test duty. And in typical Australian fashion, nor were they going to. Finally sanity prevailed and in 1983 the international regulations were updated and clubs were forced to make their New Zealand imports available for international football.

During Sorensen's exile, New Zealand had played 18 internationals. By this time, Graham Lowe had taken control of the New Zealand team from Ces Mountford. Lowe was a huge Sorensen fan. Indeed, the master coach selected him for 17 of the 19 tests in which he prepared the Kiwis. "I can't give Kurt enough wraps," says Lowe. "I saw him as a strike player. He epitomised the raw, explosive power and high skill level of New Zealand players. But he was one out of the box. I liked to use him and Mark Graham as the strike players in our forward pack. Therefore it was pretty important the other second rower was a bit of a workhorse so it could leave Kurt and Mark free to make an impact in attack. But having said that, neither of those blokes ever shirked their defensive requirements. Quite the opposite, in fact."

Sorensen's return to the black jersey came against Australia and he was delighted to mark his comeback with victory over the old enemy in the second test at Brisbane's Lang Park. One of New Zealand's most potent attacking ploys against the world champions came in a partnership forged by Sorensen and slick midfield back James Leuluai, regarded as one the finest finishers in the history of the New Zealand game. John Coffey from the *Christchurch Press*, the doyen of league writers in New Zealand, recalls this tremendous partnership in his book *Modern Rugby League Greats*.

"They (Sorensen and Leuluai) conspired to produce New Zealand's first try against Australia for five Test matches, at Carlaw Park in 1983," Coffey wrote. "But it was the second 'try' created by Sorensen and completed by Leuluai (who was ruled offside by English referee Robin Whitfield) which had a greater influence on the result. A little later massive Australian wing Eric Grothe ran away for the try which turned the test in his team's favour. Whitfield was the first of several internationally ranked referees to find fault with Sorensen's delivery to Leuluai. The transfers were made in the twinkling of an eye, usually at close quarters as Sorensen committed the defender and Leuluai scythed through the gap at full pace. They were simply too quick for some referees to keep up with them."

Sorensen was to gain his revenge against the Australians at Lang

Fast, rugged and uncompromising...Sorensen v France, 1985.

Park in the return international. He set up the match-clinching try by roving wide yet again and putting winger Joe Ropati across. As to be expected with the Australians when they are unexpectedly trailing on the scoreboard, the match had its spiteful moments. Sorensen had been particularly effective in defence with his ball-and-all tacklers preventing the key Australian playmakers from getting the leather away. Afterwards there were bitter complaints from the home side about Sorensen.

It wasn't to be the last time the Australians complained of Sorensen's tactics in a test match. He frequently tangled physically and verbally with the hard men of the Kangaroo pack, notably Steve "Blocker" Roach with whom he fought a running battle at both international level and in the Sydney competition. Others he had run-ins with included Greg Dowling and Les Boyd. "Les Boyd was a guy I seemed to tangle with a lot," he says. "When I first went to Sydney in '79, he'd just come back from England with the Australian team and he was the all-time hero. One of the first games I had for Cronulla was against Wests (Boyd's team then) and I absolutely pooped on him. At the time, I remember wondering why there was so much hype about the guy. He was all mouth, he was always talking but a lot of it was bluff. They called him a hard man but I really couldn't see it."

But it was Roach who really seemed to get Sorensen's dander up. The pair's feud over years in the Sydney premiership frequently appeared in the Australian headlines (most often with Sorensen painted as the culprit. Roach was very much a "media pet" during his playing days) and almost inevitably resurfaced when the pair faced each other with one wearing a green and gold jersey and the other black. Sorensen admits he and Roach rubbed each other the wrong way from the outset. Asked why, the Kiwi is typically blunt. "Well, I probably don't like big-mouthed people who are overrated," he replies. "I respect a really tough player but I always felt he got more press than he really deserved."

Graham Lowe, while freely admitting Sorensen was no angel, says the rugged forward's reputation across the Tasman as a hot-head developed because the Australians simply did not like it when a player stood up to them. "At that time, much of the Australian game was built around intimidation," he explained. "When I first took over the coaching job, my greatest difficulty was getting the players to accept they were the equal of the Australians. That wasn't a problem for blokes like Kurt and Mark Graham because they were already playing these guys week in and week out in Sydney. But some of the younger guys were daunted by the reputations of the Aussies. Then Australia would play on that even further by adopting a very rugged physical approach in the first 10 minutes. Given that Mark was our chief playmaker and we didn't want him taken out early in the piece, much of the responsibility of standing up to the Aussies fell to Kurt. In fact, I squarely put it on him to take that role in the '83 series. That was a big responsibility, especially with Kevin Tamati unavailable that year. The reason Kurt got such bad press in Australia during that series was that he stood up to the Aussies. He didn't take any of their rubbish and if they belted him, he gave it right back to them. That was his only crime. Any whinging about him in the Australian press was purely sour grapes."

Sorensen agrees with Lowe's theory. "In fact, at times I was probably a little bit disappointed that some of my fellow New Zealanders

Sorensen was a man who took a power of stopping. World Cup final, 1988.

didn't join in with me," he says. "Probably deep down I felt the main way we could beat Australia was to throw that physical stuff back at them and try and intimidate them. To do that you had to hit them hard early. Australia always seemed to start games so well and if they got a head start on you, they were so talented that most times you couldn't pull them back. That's why I always felt it was so important to start well against them every time. If you look back at the times New Zealand have beaten Australia, it's always been because we got away to a good start. To do that often meant upsetting and frustrating them and I guess I took that role upon myself. Looking back, I've always stood up for myself. It's been one of my strongest traits."

The following year the Kiwis were to clean sweep the touring Great Britain side 3-0 with Sorensen once again outstanding. And again, he had his share of run-ins with the more abrasive Pommie forwards. Ironically, he was soon to find himself playing in the Mother Country. At the end of the 1983 Australian season, he accepted an offer to swap clubs and join Eastern Suburbs. The Roosters were keen to exploit his pace and bulk by playing him in the centres. But Sorensen was dissatisfied with the positional change and when English club Widnes approached him to spend an off-season with them, he jumped at the chance. It was a successful partnership. Sorensen was to have another season with Cronulla in 1985, but his long term future was to be at Widnes.

He joined the English club fulltime after the Kiwis' '85 tour of Great Britain. But before that was to be one of the highlights of Sorensen's international career. He played in all three tests against Australia that year. But the high point was the 18-0 shut-out of the Australians in the third test at Carlaw Park. Sorensen's only regret from the match is that Dane was not involved. He had suffered a knee injury earlier in the season and was ruled out of the entire series. Later Graham Lowe was to publicly state that had Dane been available, he would have made the difference between a won and lost series.

Sorensen played all five tests on the '85 tour of England and France. It was an exciting and often brutally physical series. The Poms went after Mark Graham, determined to put New Zealand's key playmaker on the sidelines. Sorensen resented the tactics and fought a running battle with several Great Britain forwards throughout the series. In the third test, drawn following a controversial last-minute Great Britain penalty, thus squaring the series, Sorensen spent two stints in the sin bin after tangling with Andy Goodaway and Jeff Grayshorn. Like Steve Roach, Wigan's Goodaway seemed to light a fuse with Sorensen. The pair again swapped angry swipes at each other in the first test of the 1989 Kiwi tour of Great Britain, earning another stint each in the sin-bin.

After the tour Sorensen joined Widnes. He was to spend eight seasons at the club, establishing himself as one of the greatest players in the proud history of Widnes. He helped them to two first division league championships, in 1987-88 and again the following season. Another high was a 30-18 thumping of the Canberra Raiders at Old Trafford in the inaugural World Club Championship clash in 1989 between the reigning Winfield Cup premiers and the British champions.

During his lengthy stint with Widnes, the club was locked in a perpetual struggle with Wigan to break the Riversiders' monopoly of the major English trophies. Sorensen's dream was to play in a Challenge Cup final at Wembley. But the most prized trophy in English league was seemingly the exclusive domain of Wigan. Widnes were to be bundled out of the Cup at the semi-final stage by St Helens in both 1989 and 1991. Sorensen was beginning to despair that he would never gain the chance to experience the unique feeling of playing at Wembley that so many of his Kiwi team-mates like Dean Bell, Kevin and Howie Tamati, Gary Kemble and others had savoured. But just when it looked as if Wembley had escaped Sorensen's clutches forever, Widnes reached the Challenge Cup final against Wigan in 1993.

"For a while, I despaired over whether I would ever get there," he said. "I have to admit I stayed on longer in the game simply because I wanted to get to Wembley. Wembley is all about timing. Some players go through their entire career without getting there while others swap clubs one year and are there the next. I guess my hunger was increased by losing three Cup semi-finals. To know you were just one game away and you missed out is hard to take. Our form was often great leading up to each semi but then something would go wrong, often just little things, and we wouldn't make it. So that made me more determined that I would play at Wembley before I retired. Ivan Lendl had Wimbledon. I guess I had Wembley."

Wigan ended up beating Widnes 20-14 in the '93 final. Sorensen was on the bench but was injected into the game by coach Doug Laughton during the second half. The hallowed turf he had so longed to tread had an almost instantaneous inspirational effect on Sorensen. Millions of television viewers watched the Kiwi war horse score one of the best tries of his career, a typically blockbusting effort where he powered through Wigan's defence. It wasn't enough to win the final but Sorensen felt curiously fulfilled afterwards. "I wasn't let down at all," he says. "I was just glad to have got out there. I had been around so many people who had played at Wembley, many of them old friends and team-mates. Each of them had fed me little bits of trivia about Wembley and Challenge Cup day and I felt like I knew what to expect. The strange thing was that it all happened exactly as I had expected. Sure, we didn't win, but I have no regrets. I felt privileged to have been there."

Playing out his career in England and not wanting to return to New Zealand in the off-season meant Sorensen was unavailable for the Kiwis in 1987. It was the same for most of the 1988 season until New Zealand defeated Great Britain 12-10 in Christchurch to reach the World Cup final against Australia in October. The Kiwis had defeated Australia in their last clash, the previous year, with a largely untried and unknown team that gave new coach Tony Gordon a fantastic baptism into international football. But there was a feeling within New Zealand that if the Australians were to be rolled in the Cup final, more experienced heads were needed. It wasn't long before the local press started speculating about Mark Graham and Kurt Sorensen being drafted back into the team for the most important game in New Zealand's league history.

For Sorensen, one last tilt at the old enemy was a temptation too good to resist. After being discreetly sounded out about his availability, the warhorse decided to put his hand up. The World Cup final had an unprecedented media build-up. The entire country became caught up in the obsession of defeating the Wally Lewis-led Australians. The visitors played the hype game adroitly, cleverly manoeuvring themselves into the role of underdogs. No Australian league team ever has the right to underdog status in any test but Wally's men got it and all the pressure was heaped on the shoulders of the Kiwis. "They did the media bit really well," Sorensen said of the lead-up to the final. "That resulted in a lot of pressure being put on us. We had a lot of young guys in the team and we were playing at Eden Park for the first time. The Aussies were sitting back in their hotel rooms laughing. I remember afterwards talking to a couple of my mates in the

Australian team like Gavin Miller and they told me they couldn't believe the pressure we were under. In contrast, they were totally relaxed."

But the Australians hadn't finished their psychological warfare. They also wanted to humble the two men they believed could bring them undone...Sorensen and Mark Graham. It appeared they had two distinct plans as well. Graham was dealt with on the field of play where, within the first 15 minutes, he'd been hit from behind late and high by Steve Roach. He played the rest of the game, won handsomely by the Kangaroos, in a daze.

The plot to undermine Sorensen was a little more subtle, however. In the final days leading up to the match, the Australians casually let slip to their media that they had held a special players' meeting to voice their concern about one particular Kiwi forward who had a habit of "causing mayhem" on the field. The player wasn't publicly named but the Australians made it clear to their loyal pressmen exactly who they were talking about. And the Aussie media had no qualms in pointing the finger at Sorensen. Predictably, the media firestorm quickly reached this side of the Tasman and Sorensen found his playing style acutely analysed.

Also undoubtedly perusing the media analysis was the World Cup final referee, Graham Anui, a policeman from Papua-New Guinea. Unfortunately, Anui was to prove woefully out of his depth handling such an important match. It would be churlish to suggest Anui cost the Kiwis the match. New Zealand did enough wrong to take almost total blame for the debacle that followed. But Anui also contributed by penalising the home team off the park in the opening minutes. Sorensen was also baited relentlessly by the Australian forwards, in particular his old sparring partner Steve Roach. The pair tangled on several occasions while Sorensen was also involved in a few other skirmishes. Although New Zealand were guilty of plenty of offending, history had judged them as the sole offenders. This rankles with Sorensen, who says the Australians also put themselves about during the match.

Sorensen was to tangle one more time with the team he most loved to beat. The Kangaroos toured the United Kingdom in 1992 and it was Widnes who provided them with their toughest match outside the tests. And it was no surprise to see who was leading the charge. Sorensen had a blinder. But afterwards the match was to explode into controversy with the Australians accusing Sorensen of eye-gouging. The charges were levelled by Kangaroo coach Bob Fulton and, surprise, surprise, Steve Roach. It was a strange turnaround for Fulton who, all those years earlier, had praised Sorensen in his *Daily Mirror* newspaper column and remained a staunch admirer since.

Sorensen theorises that Fulton wanted to take the heat off a less than impressive Australian display and that the eye-gouging allegations were a convenient excuse. "I actually had friends of mine in Australia ringing me and telling me I should sue Fulton for what he was saying in the press back there," he says. "They seized on a minor incident and tried to blow it up. Paul Sironen had hit the ball up and I had tackled him high. When I went in for the tackle, my fingers actually went into his eye accidentally. I knew straight away, when he went down, and I said to the referee that it was an accident. The ref was right there and he agreed. Eye-gouging was never my go. I mean if you're going to do that, you would do it when the guy is on the ground not when he's coming straight at you. It was a ridiculous allegation but pretty much what you would expect from the Australians. That's the way they've always worked. Whenever they've lost, they have always made excuses. But I guess that's something New Zealanders have been brought up with. We're brought up to try and win, but if we lose, we cop it sweet. The Aussies always seem to have an excuse, though. But I'm not telling you anything any Kiwi doesn't already know."

Sorensen's last test came in 1989 against France. By the time he had stood down from international football, he had set a New Zealand record for length of time between the start of his test career and the end. Retirement, even from club football, did not come easy. "I had been agonising over it for three years or so before I finally went through with it (at the end of 1993-94 season). I felt I had to put the whole thing in perspective. I've been really lucky that I haven't suffered any major injuries during my career. That was part of the reason I was able to keep going for so long. I'd really had a lot of great successes and I just wanted to have a life after football. My wife was bugging me to take her skiing and things like that and I felt like the time had come to give it away."

When Kurt Sorensen did retire, it cut one of the last links with the great era of the 1980s. Only Dean Bell remains still playing. Sorensen is gone, but definitely not forgotten.